MASCULINITIES IN HIGHER EDUCATION

Masculinities in Higher Education provides empirical evidence, theoretical support, and developmental interventions for educators working with college men both in and out of the classroom. The critical philosophical perspective of the text challenges the status quo and offers theoretically sound educational strategies to successfully promote men's learning and development.

Contesting dominant discourses about men and masculinities and binary notions of privilege and oppression, the contributors examine the development and identity of men in higher education today. This edited collection analyzes the nuances of lived identities, intersections between identities, ways in which individuals participate in co-constructing identities, and in turn how these identities influence culture.

- Section A provides practitioners and scholars perspective in placing the current problems associated with men's engagement and developmental difficulties in socio-historical context.
- Section B helps educators and researchers understand the complexities associated with men's development and the multi-dimensional, contextual, and highly interconnected aspects of men's identities.
- Section C contains practical advice and resources for student development professionals and educators and has a theory-to-practice focus.

While there are books that address men's issues globally or focus on the development of elementary or secondary school boys, there is a lack of conceptual guidance for working specifically with college men. *Masculinities in Higher Education* is a unique resource for graduate students and professional post-secondary educators looking for strategies to effectively promote college men's learning and development.

Jason A. Laker is the Vice President for Student Affairs and Professor within the Connie L. Lurie College of Education at San José State University.

Tracy Davis is Professor and Program Coordinator of the College Student Personnel graduate program at Western Illinois University.

MASCULINITIES IN HIGHER EDUCATION

Theoretical and Practical Considerations

Edited by Jason A. Laker, SAN JOSÉ STATE UNIVERSITY

and Tracy Davis, WESTERN ILLINOIS UNIVERSITY

Routledge
Taylor & Francis Group

NEW YORK AND LONDON

First published 2011
by Routledge
711 Third Avenue, New York, NY 10016

Simultaneously published in the UK
by Routledge
2 Park Square, Milton Park, Abingdon, Oxon OX14 4RN

Routledge is an imprint of the Taylor & Francis Group, an informa business

Library of Congress Cataloging in Publication Data
Masculinities in higher education : theoretical and practical considerations / Jason A. Laker, Tracy Davis [editors].
   p. cm.
   Includes bibliographical references and index.
   1. Men—Education (Higher)—United States. 2. Education, Higher—United States—Philosophy. 3. College students—United States—Social conditions. 4. College students—United States—Attitudes. 5. Masculinity—Social aspects—United States.
I. Laker, Jason A. II. Davis, Tracy.
LC1397.M37 2011
378.1'9821—dc22
2010045396

ISBN13: 978-0-415-87463-2 (hbk)
ISBN13: 978-0-415-87464-9 (pbk)
ISBN13: 978-0-203-83305-6 (ebk)

Typeset in Bembo and Stone Sans by
EvS Communication Networx, Inc.

Printed and bound in the United States of America on acid-free paper by
Walsworth Publishing Company, Marceline, MO

SUSTAINABLE FORESTRY INITIATIVE
Certified Sourcing
www.sfiprogram.org
SFI-00555
The SFI label applies to the text stock.

CONTENTS

Foreword by Dr. Jane Fried   *vii*

Introduction by Tracy Davis and Jason Laker   *xi*

SECTION A
Theoretical and Historical Perspectives   **1**
Section Editor, Jason Laker

1   Mapping Guyland in College   3
    Michael S. Kimmel and Tracy Davis

2   Using the Psychology of Men and Gender Role Conflict Theory
    to Promote Comprehensive Service Delivery for College Men:
    A Call to Action   16
    James M. O'Neil and Bryce Crapser

3   The Situation of Men, and Situating Men in Higher Education:
    A Conversation about Crisis, Myth, and Reality about College
    Students Who Are Men   50
    Frank Harris III and Ryan P. Barone

4   Inviting and Inspiring Men to Learn: Gendered Pedagogical
    Considerations for Undergraduate Teaching and Learning
    Environments   63
    Jason Laker

SECTION B
Identity Intersections with Masculinities   **79**
Section Editor, Tracy Davis

5 Man of Multiple Identities: Complex Individuality and Identity
   Intersectionality among College Men   81
   Shaun R. Harper, Cameron C. Wardell, and Keon M. McGuire

6 Queer Masculinities in Higher Education   97
   Beth Berila

7 Socio-Economic and Work Identity Intersections with Masculinity
   and College Success   111
   Brian D. Reed

8 Disability Identity Intersections with Masculinities   130
   Thomas J. Gerschick

SECTION C
Effective Interventions with College Men   **145**
Section Editors, Jason Laker and Tracy Davis

9   Masculinities Reviewed and Reinterpreted: Using a Critical
    Approach to Working with Men in Groups   147
    Tracy Davis, James LaPrad, and Sean Dixon

10 Using How College Men Feel about Being Men and "Doing the
    Right Thing" to Promote Men's Development   161
    Alan D. Berkowitz

11 Best Practices for Improving College Men's Health: Designing
    Effective Programs and Services for College Men   177
    Will Courtenay

12 Successful Judicial Intervention with College Men   193
    Randall B. Ludeman

13 Embracing Liberatory Practice: Promoting Men's Development as a
    Feminist Act   210
    Rachel Wagner

Index   *224*

FOREWORD

When Ruth Hawthorne, one of my first female mentors in higher education, entered Syracuse University in 1912, many people believed that too much learning dried up a woman's reproductive organs. Ruth managed to marry, raise two children and ultimately find a career as a housemother at the University of Michigan and Syracuse University. She was a feminist, a suffragist, and a person who found most socially constructed dogmas about gender roles laughable. She was still auditing courses in philosophy when I met her in 1966 and enjoyed discussing the evolution of higher education during her lifetime. At the time I was a student radical hippie, chafing under the restrictions of the Dean of Women's office at Syracuse. The Dean of Women, Marjorie Smith, had firm beliefs about appropriate behavior for women, both those under her tutelage in the master's degree program in student personnel and those undergraduate students for whom we were responsible. But the times were changing, the constructs were being deconstructed and women were becoming people capable of much larger roles in society than Ward and June Cleaver ever imagined.

A century after Ruth Hawthorne entered college, the wheel has made a complete turn. Although nobody presumably believes that higher education desiccates men's reproductive organs, many are seriously concerned about the evolving roles assigned to men in this society and their ability to create lives of meaning and contribution in the 21st century. Even though men should have no worries about connections between their virility and college attendance, they are not doing well in the academic arena. For the first time since Oxford University was founded to educate sons of feudal lords and aspiring priests, women outnumber men in our colleges. Liberal arts colleges are struggling to maintain a ratio of 60% women to 40% men in the belief that further imbalance would undermine the attractiveness of their institutions for potential students. Among people aged 30–44, there are currently more college educated women than men and women outnumber men at almost all levels of higher education from community colleges to research universities.

What's happening to men? Or more accurately, what's happening to the socially constructed notions of masculinity? The male/female binary in American culture and its ancestral cultures in Europe has been around for at least 5,000 years. Gender designations are far more complex than sex designations, which are generally determined by genitalia and chromosomes. The boundaries between gender categories have been somewhat fluid over time and have varied by race and economic class. White women may have been considered fragile flowers in the antebellum South, but Black women certainly worked as hard as men harder than White men of the landowning class.

The research on male/female biological differences is inconclusive. We may never be able to separate nature from nurture in this situation. However, we do know that our notions of masculinity and femininity have changed over time in the United States. Dean Marjorie Smith did not permit her female student deans to appear in public in slacks, and we all knew what was required of a "Syracuse girl." During the 1960s we were also clear on what was required of men—athleticism, stoicism, physical strength, dominance in relationships and autonomy. The football team was at the top of the hierarchy.

The Vietnam war rattled the rigid gender roles of the post-WWII era. Feminism, Black Power, and Gay rights movements shook the categories at an even deeper level by granting increased economic and educational opportunities to women and Black people. Women did not need to marry in order to become economically viable adults. White feminists wanted the right to work while married and Black "womanists" challenged White women's ideas about strength and power. Black women had been working outside their own homes since emancipation but had far fewer opportunities for education or career mobility than middle class white women. The challenges to the established binary were pushed further as gay and lesbian people came out of their closets and demanded to be seen as men and women regardless of their sexual orientation. The most recent development in these category collapses has been the increasing emergence of the transgender population demanding that they be seen as people worthy of respect regardless of genitalia, chromosomes, or gender presentation.

For the majority of the population that has remained within the binary, these developments are often confusing and frightening. Identity is a socially constructed phenomenon. If you can't look at a person and tell if s/he is a man or a woman, how do you know how to address that person? What changes does gender ambiguity require in building architecture and the architecture of interpersonal relationships? If men are permitted to marry men and women to marry women, how will the people who have followed all the traditional gender rules know who they are and what is right and reasonable in our cultural and social arrangements? From a broader perspective, how do we need to shift our perceptions of gender roles, family arrangements and human dignity so that all people can thrive in a rapidly changing world?

The second wave women's movement began in the 1960s and has made unquestioned progress in supporting the equality of women in the 21st century. The men's movement began much later and has sputtered. There is confusion about why men need a movement. Feminists have been so concerned about the historical dominance of men that they have failed to notice the price men pay for remaining in their historically assigned roles. Nevertheless, that price has been documented in the illnesses to which men are prone—higher incidence of work related injury, higher rates of coronary disease and stroke, earlier death rates and shorter lives following the loss of a spouse or partner. At a party celebrating the creation of a women's center at my current university, I thanked the president for his support. He then commented that we needed a men's center as well. I told him that the entire university was a men's center, which is why we needed a women's center. His remarks and mine were entirely predictable in 1998. He didn't understand male dominance and I didn't understand male vulnerability. The dominant group rarely understands its privilege and the non-dominant group rarely understands the price.

Throughout my own life, I have experienced the turning of this wheel of dominance. In 1965 I was working on eliminating curfews for women at my undergraduate college. I asked the Dean of Students why women were subject to curfews and men were not. In a typical smartass undergraduate remark, I reminded her that women could get pregnant in the afternoon. In exasperation, she tried to stop me with, "Jane, you can't fight Western civilization." Of course, I believed that I could and we could and we did. At Syracuse, I met Ruth Hawthorne who taught me about change, emancipation, suffrage, and humor. In the 1970s the rules changed because of social unrest induced by the Vietnam war, the development of The Pill and the legalization of abortion.

During that period the American College Personnel Association (ACPA) created the Standing Committee for Women (SWC) and the gender dialogue opened up in the profession of student affairs. The SCW supported the creation of the Standing Committee for Men (SCM) because the male leaders in ACPA realized that gender equity required conversation within both groups and between groups as well. Neither committee was universally supported by the membership. The existence of both committees made many people nervous. When the SCM asked the SCW for its support in applying for standing committee status, one of the SCW founders tried to hold a meeting in the ladies room of a convention hotel so that the men could not attend. With Jane Fried inside and Harry Canon outside, we propped the door open so that the dialogue could continue. The SCW did support the SCM. This book is one of the fruits of that early decision.

The wheel has turned and it's not pretty sight. Men are now the minority in higher education. Articles abound about 30 being the new 20 and the inability of males to find a focus for their lives. Women are attending graduate schools, the entryway to upper middle-class status, at higher rates than men and many men are now beginning to believe that they will be the "stay at home" parents while their wives become the breadwinners for their families. Although women on the Supreme Court are still a novelty, women in national and state legislatures are not. If men have defined themselves for the past 5,000 years as the protectors, the providers, the warriors, and the patriarchs, how will they retain their sense of identity and agency when those roles have migrated to women and been significantly transformed in the process? The "we can't call it a Depression" recession of recent memory has disproportionately thrown men out of work because the jobs lost were disproportionately and stereotypically male-manufacturing, construction and other kinds of manual labor. Service industries, which have historically employed women, have remained far more stable. Men are losing or have lost their most important anchors of identity. The binary of gender roles is almost collapsed. A balance of conversation and negotiation provides one likely path to reframing our relationships and our constructions of self. This conversation is essential if we are to continue to flourish as a society.

Social roles and gender roles build up slowly, over centuries. The current transformation in our ideas of male and female abilities, proclivities and roles has happened quickly. Things began to change during WWII with Rosie the Riveter. We tried to go back, but it didn't work well or for very long. The social justice movements that began in the 1960s continue to expand possibilities for groups that had been limited and to provoke confusion and a sense of loss in our previously most privileged group—White men who attend college. Working-class men experience the loss differently, but with equal severity. Our institutions of higher education are based on many assumptions about teaching, learning, living, and attendance that are connected in unacknowledged ways to traditional sex roles and to male dominance. It is clear that women are succeeding at higher rates than men and this imbalance will continue to disrupt society until a new equilibrium is created.

The writing in this book constitutes a significant contribution to this essential conversation. We need to replace our notions of hierarchy and privilege with notions of balance, dialogue, efficacy and equity. When one of us loses, all of us lose. The motto of the United Negro College Fund, "A mind is a terrible thing to waste," applies equally to gender and to people of color. New insights must precede new approaches to educating men and women. The essential knowledge to create new ways of educating our citizens will be constructed in the conversations that this book will provoke.

Dr. Jane Fried

INTRODUCTION

Tracy Davis and Jason Laker

Theoretical perspectives on human development in the last two decades clearly support the notion that women's gender development should be considered distinct from men's, and given particular attention both generally and in relation to other dimensions of identity. As Kimmel and Davis illustrate in Chapter 1 of this book, too often scholars and practitioners have ignored important sociological factors that shape men and women differently. Gilligan (1982), Josselson (1987), Belenky, Clinchy, Goldberger, and Tarule (1986), and Baxter-Magolda (1992), among others, have provided theoretical support for connected or relational influences on growth tied to women's cognitive and psychosocial development. An unintended consequence of the relatively recent focus on these theories is an assumption that earlier scholarship based almost exclusively on male research participants had already articulated men's development. More recently, scholars have come to understand that such research did not succeed in explaining men or their experiences in terms of their sex role socialization. In a 2002 study, Davis, for example, found that college men seldom considered how or what they have learned about becoming a man. A more striking recent example is Sax's (2008) pioneering book *The Gender Gap in College*, where, in the chapter on gender and college student development, there is an entire section on *Perspectives on Women's Development*, with no mention of the books, models and research related to the influence of gender on men's development (see chapter 1 of this book for an extensive discussion of models of men's development). Harper and Harris (2010), similarly lament that "most articles in student affairs journals that are supposedly about "gender" are almost always studies of women or statistical documentations of gender differences" (p. 6).

We'll leave it to others to debate the reasons for such exclusion, but the unsettling fact remains that ignoring the influence that sex role socialization has on men's development undermines professional effectiveness with male students and serves to reify systematic patriarchy. The proposition of featuring subjects of men and masculinities may activate skepticism among those who believe men are already centered within the academy and beyond. We contend however that explicit examination of women's, men's and trans individuals' gendered lived experiences and development is critical to dismantling hegemonic gender binaries and associated privilege and oppression. As hooks (2004) reminds us, "it may be difficult for those who have experienced subordination and who live within the web of oppression to hear emphasis placed on men being victimized by sexism; they cling to the "all men are the enemy" version of reality.... While it in no way diminishes the seriousness of male abuse and oppression of women, or negates male responsibility for exploitive actions, the pain men experience can serve as a catalyst calling attention to the need for change" (p. 558). If we understand how all people are harmed by adhering to the unconscious absorption of narrow standards that lead to confining and oppressive roles, we can begin the process of deciding for ourselves who we are and realize a more full human potential.

Fortunately, there are conceptual frameworks that help us focus on the processes that create and sustain sexism and other forms of oppression. Moreover, there are an increasing number of theories of men's development that both build an understanding of men and suggest practical strategies for promoting healthy growth and development. O'Neil's chapter in this book, Kimmel's (2008) portrayal of "Guyland," Laker's (2005) concept of "Bad Dogs," Davis' (2002) "Voices of Gender Role Conflict," Edwards' Masks of Masculinity (2007), Pollack's Boy Code (1999), Brod and Kaufman's (1994) compilation of theoretical perspectives on men, to name a few.

But accurately understanding men's development through the lenses of theoretical models and empirical evidence is only the first step. As Laker illustrates in Chapter 4, translating theory to practice requires practitioners and educators to confront complicated hurdles related to outdated assumptions and overly-simplistic notions of development and identity which invite unsophisticated approaches to professional practice with our students. Moreover, we argue throughout this book that the current discourses regarding men and masculinities are stagnated by binary and at times moralistic notions of privilege and oppression that ignore critical analysis of the nuances of lived identities, intersections among identities, ways in which both other individuals and socio-political-historical contexts serve to co-construct identities, how and why identities are performed, and in turn how identities influence culture. We hope the explicitly critical philosophical perspectives advanced in this text will provide conceptual challenges to the status-quo (which evidence suggests has not been effective), and theoretically sound educational strategies to successfully promote men's learning and development. While we believe this book provides the empirical evidence, theoretical support and developmental interventions for educators working with college men in and out of the classroom, we invite you to actively critique and discuss our perspectives.

In the first section, we begin by framing broad conceptual lenses for understanding men as gendered individuals. Chapter 1, by Kimmel and Davis demarcates the experiences and identities of the critical mass of college men in late adolescence through early adulthood. In Chapter 2, noted psychologist and Men's Studies scholar Jim O'Neil, along with Bryce Crasper contemplates the implications of men's gender identity formation on facilitation of development on campus generally and in therapeutic contexts. In Chapter 3, Frank Harris and Ryan Barone discuss the challenges for men as they navigate hegemonic messages and attempt to transcend associated crises toward a more human experience. Finally, in Chapter 4, Laker critically reflects upon the conventional wisdom and dogma in Student Affairs graduate programs and administrative departments, challenging our notions of male students and their developmental needs. Readers are invited to revisit their professional preparation and recast long-held assumptions about male students.

The second section of the book focuses on the many of the salient dimensions of mens' identity development. By highlighting multiple masculinities, the authors interrogate reductionistic perspectives on identity that tend to promote fragmented understanding and ineffective practice. In chapter 5, Shaun Harper, Cameron Wardell, and Keon McGuire capture many of the complexities associated with the multiple dimensions of an individual's identity. Through a case example they clearly illustrate how one dimension of one's identity intersects with other dimensions and how lived identity is the result of choices made through continuous interaction with contextual factors that influence what is performed and what is not. Beth Berila uses a critical approach to trouble hegemonic masculinities in order to reveal common circumstances confronting gay men in college in Chapter 6. Her powerful analysis also offers important strategies for helping students successfully navigate the challenges that gay college men often confront. While the student affairs-related literature contains models of identity development focusing on both ethnicity and sexual orientation, there is a striking paucity of empirical evidence and theory that helps us understand socio-economic class and disability, much less their intersections with masculinity. Beginning to fill this void is Brian Reed's discussion in Chapter 7 of how men's work identity and social class intersects with masculinity to sometimes inhibit development as well as reduce chances for college success. He describes how hegemonic masculinities like provision and production coalesce with low socio-economic status to create obstacles to success, often leading men away from postsecondary education and into low-paying, high-risk, and/or dwindling segments of the labor market. In Chapter 8, Tom Gerschick examines the experiences of, and challenges faced by college men with physical disabilities. He illustrates how men with disabilities negotiate acceptance, achievement, and an empowered sense of manhood by contesting hegemonic standards of masculinity.

We had anticipated including a chapter on intersections with religion and spirituality within this section. As we worked to identify individuals who could speak to this important topic, we came to see that these are still uncharted waters in the literature and lives of men. We imagined the chapter would include attention to a range of identity conflicts and tensions between religiosity and normative college activities; spiritual authenticity versus conformity within male peer groups; and, highlighting contemporary issues and debates about religious diversity (e.g., Muscular Christianity, church/state separation, religiously affiliated institutions, post-911 Muslim identities, Jewish and Zionist identities). We attempted to elicit a chapter written by a particular group of male colleagues who represent Muslim, Jewish, Atheistic, Buddhist, and Christian traditions. In the end, the difficulty of expressing an explicitly gendered message about men's religious and spiritual identities proved too difficult and unfinished. In short, it didn't work for this edition of the book. We continue to see this as an important and necessary area for further research and professional discourse, and perhaps this will stimulate new scholarship and consideration for the future.

The third section of the book takes an overtly pragmatic view, where authors highlight effective interventions for addressing common issues confronting college men. Tracy Davis, James LaPrad, and Sean Dixon challenge readers to reimagine their work with male students by incorporating a critical pedagogical approach in Chapter 9. Examples of how to successfully work with *groups* of men, including fraternities, athletic teams, psychoeducational groups, service and outdoors-learning environments are provided. In Chapter 10, Alan Berkowitz introduces innovative strategies for promoting men's growth related to social norming, normative feedback, and other skills training that address the blind adherence to hegemonic masculinity and pluralistic ignorance that serve as enemies to healthy identity development. Chapter 11 takes on the subject of men's relationships with their bodies, offering insights into health issues and promotion among male students. In Chapter 12, Randy Ludeman addresses men's overrepresentation within disciplinary proceedings on campus, and suggests ways to make the most of these teachable moments with young men. Finally, Rachel Wagner closes the volume by navigating the opportunities and challenges for women working in Student Affairs. Through narrative reflection and incisive wisdom, she offers women colleagues a pathway toward their own and male students' respective dignity and growth.

In the end, this text represents a community of practice and makes transparent our collective grappling with difficult issues. We hope readers will be motivated, liberated, and especially successful as they apply this work toward their own learning and practice.

References

Baxter-Magolda, M. B. (1992). *Knowing and reasoning in college: Gender related patterns in students' intellectual development* (1st ed.). San Francisco: Jossey-Bass.

Belenky, M. F., Clinchy, B. M., Goldberger, N. R., & Tarule, J. M. (1986). *Women's ways of knowing*. New York: Basic Books.

Brod, H., & Kaufman (1994). *Theorizing masculinities*. Thousand Oaks, CA: Sage.

Davis, T. L. (2002). Voices of gender role conflict: The social construction of college men's identity. *Journal of College Student Development, 43*(4), 508–521.

Edwards, K. (2007). *"Putting my man face on": A grounded theory of college men's gender identity development*. Unpublished doctoral dissertation, The University of Maryland, College Park.

Gilligan, C. (1982). *In a different voice*. Cambridge, MA: Harvard University Press.

Harper, S. R., & Harris, F. (2010). Beyond the model gender majority myth: Responding equitably to the developmental needs and challenges of college men. In S. Harper & F. Harris (Eds.), *College men and masculinities: Theory, research, and implications for practice* (pp. 1–16). San Francisco: Jossey-Bass.

Josselson, R. (1987). *Finding herself: Pathways to identity development in women*. San Francisco: Jossey-Bass.

Kimmel (2008). *Guyland: The perilous world where boys become men*. New York: HarperCollins.

Laker, J. (2005). Beyond *bad dogs: Toward a pedagogy of engagement of male students*. Unpublished doctoral dissertation. The University of Arizona, Tucson.

Pollack, W. S. (1999). Real boys: Rescuing our sons from the myths of boyhood. New York: Holt.

Sax, L. (2008). *The gender gap in college: Maximizing the developmental potential of women and men*. San Francisco: Jossey-Bass.

SECTION A

Theoretical and Historical Perspectives

Section Editor, Jason Laker

1

MAPPING GUYLAND IN COLLEGE

Michael S. Kimmel

STATE UNIVERSITY OF NEW YORK AT STONY BROOK

Tracy Davis

WESTERN ILLINOIS UNIVERSITY

> If men have a difficult time asking for directions when they are lost driving in their cars, imagine what it feels like to feel lost and adrift on the highway of life.
>
> (Kimmel, 2008, p. 42)

Men and masculinities are both pervasive and invisible as subjects of scientific inquiry. Like the proverbial fish in water, what we know is so immersed in our apparent surroundings that important distinguishing factors that shape men's development remain unnoticed. Meth and Pasick (1990) explain the nature of this apparent contradiction; "although psychological writing has been andro-centric, it has also been gender blind [and] it has assumed a male perspective but has not really explored what it means to be a man any more than what it means to be a woman" (p. vii). This deficit, then, is less an artifact of carelessness or conspiracy, and is more accurately understood as the result of dominant, taken-for-granted assumptions. Assumptions that, left un-interrogated, jeopardize an accurate understanding of boys and men and, moreover, threaten to main-tain a patriarchal status quo. To be clear, we use the term patriarchy to mean the institutionalized system that privileges men and serves to oppress women. According to Johnson (1997), "a society is patriarchal to the degree that it is male-dominated, male-identified, and male-centered" (p. 5). It is important to remember, as will soon be described, that a man or men in general are not patriarchy and not every man is privileged equally. Moreover, Lindsey German (1981) in "Theories of Patriarchy" has persuasively argued that it is not men who ultimately "benefit" from the oppression of women, but capital and our economic system. Patriarchy, privilege, intersectional identities, and social, economic, historical contexts are concepts related to the critical theory perspective advocated throughout this chapter and book. This chapter offers a framework for critically examining men as a subject, and masculinities as a phenomenon of inquiry. As one of the authors of this chapter has argued, "the important fact of men's lives is not that they are biological males, but that they become men. Our sex may be male, but our identity as men is developed through a complex process of interaction with the culture in which we both learn the gender scripts appropriate to our culture and attempt to modify those scripts to make them more palatable" (Kimmel & Messner, 1998, p. ix).

A central analysis that is too often missing in our study of men and masculinities, then, is the cultural influence that shapes the contours of men's development. In the United States scientific community, the 20th century was dominated by Western assumptions of rationalism and individualistic psychological development. As a result, we look to psychology to explain the outrageous, but rare occurrences of mass murder by single shooters (always male), and gang rape, drunk driving accidents, etc.—rather than the cultural influences. Only in the last 30 or so years have we begun to illuminate the sociological, institutional, cultural impacts that shape men's development. It is becoming increasingly clear that identity is socially constructed, historically situated, multidimensional, intersectional, and mutually-shaping (e.g., Abbes, Jones, & McEwen, 2007; Torres, Jones, & Renn, 2009). Susan Jones and Marylu McEwen's (2000) groundbreaking Multiple Dimensions of Identity Model illustrates this complexity.

In addition to highlighting models of men and masculinities that give salience to contextual/sociological influences, in this chapter we take an explicitly critical perspective in our presentation and analysis. Just as the psychological perspective has overshadowed cultural impact, an even more comprehensive psycho-social focus may miss the power-laden historical and political influences explicitly examined through the lenses of critical theory. The term *critical* has deeply divergent meanings and interpretations. In this chapter, we mean *critical* as a process of "unearthing, and then researching, the assumptions one is operating under, primarily by taking different perspectives on familiar, taken-for-granted beliefs and behaviors" (Brookfield, 2005, p. viii). We also adopt the distinctively political stance of critical theory by highlighting the power structures that generally privilege men and oppress women, and in our concern for providing the knowledge and understanding that will change, not just interpret, the world. In this way, theory is practical. In other words, we hope that you join us in the dialectical journey of (re)considering aspects of men's development that will move us beyond personal insight into action that liberates men and women in our common journey. An example of the sort of praxis we aspire to is illustrated in bell hooks' (1994) *Teaching to Transgress*. In describing her need to make sense of her past, she writes, "I came to theory because I was hurting—the pain within me was so intense that I could not go on living. I came to theory desperate, wanting to comprehend—to grasp what was happening around and within me. Most importantly, I wanted to make the hurt go away. I saw in theory then a location for healing" (p. 59). We believe that what follows offers theoretical background to the professional interacting with men in a way that illuminates the ways men are both privileged and harmed by the patriarchy. The models and concepts provided here offer a way of helping professionals better understand male behavior and to be conscious of potential countertransference reactions. Pollack (1990), for example, challenges us to "be sensitively aware (and less countertransferentially critical) of the particular forms of affiliative needs and capacities shown by men" (p. 318). Student affairs professionals will need to be alert to any disposition to rely on sex role expectations in deciding on developmentally appropriate challenges and supports. We are not advocating a dismissal of inappropriate or otherwise hurtful men's behavior. To the contrary, the critical approach described here promotes both individual and institutional level challenge to hegemonic masculine norms and patriarchal privilege.

Positionality

Before we outline several landmark models that describe the social construction of hegemonic masculinity, it is important to situate ourselves within this discussion of men and masculinities. It is important for several reasons. First, we assume a critical approach that requires us to be explicit and mindful about how we are positioned in relation to others: as empowered/powerless, dominant/subordinate, central/marginal. Maher and Tetreault (2001), for example, in *The Feminist Classroom,* describe "the idea of positionality, in which people are defined not in terms of fixed identities, but by their location within shifting networks of relationships, which can be analyzed and changed" (p. 164). We hope to offer important insights, and these ideas, particularly the way they are put into practice, are shaped by our positionalities. In our experience, decisions about how to effectively subvert, challenge, support, and interrogate unreflective acceptance of unhealthy norms, as well as the institutional policies, practices and procedures that promote them, are greatly impacted by our positions. Each of us is a professor and has done extensive writing on men and masculinities. While both of us are humanistic in our spirituality, one of us is currently exploring Zen Buddhism but was raised Catholic and one of us is Jewish. We are both middle-aged, able-bodied, heterosexual, White men with European ancestry who currently have upper-middle class standing. Both philosophically and pragmatically we have developed a pro-feminist perspective that has grown out of anti-patriarchal practices, activities, and research that has been positively shaped by feminist theory and practice. In some aspects of our identities. we have experienced oppression (e.g., being Jewish). The experience is mostly sensitizing, but potentially blinding. On the one hand, experiencing a Jewish identity in a predominantly Christian culture leads to *some* awareness of how other forms of oppression might be felt. While personal history and other identity dimensions intersect to mediate how oppression is individually experienced, there are some commonalities that allow for some level of understanding. On the other hand, we are at risk of acting as if we understand all oppression, forgetting the complexity and unique characteristics associated with various forms of oppression. In this way, our position is blinding. History, contemporary contexts, and even the visibility of an identity dimension, all impact felt oppression in complex ways.

Similarly, we each experience significant privilege in our current positions based on class, sex, ability, sexual orientation, and ethnic appearance. The nature of privilege is that it typically lies outside of our awareness and operates in a largely invisible, unconscious manner (Johnson, 1997; McIntosh, 2001). Suffice it for now to say that the following discussion of the socially constructed contours of hegemonic masculinities is general in nature, and we recognize that masculinity is likely experienced differently, to some extent, based on sexual orientation, ethnicity, and other identity dimensions, as well as performed uniquely based on important contextual factors. We are positioned in a manner that may influence our missing some important nuances and we certainly invite a critique that engages in discourse that leads to deeper understanding.

A Conceptual Basis for Understanding Men's Development

Developing an understanding of the construction of men and masculinities in this culture provides a map to illuminate the way toward helping men understand themselves, make self-authored choices that stand against standards of masculinity which have been unreflectively absorbed and socially reinforced, and begin to challenge the institutionalized hegemonic norms that alienate men from ourselves and other people. Too often our institutional policies and professional practices reflect simplistic and/or overly reductionist conceptions of men and masculinities. For example, while all men are privileged by patriarchy, the experience of power and privilege is based on a range of social identities. According to Kaufman (1999), "The social power of a poor man is different than a rich one, a working class Black man from a working class White man, a gay man from a bisexual man from a straight man, a Jewish man in Ethopia from a Jewish man in Israel, a teenage boy from an adult" (p. 68). The contradictory experiences of power described by Kaufman demonstrate the need to go beyond surface assumptions constructed by (a) the belief that we already know about men from past research (even though men were not studied *as* men) and (b) the related failure to develop a comprehensive theoretical base for understanding men. We attempt here to critically represent men by explicitly gendering this dominant social group, promoting a fuller critique and understanding of men, and offering ways for *translating theory to practice* that shifts attention from reductionist tendencies to a reflective practice based on a more comprehensive understanding of how men become men.

The Guy Code

Boys learn how to be a man from an early age in playgrounds, schoolrooms, religious institutions, and homes, and are taught by peers, media, parents, teachers, coaches—just about everywhere and from everyone. What is remarkable is how clear and consistent the messages are. The messages are not subtle suggestions for boys to consider, they are strict rules that must be followed and most are deeply afraid of the consequences of breaking them. In fact, James O'Neil, a leading expert in men's development, has decades of research supporting the conflict that men feel in response to the internalization of the male gender role (see Chapter 2). Gender role conflict is defined as "a psychological state occurring when rigid, sexist, or restrictive gender roles learned thorough socialization, result in personal restriction, devaluation, or violation of others or self" (O'Neil, 1990, p. 25). At the very heart of men's conflict is a fear of femininity. There is a scene in the widely acclaimed movie *The Sandlot* (1993) that clearly illustrates boys' fear of femininity. In one part of the film, the "sandlot boys" are arguing with the apparently upper-class team of boys with uniforms. Each team continues trading insults until one of the sandlot boys shouts that the boy's on the other team "play ball like a girl." There is complete silence at this "ultimate slur" indicating that a line has been crossed and there is no place left to go. A critical deconstruction of the scene implies that the worst thing or the biggest fear boys and men experience is to be considered feminine. Hundreds of studies have been conducted using O'Neil's Gender Role Conflict construct and the following four patterns related to the traditional masculine role, and the underlying fear of femininity, have emerged: (a) Success, Power, and Competition; (b) Restrictive Emotionality; (c) Restrictive Sexual and Affectionate Behavior Between Men; and (d) Conflict Between Work and Family Relations (O'Neil, Helms, Gable, David, & Wrightsman, 1986). Again, underlying these factors is a code that essentially says don't appear feminine: don't show emotions, don't show taste in art or music, watch how you dress. The guy code fits as snugly as a straightjacket. It is, however, important to recognize that while the code clearly leads to the denigration of women, it simultaneously subjugates men. Moreover, this occurs somewhat routinely, rather than resulting from some insidious conspiracy. For example, as men individuate from mother (historically most often the primary care giver in American culture), they begin to also repudiate feelings associated with maternal femininity—compassion, nurturance, vulnerability, and dependency (Chodorow, 1989).

More recently, Harvard Psychologist William Pollack (1999) defined the "Boy Code" in his book *Real Boys*. He uses the following direct quotes from boys in his study to provide evidence of the code: "even very young boys reported that they felt they must 'keep a stiff upper lip,' 'not show their feelings,' 'act real tough,' 'not act too nice,' 'be cool,' 'just laugh and brush it off when someone punches you'" (p. 23). In Pollack and Shuster's (2001) study, the researchers investigated hundreds of young and adolescent boys and found

absolute consistency between the boy code and Brannon's (1976) four fundamental rules of masculinity:

- "No Sissy Stuff!" Being a man means not being a sissy, not being perceived
  as weak, effeminate, or gay. Masculinity is the relentless repudiation of the
  feminine.
- "Be a Big Wheel." This rule refers to the centrality of success and power
  in the definition of masculinity. Masculinity is measured more by wealth,
  power, and status than by any particular body part.
- "Be a Sturdy Oak." What makes a man is that he is reliable in a crisis. And
  what makes him so reliable in a crisis is not that he is able to respond fully
  and appropriately to the situation at hand, but rather that he resembles an
  inanimate object. A rock, a pillar, a species of tree."
- "Give 'em Hell." Exude an aura of daring and aggression. Live life out on
  the edge. Take risks. Go for it. Pay no attention to what others think."

If you want to understand men and their behavior, you need to understand
these regulations. As an anecdotal illustration of the clarity and penalizing
double-standards of these rules, one of us sometimes asks in our gender presentations for women who don't mind being referred to as a "tomboy" to raise
their hands, and men who don't mind being called a "sissy" to raise their hands.
Typically 50% or better of the women in the room, but not a single man, raises
his hand.

While we are beginning to get a view of "boyland," only recently has "guyland" been mapped. In his 2008 book *Guyland: The Perilous World Where Boys
Become Men*, Michael Kimmel interviewed nearly 400 young men between the
ages of 17 and 26 and found the terrain strikingly similar to Pollack's findings
a decade earlier and Brannon's (1976) research nearly 30 years ago. The Guy
Code he uncovered is made up of the following collection of attitudes, values,
and traits that together composes what it means to be a man:

1. Boys Don't Cry
2. It's Better to be Mad than Sad
3. Don't Get Mad—Get Even
4. Take It like a Man
5. He who has the Most Toys When he Dies, Wins
6. Just Do It or Ride or Die
7. Size Matters
8. I Don't Stop to Ask for Directions
9. Nice Guys Finish Last
10. It's All Good

The unifying emotional subtext of all of these aphorisms involves never
showing emotions or admitting weakness. You must show a face that indicates that everything will be fine, that everything is under control. Win-

ning is crucial, especially when the victory is over other men who have less amazing or smaller toys. Kindness is not an option, nor is compassion. These sentiments are taboo, but are part of the rules that govern men's behavior in Guyland, the criteria that will be used to evaluate whether any particular guy measures up.

Selling and Maintaining the Guy Code

The rules of Guyland are so deeply and consistently maintained due in large part to hegemony and three underlying cultural dynamics distinctly representative of masculinity: a culture of entitlement, a culture of silence, and a culture of protection.

Hegemony and Masculinity

Hegemony is the process of influence where we learn to earnestly embrace a system of beliefs and practices that essentially harm us, while working to uphold the interests of others who have power over us. Men will fight, literally, to defend a set of regulations related to traditional masculine ideology that are essentially harmful to their own well-being. A review of the literature clearly portrays the harm of adhering to the Guy Code. The investigations into the links between traditional masculine ideology and various wellness variables, use several measures including traditional masculinity ideology, conformity to masculine norms, and gender role conflict. Each offers a slightly different focus, but all are essentially based upon the same social constructionist view of masculinity that emphasizes elements of the Guy Code. Research has consistently found a relationship between adherence to traditional masculine ideology and depression (Brewer, 1998; Cournoyer, 1994; Good & Mintz, 1990, Sharpe & Heppner, 1991), use of alcohol and other drugs as well as binge drinking (Liu & Iwamoto, 2007; Mahalik et al., 2003), anxiety (Davis, 1987; Cournoyer, 1994; Sharpe & Heppner, 1991; Wester, Vogel, Wei, & McLain; 2006), and difficulties with intimacy (Good, Robertson, Fitzgerald, Stevens, & Bartels 1996; Rounds, 1994) to name just a few.

Instead of conceiving traditional masculine ideology as a system intentionally designed to reinforce the status quo, it is more accurately viewed as embedded in our everyday practices, behaviors, and actions within relationships, institutions, and communities. Interestingly, from this perspective, both men and women participate in the construction of hegemonic masculinity (just as men are complicit in maintaining hegemonic feminine ideology). According to Brookfield (2005), "Ideology becomes hegemony when the dominant ideas are learned and lived in everyday decisions and judgments and when these ideas (reinforced by the mass media images and messages) pervade the whole existence." (p. 94) One needs only to view a few hours of prime time television to see traditional sex roles portrayed and reinforced. The ideology becomes so ingrained that we consent to it willingly.

Thus, Guyland is pervasive—it is the air guys breathe, the water they drink—each guy cuts his own deal with it as he tries to navigate the passage from adolescence to adulthood. Unfortunately, there are few guides along the way. In non-Western cultures, it is the adult men of the community whose collective responsibility it is to ensure the safe ritual passage of boys into manhood. The older men devise the rituals, they perform the ceremonies, and they confer adult male stats as only adults can. As a result, once initiated, men no longer have identity crises, wondering who they are, if they can measure up, or if they are man enough. Absent rituals, ceremonies, actively involved adult men, and other mindful strategies, hegemonic notions of masculinity become the socializing agents to shape men's sense of self and identity.

The power of hegemonic masculinity lies not only in its all-pervasive, taken-for-granted, consensual nature, but also in the fact that there seems little chance for opposing it. When a concept is seen as naturally occurring (cf. biological explanations of gender roles) and is reinforced by actions and relations one lives out on a daily basis, challenging with alternative possibilities becomes particularly difficult. While we learn masculine hegemony, we also have the capacity to become critically aware of how it works and to develop consciousness so that we transform our culture and help boys become men by being true to themselves, not some artificial code.

Three Intersecting Cultures of Guyland

The picture should be becoming increasingly clear that while men who perform harmful, illegal, or otherwise inappropriate behaviors need to be held accountable, failing to understand the cultural influences that shape, provide rationale for, and even promote behavior may help explain why real change does not occur more deeply or quickly. In other words, while many men perform healthy masculinity, those behaviors and patriarchal practices we associate with unhealthy masculine behavior remain unchallenged due, at least in part, to our failure to accurately understand the socio-cultural construction of masculinities. Therefore, in addition to hegemony, there are three distinct cultures identified by Kimmel (2008) that need to be understood as supporting Guyland. The first is a *Culture of Entitlement*. Many young men have both an alarming sense of male superiority and a diminished capacity for empathy. They grow up believing that empathy and compassion need to be suppressed in the name of achieving masculinity. Many men who engage in acts of violence—or who are bystanders to it—or who joke about it with friends, fully subscribe to traditional ideologies about masculinity. The problem isn't psychological; these guys aren't deviants. If anything, they are overconforming to the hyperbolic expressions of masculinity that they see reinforced over and over again in American culture. Kimmel tells the story of being on a television talk show with several White males who felt they had been the victims of work place discrimination. The title of the show was "A Black Woman Stole My Job." Kimmel asked the men about the word "my" and where they got the idea that it was their job to begin with. These men felt they were entitled to the job and someone else, in this case a Black woman, really took what was rightfully theirs.

The second culture is *The Culture of Silence*. If men are hurting and struggling, participate in unhealthy rituals, and perpetuate violence how, come no one says anything about it? Because men are afraid of being outcast, marginalized, or shunned. It is fundamentally against the Guy Code to complain or express feelings of hurt or anything resembling weakness, and certainly a violation of the regulations to "sell another man out" or violate the "bros before hos" rule. So they learn to keep their mouths shut, even when what they are seeing goes against their common sense and values. There is a code of silence, according to Kindlon and Thompson (2000), that requires boys to suffer without speaking about it and to be silent witness to cruelty toward others. Many boys and men learn to be silent in the face of other men's violence. Silence is one of the ways boys *become* men.

By upholding the culture of silence, guys implicitly support the harmful, inappropriate or even illegal behaviors of the men in their midst who take that silence as tacit approval. Not only does that silence support them, it also protects them. It ensures that there will be no whistleblowers, and no witnesses if victims themselves come forward. Yet, it's one thing for guys to protect each other—after all their masculinity is at stake—and quite another thing entirely when the community that surrounds these guys also protects them. When parents, teachers, girlfriends, school administrators, and city officials make the decision to look the other way, to dismiss acts of violence as "poor judgment" or as "boys being boys." This *Culture of Protection* sustains and promotes antisocial and excessive behaviors. From hazing incidents in fraternities, sports clubs, and military establishments to sexual harassment, assault and other forms of violence, there are examples in nearly every community and the underlying fuel to the fire remains largely ignored.

Time to Rebel

Given the pervasive and largely overlooked influence of the traditional masculine ideology on men's development that is deeply embedded through hegemony and supported through the cultures of entitlement, silence and protection, recent indicators showing that boys and men are in trouble should be unsurprising. No wonder boys are more prone to depression, suicidal behaviors and various other forms of out-of-control or out-of-touch behaviors than girls are. No wonder boys drop out of school and are diagnosed as emotionally disturbed four times more often as girls, get into fights twice as often, and are six times more likely than girls to be diagnosed with Attention Deficit Disorder. No wonder men are increasingly disengaged from higher education.

Our typical responses in the past, however, will not be effective. The exclusively psychological interventions of counseling boys to find a moral center, encouraging their resilience, providing adequate role models and clear messages are all necessary, but they are not enough. They assume that by helping the boys find their way out of Guyland, the social and cultural frameworks that sustain and encourage it will simply atrophy from lack of participants. Starved of individuals willing to play along, the game will end. While salutary, such efforts put the cart before the horse, ignoring the social and cultural mechanisms that sustain Guyland and underlie its persistence.

Interventions and Practical Suggestions

We need first a public discourse about masculinity that illuminates the price of blindly consuming masculine hegemony and raises consciousness so that boys and men can become the authors of their lives not some fictional character created by ghost writers. We need teachers, parents, counselors, bosses, coaches, and administrators to understand what is happening in boys and mens' lives; the pressure they feel to live up to unattainable ideals of masculinity, and the feelings of doubt, anxiety, and shame that often accompany that quest. Doing so can mitigate the deleterious effects of sexism. For example, men's insecurity about their masculinity is analogous to women's insecurity about their bodies. Each are sold a standard that few will attain and none will capture on a permanent basis. We then use violence and eating and other control mechanisms to restore a sense of self. Violence is how men are often invited to express all disappointment. The connection between shame and aggression undermines the more biological explanations typically employed to explain men's violence. According to Kaufman and Raphael (1996), "To feel shame is to feel seen in a painfully diminished sense. Our eyes turn inward in the moment of shame, and suddenly we've become impaled under the magnifying gaze of our own eyes. Even when other people are present and watching, we are watching ourselves; but we actually mistake the watching eyes as belonging to others" (p. 17). This process is socialized into us through affects, scenes, and script (imprinting). Moreover, James Gilligan (1997) argues, "The emotion of shame is the primary or ultimate cause of all violence. The purpose of violence is to diminish the intensity of shame and replace it as far as possible with its opposite, pride, thus preventing the individual from being overwhelmed by the feeling of shame" (p. 110). Programs, counseling strategies, and professional preparation curricula aimed at inhibiting violence need to incorporate an awareness of the shame-violence connection and deliberately infuse this dimension of masculine identity development in any attempt to decrease in sexism and physical aggression.

Second, the need for a band of brothers is stronger than ever. Boys and men need a place where they can be vulnerable, honest, and open with each other and learn how to become men. A facilitated discussion of the negative consequences of gender role conflict may be a promising way to begin to loosen strict adherence to traditional gender roles which has been associated with so many negative outcomes. According to O'Neil, Egan, Owen, and McBride (1993), gender role transitions can "occur from increased awareness of how restrictive gender roles and sexism negatively affect personal growth and development" (p. 169). Such awareness, if not presented from a "men-as-victims perspective," can lead to gender role transitions which help individuals redefine or integrate their thoughts, feelings, and behaviors in a more healthy, adaptive, self-authored manner.

Third, we need to think and act creatively in designing new rituals and ceremonies demarcating men's rites of passage. Traditional markers of manhood—being the head of household, having a steady job, providing for the material needs of a family—are fading. Today's young men are coming of age in an era with no road maps, no blueprints, and no primers to tell them what a man is or how to become one. Moreover, initiations in Guyland currently have nothing to do with integrity, morality, doing the right thing, swimming against the tide, or standing up for what is right despite the odds. In fact, initiations in Guyland are about drifting with the tide, going along with peer pressure even though you know it's stupid and cruel, enabling or performing sometimes sadistic assaults against those who have entrusted their novice/initiate status into your hands. We need adult men who are deeply involved in boys' lives, otherwise boys turn to each other for initiation into manhood.

Finally, although we have highlighted cultural influences and structural solutions, boys and men individually have a role in transforming themselves and Guyland. One of the archetypes of traditional masculinity is the rebel; the self-made man who rejects outsider influence. How ironic, then, that so many boys and men fall passively into accepting socially constructed and culturally sold standards of behavior. After highlighting the institutionally sold messages and raising consciousness about cultural hegemony, we need to hold men individually accountable for the decisions they subsequently make to either be complicit with or work toward liberation from the hegemonic matrix. For example, using video clips from sitcoms, commercials, and films that highlight the hard sell of hegemonic masculinity can be effective tools for building men's capacity to critique what they consume. Following each clip with appropriate facilitated discussion can model processes necessary for developing self-authorship. Laker (Chapter 4) also provides some practical strategies for taking advantage of the rebel archetype. Our goal is helping guys find a path of emotional authenticity, moral integrity, and physical efficacy, and thereby ease themselves more readily into an adulthood in which they can stand tall.

Conclusion

Men as a category and masculinity as a phenomenon needs to be deconstructed and interrogated as historically, culturally, and ideologically situated. As Brod (1987) argues, "leaving men's lives unexamined leaves male privilege unexamined, and hence more powerful" (p. 272). Learning to recognize and challenge hegemony can both raise individual consciousness and lead to broader social movements that fight oppression, sexism, racism and homophobia. We can no longer rely on dualistic or reductionistic notions of power, privilege, and gender. A critical perspective that incorporates both psychological and sociological aspects of men's development offers the best hope for transforming Guyland.

There are many barriers to such transformation. But just as one can support the troops but oppose the war, so too can one appreciate and support individual guys while engaging critically with the social and cultural world they inhabit. In fact, we believe that only by understanding this world can we truly be empathic to the guys in our lives. Only by understanding this world can we begin to change it.

References

Abbes, E., Jones, S., & McEwen, M. (2007). Reconceptualizing the model of multiple dimensions of identity: The role of meaning-making capacity in the construction of multiple identities. *Journal of College Student Development, 48*, 1–22.

Burg, M., & Zsand Iotarpas, C. (Producers), & Evans, D. M. (Director). (1993). *The sandlot* [Videotape]. USA: 20th Century Fox.

Brannon, R. (1976). The male sex role: Our culture's blueprint of manhood, and what it's done for us lately. In D. D. Brannon & R. Brannon (Eds.), *The forty-nine percent majority: The male sex role* (pp. 1–45). Reading, MA: Addison-Wesley.

Brewer, A. M. (1998). The relationship among gender role conflict, depression, hopelessness, and marital satisfaction in a sample of African-American men (Doctoral dissertation, Kent State University). *Dissertation Abstracts International, 59*, 3049.

Brod, H. (1987). A case for men's studies. In M. S. Kimmel (Ed.), *Changing men: New directions in research on men and masculinity* (pp. 263–277). Thousand Oaks, CA: Sage.

Brookfield, S. D. (2005). *The power of critical theory: Liberating adult learning and teaching.* San Francisco: Jossey-Bass.

Cournoyer, R. J. (1994). A developmental study of gender role conflict in men and its changing relationship to psychological well-being (Doctoral dissertation, Boston College). *Dissertation Abstracts International, 54*, 6476.

Chodorow, N. (1989). *Feminism and psychoanalytic theory.* New Haven, CT: Yale University Press.

Davis, F. (1987). *Antecedents and consequences of gender role conflict: An empirical validation of sex role strain analysis.* Unpublished doctoral dissertation, The Ohio State University, Columbus.

German, L. (1981). Theories of patriarchy. *International Socialism.* http://www.isj.org.uk/index.php4?id=240

Gilligan, J. (1997). *Violence: Reflections on a national epidemic.* New York: Vintage.

Good, G. E., Robertson, J. M., Fitzgerald, L. F., Stevens, M., & Bartels, K. M. (1996). The relation between masculine role conflict and psychological distress in male university counseling center clients. *Journal of Counseling and Development, 75*, 44–49.

Good, G. E., & Mintz, L. M. (1990). Gender role conflict and depression in college men: Evidence for compounded risk. *Journal of Counseling and Development, 69*, 17–20.

hooks, b. (1994). *Teaching to transgress: Education as the practice of freedom.* New York: Routledge.

Johnson, A. G. (1997). *The gender knot: Unraveling our patriarchal legacy.* Philadelphia: Temple University Press.

Jones, S. R., & McEwen, M. K. (2000). A conceptual model of multiple dimensions of identity. *Journal of College Student Development, 41*(4), 405–414.

Kaufman, M. (1999). Men, feminism, and men's contradictory experiences of power. In J. A. Kuypers (Ed.), *Men and power* (pp. 142–164). Halifax, Nova Scotia: Fernwood Books.

Kaufman, G., & Raphael, L. (1996). *Coming out of shame: Transforming gay and lesbian lives.* New York: Broadway Books.

Kimmel, M. (2008). *Guyland: The perilous world where boys become men.* New York: HarperCollins.

Kimmel, M., & Messner, M. (Eds.). (1998). *Men's lives.* Boston: Allyn and Bacon.

Kindlon, D., & Thompson, M. (2000). *Raising Cain: Protecting the emotional life of boys.* New York: Ballantine Books.

Liu, W. M., & Iwamoto, D. K. (2007). Conformity to masculine norms, Asian values, coping strategies, peer group influences and substance use among Asian American men. *Psychology of Men & Masculinity, 8*, 25–39.

Mahalik, J. R., Locke, B. D., Ludlow, L. H., Diemer, M. A., Scott, R. P. J., & Gottfried, M. (2003). Development of the Conformity to Masculine Norms Inventory. *Psychology of Men and Masculinity, 4*, 3–25.

Maher, F., & Tetreault M. K. (2001). *The feminist classroom.* Lanham, MD: Rowman & Littlefield.

McIntosh, P. (2001). White privilege and male privilege: A personal account of coming to see correspondences through work in women's studies. In M. L. Andersen & P. Hill Collins (Eds.), *Race, class, and gender: An anthology* (pp. 98–102). Belmont, CA: Wadsworth.

Meth, R. L., & Pasick, R. S. (1990). *Men in therapy: The challenge of change.* New York: Guilford Press.

O'Neil, J. M. (1990). Assessing men's gender role conflict. In D. Moore & F. Leafgren (Eds.), *Problem-solving strategies and interventions for men in conflict* (pp. 23–38). Alexandria, VA: American Counseling Association.

O'Neil, J. M., Egan, J., Owen, S. V., & McBride, V. (1993). The gender role journey measure: Scale development and psychometric evaluation, *Sex Roles, 28*, 167–185.

O'Neil, J. M., Helms, B. J., Gable, R. K., David, L., & Wrightsman, L. S. (1986). Gender role conflict scale: College men's fear of femininity. *Sex Roles, 14*, 335–350.

Pollack, W. S. (1990). Men's development and psychotherapy: A Psychoanalytic perspective. *Psychotherapy, 27*, 316–321.

Pollack, W. S. (1999). *Real boys: Rescuing our sons from the myths of boyhood.* New York: Holt.

Pollack, W. S., & Shuster, T. (2001). *Real boys' voices.* New York: Random House.

Rounds, D. (1994). *Predictors of homosexual intolerance on a college campus: Identity, intimacy, attitudes toward homosexuals and gender role conflict.* Unpublished Master's thesis, Department of Psychology, University of Connecticut, Storrs.

Sharpe, M. J., & Heppner, P. P. (1991). Gender, gender-role conflict, and psychological well-being in men. *Journal of Counseling Psychology, 38*, 323–330.

Torres, V., Jones, S. R., & Renn, K. A. (2009). Identity development theories in student affairs: Origins, current status, and new approaches. *Journal of College Student Development, 50*(6), 577–596.

Wester, S. R., Vogel, D. L., Wei, M., & McLain, R. (2006). African American men, gender role conflict, and psychological distress: The role of racial identity. *Journal of Counseling and Development, 84*, 419–429.

2

USING THE PSYCHOLOGY OF MEN AND GENDER ROLE CONFLICT THEORY TO PROMOTE COMPREHENSIVE SERVICE DELIVERY FOR COLLEGE MEN

A Call to Action

James M. O'Neil and Bryce Crapser

UNIVERSITY OF CONNECTICUT

A call to action is made in this chapter to the student affairs profession. We advocate for increased campus programming and services for men at colleges and universities. Services and programs for men have not been institutionalized very well in student affairs and higher education. Limited theory and research on men and denial about men's problems have inhibited comprehensive service delivery for men. We critically evaluate the status of men's services in higher education and conclude that a need exists for more expansive programs for men. Moreover, we present theory and research from the psychology of men that justifies these programs. A new conceptual model is presented to explain relationships between college student development theory and the psychology of men. Another model depicts a systematic way to do campus programming and includes 30 thematic areas for psychoeducational programming for men. These models are designed to foster greater campus programming for men and promote more activism by student affairs professionals in delivering these services.

The goals of the chapter are to (a) evaluate the past programming for men in student affairs, (b) discuss why programs for men have not been developed, (c) review recent theory in the psychology of men that could provide a rationale for future programming, (d) document men's personal problems related to gender roles, (e) document empirically that men's problems relate to masculinity ideology and gender role conflict, (f) present a conceptual model that integrates Chickering and Reisser's (1993) identity vectors with concepts in the psychology of men, (g) discuss the contextual dilemmas in doing campus programming, (h) present a preventive and psychoeducational delivery model for providing services for men including 30 programming themes.

Men's Programming (1979–Present): How Well Have We Done?

Campus programming for men dates back to the late 1970s when the Men's Caucus (Scher, Sherrard, Canon, & O'Neil, 1980) and the Standing Committee on Men in American College Personnel Association (ACPA) were first formed. In the late 1970s, the question was how do we make men's issues a central part of student development and student affairs work. Thirty years later this question remains largely unanswered in student affairs. Our own answer to the question is the same as it was 30 years ago. We need data based, theoretically driven, psychoeducational-preventive programs for college men to be systematically implemented by trained student affairs professionals. We feel programming for men has not been developed, and therefore we make a call for action by student affairs professionals.

Evaluating a discipline's performance on service delivery over a thirty year period is a difficult but not an impossible task. If we gave a letter grade to student affairs for their programming for men over the last three decades, what letter grade would we assign? This is a speculative assessment, but in our opinion a C− would probably be very generous. On what criteria do we grade student affairs so low regarding service delivery for men? Based on our literature reviews, we found very few examples of programs for men at colleges and universities in the United States. This lack of service for men stands in stark contrast to what was accomplished for women in the 1980s and 1990s. Most every college and university has a women's center and active programming on women's lives. Furthermore, it appears that very few institutions annually assess men's needs or do systematic programming for men. We found very few empirically tested or validated programs in the literature that specifically help men with their psychosocial development. Moreover, very little theoretical literature exists on how men's issues relate to college student development paradigms. Additionally, we found no examples of student affairs inservice training programs that sensitize college student personnel workers, faculty, administrators, and resident assistants to the hazards of being male during the college years.

We did find a few excellent published papers scattered over the decades in the *Journal of College Student Development* and the *NASPA Journal*. We also found notable exceptions to our low grading of institutional programming for men. Extensive and ongoing programming for men has been institutionalized at Saint John's University, Hobart and William Smith College, and Morehouse College (Kellom, 2004). Nonetheless, there is little theoretical knowledge and empirical research on college men that could justify our call to action for greater services for men. Creating services for men in higher education has been an upstream battle and one wonders why.

Why Has Men's Programming Been So Difficult: Denial, Dubious Assumptions, and Lack of Consciousness About Men

There are numerous explanations why services for men have not been developed at our colleges and universities. First, student affairs professionals may be unaware of how restrictive gender roles and sexism negatively affect men's lives. This unawareness may be caused by a lack of knowledge about men's issues or unconscious denial about men's problems with their socialized gender roles. Admitting that men have problems with gender roles can raise uncomfortable questions about how boys are socialized in families and schools and therefore threaten the patriarchial system. When traditional gender roles are deconstructed and patriarchy, sexism, and destructive capitalism are boldly exposed, it can threaten people's allegiance to traditional gender roles. This kind of threat can produce reactive support of the status quo and denial about obvious problems men experience.

Furthermore, false assumptions about boys and men reinforce our denial about college men's problems. The first assumption is that "boys will be boys," meaning that boys and men develop irresponsible and dysfunctional behavior. Furthermore, these problems are considered normal, expected, and not really that significant. This slogan usually implies that boyhood problems are only short term and remediated as the boy matures in adulthood. The "boys will be boys" assumption is flawed because it reflects only a superficial assessment of boys' lives and does not capture the deeper and unidentified sources of adolescent conflicts. Many boys and men appear normal on the outside, but underneath their defensive masks (Lynch & Kilmartin, 1999) is turmoil, trouble, and gender role conflicts (O'Neil, 2008a,b). Many of boys' unidentified adolescent problems surface in adulthood specifically during the college experience.

Denial is also reinforced by the belief that male behavior is primarily influenced by innate, biological and hormonal development. Those embracing this assumption conclude that you should not interfere with biological imperatives shaping male behavior. For those believing in biological imperatives, psychoeducational programming for college men is unnecessary and could even create unnecessary turmoil. Biology does play a part in a boy's development, but it does not adequately explain how men's problems develop or how to help men cope with their gender role transitions.

Another dubious and sometimes unconscious assumption is that education about gender roles could negatively affect men's gender role identity and sexual orientation. Student affairs educators may erroneously conclude that programs on gender roles can feminize college men at the very time when they are focused on their masculine identities. These conscious or unconscious assumptions are unwarranted and represent confused, uninformed, and sometimes homophobic thinking. Educational programming on men's issues is not specifically focused on sexual orientation nor does it support the femininization of men. Education about gender roles facilitates a young man's positive views of what it means to be a man in terms of healthy character development, maximizing one's human potential, and discerning ways to serve humankind.

The lack of knowledge about men's gender role development is another problem. Many educators and parents may not perceive young men as gendered persons or understand the negative effects of learned gender role stereotypes. Student affairs workers may not understand how boys and young men learn sexist stereotypes and masculinity ideologies at an early age in families, in schools, and with peers. These stereotypes and restrictive masculinity ideologies can produce gender role conflicts (O'Neil, 2008a,b) that negatively affect academic performance, equitable interpersonal relationships, and proactive career planning. Educators may not understand the complex problems that college men face academically and interpersonally without some knowledge about masculinity ideology and gender role conflict.

Another problem that affects developing services for men is a lack of curriculum and programming options to teach men about themselves. Many student affairs workers recognize that men have problems, but do not know how to create psychoeducational and preventive interventions to them. Important information on men's lives and effective ways to do programming have not been fully described in the student affairs literature. Therefore, comprehensive service delivery for men has been underdeveloped on our campuses.

Finally, resistance to programming may come from administrators and other campus leaders. The critics may charge that this kind of programming is too expensive, irrelevant, or does not support the institution's important priorities. As we will document in later sections of the chapter, men's gender role conflicts have been empirically related to serious problems that administrators frequently struggle with. These problems include alcohol abuse, academic dismissal, conduct violations, sexual violence, and male suicide. Men's programming is not just a tangential issue but a central responsibility of any institution committed to educating the whole person.

In summary, knowledge about college men's experiences of being male have been conspicuously absent in higher education. We believe that preventing men's problems on our college and university campuses deserves a call to action. In the subsequent sections of the chapter, we will review theory and research that provides a rationale for this neglected area in student affairs. We also propose conceptual models that may help develop future services for college men.

Do Boys and College Men Really Have Problems?: Statistical Findings

What evidence exists that boys and men have problems? Reviews of the statistics from reliable national sources document the problems that boys and men experience in our society. Consider the following statistical facts about boys and men: (a) boys are three times more likely to be enrolled in a special education class than the typical girl (United States Census Bureau, 2005); (b) 16 % of school-age boys have been diagnosed with attention deficit disorder (Centers for Disease Control, 2005); (c) three times as many boys are expelled from public schools compared to girls (National Center for Education Statistics, 2005); (d)14% of 18- to 24- year-old males are high school dropouts (United States Census Bureau, 2005); (e) 12% of high school boys report being threatened or injured with a weapon on school property (Centers for Disease Control, 2007a); (f) a significantly disproportionate number of males compared to females go through universities' conduct review system because of problematic behavior; (g) college men compared to women spend more time partying, skipping classes, and watching television (Sax, 2008); (h) in a nationwide study, 14% of college men report depression in the past school year; (i) college men on average consume 8.41 drinks per week compared to women's 3.62 drinks per week; (j) 25% of college men report engaging in some type of sexual assault (Fisher, Cullen, & Turner, 2000; Koss, Gidycz, & Wisnieswki, 1987); (k) 75% of deaths of people between 15 and 24 years of age are men; (l) five times as many 15- to 24-year-old males commit suicide compared to females (Centers for Disease Control, 2007b); (m) 95% of state and federal prisoners under the age of 25 are male (Harrison & Beck, 2006). These are sobering data and do not reflect the unreported problems that boys and men have. These data suggest that not every boy is in personal crises, but many young men face significant problems during the first 25 years of life.

The Theoretical Case for Campus Programming: Masculinity Ideology and Masculine Norms, and Gender Role Conflict and Strain

Any call for action to alleviate the male problems delineated above needs established theories or conceptual paradigms about men and masculinity. Theory driven programming is more likely to result in greater understanding and commitment to men's issues on campus. Theory generated over the last two decades in the psychology of men can provide a basis for comprehensive campus programming. Two theoretical areas include masculinity ideology, norms, and conformity and gender role strain, conflict, and stress theory. These concepts have been defined and reviewed more comprehensively elsewhere (O'Neil, 2008a,b, 2010; Pleck, 1981, 1995) and only brief summaries are found below.

Pleck's Gender Role Strain Paradigm

This model describes how restrictive gender roles can be detrimental to psychological health (Garnets & Pleck, 1979; Pleck, 1981, 1995). Pleck (1995) states that violating gender role stereotypes is common and can lead to social condemnation and negative evaluations from others. Additionally, gender roles are psychologically dysfunctional for both sexes in their works and family roles. Pleck specifies three subtypes of male gender role strain: discrepancy strain, trauma strain, and dysfunction strain. *Discrepancy strain* implies that stereotypic gender role standards exist and that individuals attempt to conform to them in varying degrees. Pleck's assumption is that "not conforming to these standards has negative consequences for self esteem and other outcomes reflecting psychological well-being because of negative social feedback as well as internalized negative self judgments" (1995, p. 13). This assumption suggests that nonconformity to masculinity ideology can produce negative feelings in self (gender role self-devaluations) because of people's critical judgments. Second, *gender role trauma strain* results from traumatic experiences during men's gender role socialization that can have serious negative consequences (Pleck, 1995). Gender role trauma has not been fully conceptualized in the literature, but theorists have discussed a boys' separation from mothers and having an absent fathers as traumatizing (Levant, 1995). *Dysfunction strain* is Pleck's third subtype and implies that the fulfillment of masculine gender roles norms can have negative consequences for the man and others. This kind of strain exists when men feel they have to live up to sexist stereotypes in order to be a man. Many times the man has to prove his masculinity to others usually with exaggerated masculine attitudes and behavior that involve hypermasculine and macho presentation of self. When the man exhibits these attitudes and behaviors, they produce stress since many of the stereotypes cannot be fully realized. He becomes dysfunctional with others and experiences emotional stress internally.

Masculinity Ideology, Male Role Norms, and Conformity to Masculine Norms Paradigms

Masculinity ideology represents the primary values and standards that define, restrict, and negatively affect boy's and men's lives (Levant et al., 1992; Mahalik, Good, & Englar-Carlson, 2003; Pleck, 1995; Pleck, Sonenstein, & Ku, 1993; Thompson & Pleck, 1995). Masculinity ideology refers "…to beliefs about the importance of men adhering to culturally defined standards for male behavior" (Pleck, 1995, p. 19). Masculinity ideology is learned when men internalize masculine stereotypes that result in masculine norms and roles (Levant et al., 1992; Thompson & Pleck 1986) and masculine conformity or nonconformity (Mahalik et al., 2003). Masculinity ideologies are restrictive because rigid gender roles produce negative consequences for men and create dysfunctions in their interpersonal relationships. Examples of masculinity ideology include statements like: (a) emotions are feminine and should be avoided; (b) success, status, control, and power are essential to be man; (c) weakness, vulnerability, and intimacy are not masculine and should be avoided; (d) sexual activity is a sign and measure of one's masculinity.

Masculine norms are specific aspects of masculinity ideology. They are standards for how men should act, think, and feel and can restrict a man's behavior in unhealthy and inappropriate ways (Mahalik et al., 2005). Examples of masculine norms from the empirical literature include: status, toughness, anti-femininity/avoidance of femininity, fear and hatred of homosexuals, self-reliance, aggression, obsession with achievement/status, non relational attitudes toward sex, and restrictive emotionality (Levant et al, 1992; Thompson & Pleck, 1986). Conformity to masculine norms is defined as meeting societal expectations of masculinity in one's public or private life whereas nonconformity is not meeting these societal expectations (Mahalik et al., 2003). Mahalik's conformity paradigm is based on both societal and individual men's masculine expectancies that are either accepted (conformity) or rejected (nonconformity). Mahalik et al.'s norms include: winning, emotional control, risk taking, violence, power over women, dominance, playboy, self-reliance, primacy of work, disdain for homosexuals, pursuit of status (Mahalik et al., 2003). Masculine norms and ideologies are important because young college men base their male identity and their presentation of self on these defined standards of behavior.

Gender Role Conflict (GRC) Paradigm and Research

GRC is defined as a psychological state in which socialized gender roles have negative consequences for the person or others. GRC occurs when rigid, sexist, or restrictive gender roles result in restriction, devaluation, or violation of others or self (O'Neil, Good, & Holmes, 1995). The ultimate outcome of GRC is the restriction of a person's human potential or the restriction of another person's potential. GRC is operationally defined by four psychological domains, numerous situational contexts, and three personal experiences. The domains, contexts, and experience of GRC represent the complexity of GRC in people's lives and are defined in earlier publications (O'Neil, et al., 1995; O'Neil, 2008a,b). The psychological domains of GRC imply cognitive, affective, unconscious, or behavioral problems caused by socialized gender roles learned in sexist and patriarchal societies. The four domains of GRC include: cognitive—how we think about gender roles; affective—how we feel about gender roles; behavioral—how we act, respond, and interact with others and ourselves because of gender roles; and unconscious—how gender role dynamics beyond our awareness affect our behavior and produce conflicts (O'Neil et al., 1986; O'Neil et al., 1995). The complexity of these situational contexts can be reduced to four categories: (a) GRC caused by gender role transitions, (b) GRC experienced intrapersonally (within the man), (c) GRC expressed towards others interpersonally, and (d) GRC experienced from others. Recently, the complex dimensions of GRC have been expanded to include seven contextual domains for future research and conceptual analysis (O'Neil, 2008a,b).

Four empirically derived patterns of gender role conflict are: success, power and competition (SPC); restrictive emotionality (RE); restrictive affectionate behavior between men (RABBM); conflict between work and family relations (CBWFR) (O'Neil, 2008a,b; O'Neil, Helm, Gable, David, & Wrightsman, 1986). GRC has been significantly correlated with many psychological and interpersonal problems that produce dysfunction strain and pain in men's lives because of socialized gender roles (O'Neil, 2008a,b).

Research on Boys and Men: The Empirical Case for Campus Programming

A single question is critical in determining whether men's programming is needed and justified on colleges and university campuses. Is there empirical evidence that college men's emotional and psychological problems are related to masculinity ideology and gender role conflict? If evidence exists, what are the implications for student affairs professionals? These questions are addressed below.

A comprehensive review of the literature was completed on empirical research related to masculinity ideology, gender role conflict and stress, and other masculinity constructs (O'Neil, 2010, in press). In the review, the research questions was: Does empirical evidence exist that masculinity ideology, gender role conflict and stress, hypermasculinity, and reference group identity dependence significantly correlate with men's psychological and interpersonal problems?

To answer this question empirical studies that used the following 10 psychology of men measures were reviewed: Masculine Role Norms Scale (MRNS; Thompson & Pleck, 1986), Male Role Norm Inventory (MRNI; Levant et al., 1992), Conformity to Masculine Norm Inventory (CMNI; Mahalik et al., 2003), Masculine Gender Role Stress Scale (MGRS; Eisler, Skidmore, & Ward, 1987), Gender Role Conflict Scale (O'Neil, 2008a,b; O'Neil et al., 1986), Gender Role Conflict Scale for Adolescents (Blazina, Pisecco, & O'Neil, 2005), Adolescent Masculinity Ideology Relationships Scale (Chu, Porche, & Tolman, 2005), Hypermasculinity Inventory (HMI; Mosher & Sirkin, 1984), Auburn Differentiated Masculinity Inventory (ADMI; Burk, Burkhart & Sikorski, 2004), and Reference Group Identity Dependence Scale (RGIDS; Wade & Gelso, 1998).

Table 2.1 summarizes the studies reviewed for the 10 masculinity scales. For each study, every dependent variable that significantly correlated with a masculinity subscale is enumerated. Two hundred and forty-nine studies were reviewed. The summary of the masculinity ideology scales (MRNS, CMNI, & MRNI) indicate that attitudes about masculine norms have been statistically correlated with a wide variety of psychological and interpersonal problems in 26 studies. Over 58 dependent variables related to men's problems have been significantly correlated with masculinity ideology, norms, and conformity.

TABLE 2.1 Men's Psychological and Interpersonal Problem Areas That Significantly Correlated With Ten Measures In the Psychology of Men

1. Pleck's Male Role Norm Scale (MRNS)

Subscales: Status Norm, Toughness Norm, Anti-femininity Norm

Number of Studies = 9

Men's Problems Significantly Correlated with the MRNS:

Negative Attitudes Lesbians; Hostile Sexism; Negative Attitude toward Women; Opposition to the ERA; Preference for Virgin Wife, Ethnic Belonging Suspension from School; Drinking and Use of Drugs; being Picked Up by Police; Being Sexually Active; Coercive Sex, Increased Sexual Risk, Loneliness, Separation-Individuation Problems, Restricted Affectionate Behavior between Men, Fear of Appearing Feminine, Antigay Attitudes, Overt Hostility and Aggression, Adversarial Sexual Beliefs, Rape Myths, Psychological Violence

2. Mahalik's Conformity to Male Role Inventory (CMNI)

Subscales: Winning, Emotional Control, Risk Taking, Violence, Power Over Women, Dominance, Playboy, Self-Reliance, Primacy of Work, Disdain for Homosexuals, Pursuit of Status, Total Conformity

Number of Studies = 13

Men's Problems Significantly Correlated with the CMNI:

Positive Relations With Others, Unhealthy Alcohol Use; Neglecting Preventive Skin Care; Health Screenings; Not Seeking Help With Emotional; Difficulties, Not Going to Health Care Appointments; Getting into Physical Fights; Difficulty Managing Anger; Taking Risks; Risky Behavior With Automobiles & Sexual Practices Substance Use; Marijuana Use; Binge Drinking, Responses to Depression, Health Risks, Few Health Promotion Behaviors, Sexism, Health Promotion Behaviors, Internalized Homophobia; Masculine Body Ideal Distress, Poor Sexual Functioning, Racial Identity: Pre- encounter Phase; Lower Self Esteem; Psychological Distress, Attitudes About Help Seeking, Shocks Given During Competition

3. Levant's Male Role Norms Inventory (MRNI)

Subscales: Avoidance of Femininity; Fear and Hatred of Homosexuals; Self Reliance; Aggression; Achievement/Status; Non Relational Attitudes Toward Sex; Restrictive Emotionality

Number of Studies: 4

Men's Problems Significantly Correlated with the MRNI:

Alexthymia, Negative Attitudes about Racial Identity and Women's Equality; Attitudes toward Condoning Sexual Harassment of Women, Racial Group Marginalization, Ethnocentrism, Negative Attitudes toward Help Seeking

4. Eisler's Masculine Gender Role Stress Scale (MGRSS)

Subscales: Physical Inadequacy; Emotional Inexpressiveness; Subordination to Women; Intellectual Inferiority; Performance Failure

Number of Studies: 10

Men's Problems Significantly Correlated with the MGRSS:

Increases in Systolic Blood Pressure; Impaired Cognitive Performance, Higher State Anger; Negative Intent Attributions; Verbal Aggression, Greater Negative Intent; Greater Irritation, Anger, Jealousy, & Aggression; Anger; Increases in Anxiety; Poorer Health Habits; Greater Systolic Blood Pressure, Lower Work Satisfaction, Negative Attributions & Negative Affect; Verbal Aggression, Alexithymia; Social Support, Overt Hostility and Aggression, Controlling behaviors; Fearful Attachment

5. O'Neil's Gender Role Conflict Scale (GRCS)

Subscales: Success, Power and Competition; Restrictive Emotionality; Restrictive Affectionate Behavior Between Men; Conflict Between Work and Family Relations

Number of Studies: 203

Men's Problems Significantly Correlated with the GRCS:

Self Esteem, Anxiety, Depression, Stress, Shame, Help Seeking Attitudes, Alexithymia, Alcohol and Substance Use and Abuse, Hopelessness, Coping, Psychological Strain, Traditional Gender Role Attitudes, Machismo, Psychological Well Being, Homonegatively, Self Silencing, Body Image, Family Problems, Family Stress, Conduct Problems, Problems With Anger, Physical Strain, Health Risk Taking, Problem Solving Attitudes, Anger, Suicide, Physical Health Problems, Drive for Muscularity, Interpersonal Problems and Competence, Self Disclosure, Shyness, Attachment, Intimacy, Friendship, Marital Satisfaction, Family Enmeshment/ Disengagement, Family Conflict/ Avoidance, Family Cohesion, Fathering Self Efficacy, Parenting Satisfaction, Women's Psychological Health, Women's Depression and Anxiety, Women's Marital Happiness and Adjustment, Women's Negative Affect, Couple's Marital Adjustment & Depressive Symptoms, Gender Role Stereotyping, Stereotypic Beliefs About Man's Emotions, Attitudes Towards Women, Sex Role Egalitarianism, Racial Bias, Attitudes Towards African Americans, Anti-Gay Attitudes & Beliefs, Homophobia, Abusive Attitudes and Behaviors, Hostile Sexism, Hostility Towards Women, Attitudes Toward Sexual Harassment, Rape Myth Attitudes, Dating Violence, Sexual Aggression & Coercion, Men's Entitlement, Victim Blaming, Violence Against Women and Other Men

6. Mosher & Sirkin's Hypermasculinity Inventory (HMI)

Subscales: Violence, Danger, & Calloused Sex

Number of Studies: 1

Men's Problems Significantly Correlated with the HMI:

Self Reported Drug Use, Aggressive Behavior, Dangerous Driving Following Alcohol Consumptions, Delinquent Behaviors During High School Years.

(continued)

TABLE 2.1 Continued

7. Burk, Burkhart & Sikorksi's Auburn Differential Masculinity Inventory (ADMI)

Subscales: Hypermasculinity, Sexual identity, Dominance & Aggression, Conservative Masculinity, Devaluation of Emotion

Number of Studies: 3

Men's Problems Significantly Correlated with the ADMI:

Hostility Toward Women, Antisocial Practices, Negative Self-esteem, Sensation Seeking, Anxiety, Anger, Contempt, Acceptance of Interpersonal Violence, Beliefs that Women are Manipulators, Hedonism, Not Loving, Social Acceptance, Dominance, Sexual Competence, Consensual Sexual Experiences, Ignoring Partner's Protests to Obtain Sex, Use of Low Physical Force to Obtain Sex, Desired Orgasms Per Week, Number of Sexual Partners, Likelihood to Use Force to Obtain Sex, Likelihood to Commit Rape, Negative Sexual Satisfaction.

8. Wade and Gelso's Reference Group Identity Scale (RGIDS)

Subscales: Reference Group Nondependent, No Reference Group, Reference Group Dependent

Number of Studies: 3

Men's Problems Significantly Correlated with the RGIDS:

Identity Diffusion, Social Anxiety, Low Self-Esteem, Anxiety, Depression, Negative Attitudes About Racial Diversity & Women's Equality, Positive Attitudes Toward Sexual Harassment, Health Related Behaviors, and Personal Wellness.

9. Chu, Porche, & Tolman's Adolescent Masculinity Ideology Relationships Scale (ADMI)

Single Scale: Adolescent Masculinity Ideology in Relationships

Number of Studies: 1

Boy's Problems Significantly Correlated with the ADMI:

Restrictive Emotionality, Inhibited Affection, Exaggerated Self Reliance, Negative Attitudes Toward Women, Low Self-esteem, Acting Out, Gender Role Conflict, Need for Achievement and Success, Restrictive Affectionate Behavior Between Men, Status and Anti-femininity Norms, Engaging in Sexual Relations

10. Blazina, Pisecco, and O'Neil's Gender Role Conflict Scale for Adolescents (GRCS-A)

Subscales: Restricted Affection Between Men, Restrictive Emotionality, Conflict Between Work, School, & Family; Need for Success and Achievement

Number of Studies: 2

Boy's Problems Significantly Correlated with the GRCS-A:

Emotional, Family, & Anger Management Problems, Conduct Problems, Family Stress, Emotional & Psychological Stress, Masculinity Ideology, Anti-femininity Norms, Sexual Relations.

Adapted with permission from Altmaier, E. M., & Hansen, J. C. (Eds.) (2010). *The Oxford Handbook of Counseling Psychology*. New York: Oxford University Press.

A similar pattern is evident with the GRCS and MGRSS studies. The 10 MGRSS studies correlated with 19 dependent variables and the 203 GRCS studies correlated with 87 separate indices of men's personal and interpersonal problems. The four studies using hypermasculinity scales (HMI & ADMI) indicate that extremes in masculinity ideology are significantly correlated with 25 negative variables. Furthermore, three studies using the RGIDS found relationships between reference group status and eight male problems. Finally, three studies using the GRCS-A and ADMI indicated that masculinity problems and GRC relate to 17 negative outcomes for adolescent boys.

The results in Table 2.1 represent the first summary of empirical research that indicates that masculinity ideology and masculine gender role conflict/ stress significantly correlates with men's psychological and interpersonal problems. A careful study of Table 2.1 reveals some sobering associations between specific masculinity constructs and dysfunctional problems for men and boys. The results of the 249 studies in Table 2.1 provide a rather convincing case that the operationalized aspects of the masculinity construct have significant relationships to men's and boy's psychological and interpersonal problems.

These findings are important because until recently empirical research has not confirmed that men's psychological problems relate to masculinity constructs. The "hazards of being male" is no longer just a title of a once popular paperback (Goldberg, 1977), but a documented scientific finding in the research. One thing is known now empirically that wasn't known before: operationalized aspects of masculinity constructs predict the hazards of being male. The male gender role is dangerous to men's emotional and interpersonal health. This has never before been empirically documented. These findings need to be seriously considered by student affairs professionals who work with men.

Integrating Chickering and Reisser's Identity Vectors With Masculinity Ideology and Gender Role Conflict Theoretically and Empirically

Another issue to address in this call to action for campus professionals is the theoretical link between the psychology of men and student development theory. As mentioned earlier, how men's problems relate to student development theories is conspicuously absent in the literature. The link between men's documented problems and student development theory needs to be established. The critical question is how can this link be made? Chickering and Reisser's (1993) identity vectors of student development, one of the seminal works in the field, are clearly relevant to the masculinity constructs reviewed earlier and to any service delivery model for college men. Chickering and Reisser indicate that the broad conceptual nature of the vector model allow practitioners "... the option of putting their own understanding and interpretation into it and applying it within their own contexts (p. 44). The context we used in this chapter with the vector model is college men's masculinity ideologies and gender role conflict.

The seven identity vectors are well known by student affairs practitioners and include: (a) developing competence, (b) managing emotions, (c) moving through autonomy toward independence, (d) developing mature interpersonal relationships, (e) establishing identity, (f) developing purpose, and (g) developing integrity. Developing optimal student development outcomes with Vectors 1–4 result in gains in personal identity, purpose, and integrity in Vectors 5–7. These vectors, although well known, have not been fully operationalized in terms of how they relate to psychological and emotional growth. Furthermore, how gender role socialization and sexist attitudes and values affect these identity vectors has gone unexplored. Therefore, we provide theoretical explanations that may help connect college student development theory with the psychology of men and male gender role socialization.

The identity development vectors are conceptually related to the psychology of men by two assumptions: (a) men who endorse restrictive masculinity ideology or experience gender role conflicts experience greater problems developing competence, managing emotions, moving from autonomy to interdependence, and developing mature relationships (Vector 1–4); (b) men who endorse restrictive masculinity ideology or experience gender role conflicts have greater problems establishing their identities and developing purpose and integrity (Vectors 5–7).

The seven developmental issues in the vector model are more difficult to accomplish if you are sexist, experiencing gender role conflict or living out a restrictive masculinity ideology. The seven identity vectors are discussed below in the context of the masculinity ideology, masculine norms, and gender role conflict defined earlier in the chapter. Our integration of the vector model with the psychology of men concepts includes: (a) definition of the identity vector, (b) explanations of how masculine norms and GRC conceptually relate to the vector, (c) research from Table 2.1 that directly or indirectly links men's identity development with men's gender role problems. Theory and empirical evidence that connects gender role conflict and masculinity ideology to Chickering and Reisser's (1993) identity vectors is critical to develop a full rationale for any call to action for expanding men's services on campus.

Developing Competence

Risk taking, self-trust, and facing fears about failure are all important in developing competence. When you feel competent, you experience positive self-esteem and like yourself. Developing competence requires managing feedback from others without defensiveness and being able to share power and personal control. Confidence in one's skills develops if the young man is open to growth and not defensive about it. Numerous masculinity norms and gender role conflicts can negatively affect the development of competence. Table 2.1 enumerates some of the masculine norms and gender role conflicts from the psychology of men that may negatively affect competence including: performance failure, physical inadequacy, intellectual inferiority, winning, pursuit of status, achievement/status, success/power/competition, and the need for success and achievement.

Competence is more difficult to develop if a young man experiences these masculinity problems or conflicts. Furthermore, failure is the opposite of competence and can cause shame and humiliation. A man who has rigid and restrictive masculinity ideology and believes that "real men" should never fail will struggle with developing competence and gaining confidence. Furthermore, everyone fails at something along the way to adult maturity and experiences strong emotions. Men who believe that emotions are feminine are likely to avoid feelings related to failure. No one can process failures and develop competence without managing their emotions. Dealing with the fears of failure requires processing emotions without feeling emasculated or diminished.

Competence is also difficult to achieve if you are obsessed with proving your masculinity (Kimmel, 2006) through always winning, succeeding, and being in control. Competence also relates to how men feel about their intellectual abilities, physical strength, and body image. Distortions about any of these may cause a false sense of self by under estimating or over estimating one's physical and intellectual abilities. These kinds of gender role conflicts may contribute to a man's masculine façade and interpersonal distance. Defensiveness may occur to mediate any threats to competence or one's masculine identity. Psychosocial development is difficult for college men under these circumstances and therefore a potential area for intervention for college student development professionals.

Research demonstrates that masculinity ideology and gender role conflict relate to issues of developing competence. Both GRC and restrictive male norms have been significantly correlated with lower self-esteem. Gender role conflict/stress research has also been significantly correlated with impaired cognitive performance, ineffective problem solving attitudes, and negative attitudes toward help seeking. All of these have implications for developing competence or at least being open to increasing one's self-efficacy.

Managing Emotions

The ability to label, experience, and express feelings and responding to other people's feelings in effective ways is what managing emotions is about. Managing emotions may be difficult for men whose masculinity ideology includes devaluing feelings because affect is considered feminine. Restrictive emotionality is a primary source of male anxiety, depression, stress, and substance abuse (O'Neil, 2008a,b). Recognizing that emotions are human and necessary for effective functioning is one of the most important milestones to male maturity. Constructs in the psychology of men related to managing emotions include emotional control, restrictive emotionality, emotional inexpressiveness, devaluation of emotions, and alexthymia (see Table 2.1).

The emotionally controlled and inexpressive man deprives himself of feelings needed to discover personal truths that promote identity development. The ability to label, experience, and express emotions is critical to any growth processes, particularly during the college years. Strong emotions like anger, fear, hurt, longing, boredom, anxiety, anger, depression, guilt, and shame can disrupt a man's learning processes. No one can study or grow if they are experiencing these heavy emotions. When these feelings go unexpressed and accumulate over time, emotions can be overwhelming and disruptive of sleep and daily problem solving. College men who endorse a restrictive masculinity ideology by saying that "everything is okay" even if they are in pain and suffering, are at high risk for emotional and interpersonal problems. Emotional intelligence is needed to process feelings before they negatively affect the learning process or spoil important relationships. College men need to recognize that emotions are not masculine or feminine but human qualities that need to be courageously faced. Unfortunately, many men come to campus with deficits in emotional intelligence at the very time when they need to face feelings that can help them with identity development, maturity, and academic achievement.

Empirical research indicates that GRC and restrictive masculinity ideologies correlate with significant emotional problems (see Table 2.1). In terms of managing emotions, GRC has been correlated with depression in 25 studies. Eight studies have shown that anxiety and stress are related to gender role conflict. Gender Role Stress has been correlated with increases in systolic blood pressure, higher states of anger, verbal aggression, and increases in anxiety, negative affect, alexithymia, overt hostility and aggression. Furthermore, masculinity ideology and norms have been correlated with difficulty in managing anger, psychological distress, and alexithymia. The gender role research on men's emotional problems provides convincing evidence that justifies special programs for men during the college years.

Moving From Autonomy to Interdependence

Autonomy implies developing self-sufficiency, choosing your goals responsibly, and having less dependence on other's opinions, by discerning your own truths. Autonomy is the development of self-reliance and being emotionally and behaviorally on your own. Interdependence means that there is awareness of the limits to self-reliance because we all depend on each other in important ways. Two masculinity measures in Table 2.1 have self-reliance subscales that are theoretically related to the autonomy and interdependence identity vector. Furthermore, resolving problems with parental attachment or separation issues are important to develop autonomy. The young man works through the need for approval from parents and other authority figures and affirms himself as well as learns how to solve his own problems. Additionally, interdependence is recognized as a necessary and important part of life. None of us can do everything alone and the maturing man recognizes that we are all connected and interdependent.

When reliance on others is viewed as masculine weakness, healthy autonomy and interdependence become difficult to develop. Furthermore, positive attitudes toward help seeking are difficult to develop when autonomy and interdependence questions go unresolved. Men do not seek help as often as women because of unresolved issues with autonomy and interdependence. Furthermore, some men have stigmatized help seeking and believe that needing assistance with life's problems is not masculine. Macho self-reliance and denial about inevitable interdependence can be barriers to identity development and men's growth during the college years.

Masculinity ideology and GRC have not directly been correlated with autonomy and interdependence. They have been indirectly connected through negative attitudes towards help seeking, problems with attachment to parents, and negative problem solving attitudes. For example, gender role conflict has been correlated with negative attitudes toward help seeking attitudes in 16 studies. Ineffective problem solving attitudes have been correlated with GRC in two studies. Eleven studies have significantly correlated gender role conflict to problems with attachment to mothers and fathers in terms of separation, individualization, dis-identification, and conflictual independence. Gender role stress has also been correlated with fearful attachments and finally masculine norms have significantly correlated with negative attitudes toward help seeking and separation and individualization problems. Overall, the collective evidence suggests that masculinity issues have been correlated with critical issues related to autonomy and interdependence.

Developing Mature Relationships

Mature interpersonal relationships imply appreciating individual differences and having capacities for human intimacy with others. Numerous masculinity concepts in Table 2.1 negatively affect developing mature relationships. These include antifemininity norms, power over women, dominance, playboy, disdain for homosexuals, avoidance of femininity, fear and hatred of homosexuals, non relational attitudes toward sex, subordination of women, success/power/ competition, restrictive affectionate behavior between men, dominance, and aggression. Boys and men's restrictive gender role socialization can contribute to this long list of negative attitudes toward others. Therefore, GRC and masculinity ideology are central to understanding men's problems with other men, women, gay, lesbian and bi-sexual people, and racial minorities.

Empathy, altruism, and acceptance of others are critical parts of developing mature relationships. Accepting people for who they are, free from stereotypes, in both the interpersonal or intercultural realms requires an emerging sense of self-identity. Furthermore, not accepting others who deviate from masculine and feminine norms because of their age, sexual orientation, race, and ethnicity can result in discriminatory attitudes that are devaluing and hostile towards others. Under these conditions, developing mature interpersonal relationships is nearly impossible and likely to produce sexist, racist, homophobic, and ethnocentric interpersonal interactions that can produce conflict, abuse, harassment, and even violence.

The capacity for intimacy in mature relationships implies making commitments based on honesty, responsiveness, and unconditional positive regard. Intimacy does not imply dominance or dependency but the development of interdependence between two equals. There is an acceptance of each other's flaws and personal assets and a commitment to long term relationships that last through difficulties and separations. Masculinity ideology and norms that conform to rigid stereotypes of masculinity and femininity can inhibit the development of capacities for intimacy in relationships. Celebrating diversity means appreciating the diversity of human beings. When this happens, mature relationships flourish and enrich people's lives. Furthermore, this appreciation helps reduce stereotypic biases, ethnocentric values, and racist attitudes that oppress people and human communities.

Many studies indicate that gender role conflict is correlated with difficulties in relationships including poor interpersonal functioning, marital/relationship dissatisfaction, problems with intimacy, limited self-disclosure, spousal criticism, stereotypic thinking towards women, homophobic and anti-gay attitudes, and negative attitudes toward African Americans (see Table 2.1 and O'Neil, 2008a,b). Twenty-two studies have shown that GRC has been correlated with men's negative or violent attitudes toward women including positive attitudes toward sexual harassment, rape myths, hostile sexism, and self-reported sexual and dating violence. Gender role stress has been correlated with greater irritation with others, anger, jealousy, and controlling behaviors.

A similar pattern of research is found with masculinity ideology and norms. A restricted view of masculinity has been correlated with men's anti-gay attitudes, positive attitudes toward sexual harassment, rape myths, hostile sexism, negative attitudes toward women, negative attitudes toward lesbians, coercive sex, overt hostility, aggression, adversarial sexual beliefs, psychological violence, getting into physical fights, internalized homophobia, and poor sexual functioning. These research studies are sobering and help explain how men's gender role socialization relates to emotional abuse, sexual violence, and men's victimization of others.

Developing Identity, Purpose, and Integrity

The first four vectors for student development are critical in establishing purpose, integrity, and identity (Vectors 5–7). There is also a theoretical connection between Vector 5–7 and masculinity constructs. All of the masculinity ideology and GRC issues that affect Vectors 1–4 significantly affect the development of purpose, integrity, and identity. *Developing Purpose* includes setting goals and being intentional with relationships, career plans, and one's family and community. Integrity is closely related to establishing purpose by internalizing humanistic values and ethical standards. This means mediating rigid and uncompromising gender role beliefs about life and having congruence between one's personal values and socially responsible behavior. *Integrity* involves principled thinking that mediates conflicts between personal self-interests and other people's needs. Personal values and beliefs are expressed when respecting other people's points of view. *Establishing overall identity,* according to Chickering and Reisser (1993), relates to many issues that have gender role implications including comfort with body and appearance, gender and sexual orientation, self-concept, self-understanding, self-acceptance, self-esteem, understanding one's sexuality, family of origin, ethnic, religious, and cultural heritage. All of these issues can be directly tied to masculinity constructs in one way or another.

Summary of the Seven Identity Vectors and Developmental Directions

In summary, there is substantial theoretical overlap between Chickering's and Reisser's (1993) identity vectors and the emerging concepts in the psychology of men. Over 25 different masculinity constructs were theoretically reviewed that relate to the first four identity vectors for college students. Furthermore, the empirical research reviewed does support the idea that masculine ideology and gender role conflict/stress are significantly correlated with the developmental directions of Chickering and Reisser's (1993) identity vectors. Clearly, the masculinity constructs in the psychology of men are theoretically and empirically related to identity outcomes and strongly support any call for action for increase campus programming for men.

Conceptual Paradigm to Understand Male College Students: Integrating the Psychology of Men and Chickering and Reisser's Identity Vectors

In this section, the theory and research in the psychology of men reviewed earlier are integrated with Chickering and Reisser's (1993) identity vectors with a single conceptual paradigm. This conceptual paradigm represents a new way to understand college men in the student development literature. Furthermore, the paradigm provides a conceptual framework to organize our call to action for comprehensive campus programming for men.

Figure 2.1 shows six conceptual areas from the psychology of men that are theoretically related to college men's gender role identity and Chickering and Reisser's (1993) seven identity vectors shown at the bottom of the paradigm. The directional and bi-directional arrows in Figure 2.1 imply complexity with college men's masculinity dynamics and require thinking outside of the status quo's view of college student development. Each arrow implies possible educational programming possibilities as well as empirical research on college men.

At the top of the conceptual paradigm, the larger patriarchal society, sexism, and stereotypes are shown as organizers of society. Patriarchy instills sexist values and stereotypes that influence how men relate women, other men, and themselves. With society organized this way, it is not surprising that men come to campus with distorted or ambivalent view of masculinity, femininity, and themselves. In the top-right corner of Figure 2.1, men's gender role socialization and specifically, the masculinity ideology and norms are shown. As documented earlier (see Table 2.1), narrow, rigid, and sexist masculinity ideologies represent significant emotional and interpersonal problems for boys and men.

Gender- role identity, construed as a subset of Chickering and Reisser's (1993) overall notion of human identity, is shown as the dominant issue for college men. All six of the conceptual areas impact college men's gender role identity. Gender role identity is the "Who am I, as a man" question that consciously or unconsciously emerges during adolescence and the college experience. Gender role identity is formed by many factors, but the patriarchal system and men's socialization in families and schools are significant contributors. Masculine gender-role identity is defined as a man's total conception of his masculine roles, values, functions, expectations, and belief system (O'Neil & Nadeau, 1999). This includes how biological sex, social learning, and stereotypes of masculinity and femininity shape the man's sense of self over the lifespan. Masculine gender role identity is everything that the man says and does that communicate his masculine and feminine dimensions. Men have both a conscious and unconscious aspect of their masculine gender role identities. Consequently, coming to terms with masculine identity can be difficult, elusive, and confusing. This makes campus programming for men critical and an important part of student affair's mission.

Gender role identity is continually shaped by the many interacting and socializing dynamics shown in the paradigm. Distorted gender-role schemas develop from masculinity ideologies and norms learned in our sexist society. Distorted gender-role schemas are exaggerated thoughts and feelings about the role of masculinity and femininity in a man's life. Boys and men internalize these distortions when they learn stereotypes of restrictive masculinity ideology from society, in families, and from peers. Distortions occur when a man experiences

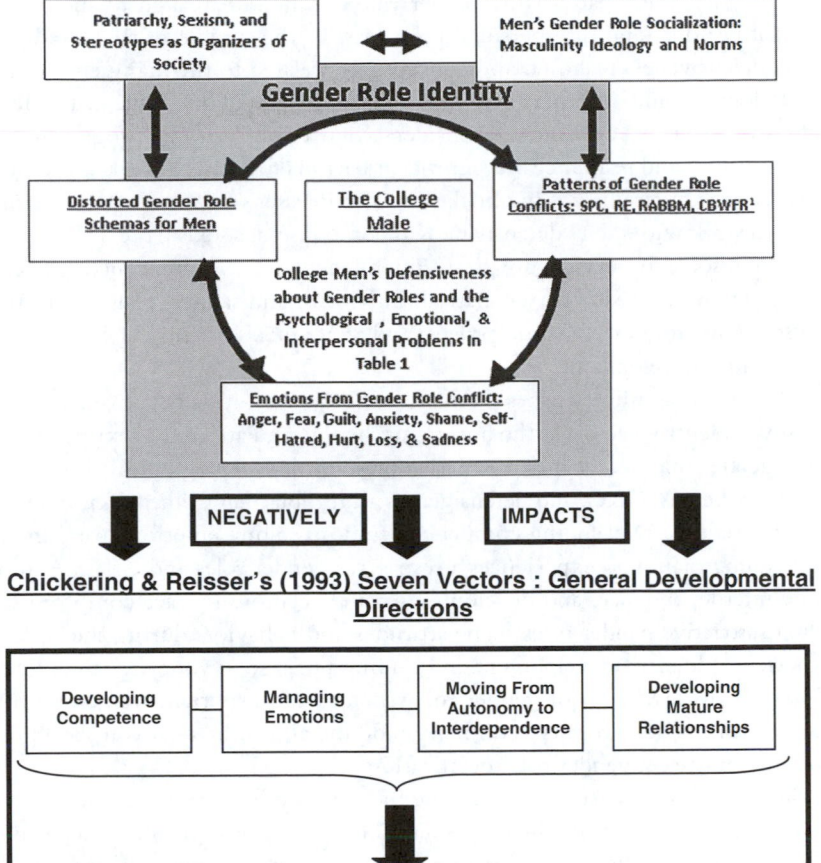

[1]SPC = Success, Power, Competition; RE=Restrictive Emotionality; RABBM=Restrictive Affectionate Behavior Between Men; CBWFR = Conflict Between Work and Family Relations

FIGURE 2.1 A conceptual paradigm explaining college men's gender role conflict impacting seven developmental vectors.

an intense pressure to meet stereotypic notions of masculinity and prove his masculinity (Kimmel, 2006). This results in fears and anxieties about not measuring up to traditional gender-role expectations (O'Neil & Nadeau, 1999).

On the right side of Figure 2.1, the four patterns of GRC are shown including success, power, and competition (SPC), restrictive emotionality (RE), restrictive affectionate behavior between men (RABBM), and conflict between work and family relations (CBWFR). The research in Table 2.1 provides strong evidence that these patterns of gender role conflict are related to men's significant personal and interpersonal problems. In the middle of the paradigm, men's defensiveness is shown and conceptually related to the many emotional, psychological, and interpersonal problems enumerated in Table 2.1. Men's defensiveness is a key issue to consider when doing campus programming. Defensiveness and resistance are significant barriers for men to work through as they face the critical issues in Chickering and Reisser's (1993) identity vectors. How to work with men's defensiveness and unconscious sexism are challenging issues to resolve for service providers. Finally, negative emotions, such as anger, fear, guilt, anxiety, shame, self-hatred, hurt, loss, and sadness result from this sexist gender-role socialization process and affect men's developmental growth and identity development.

All of the masculinity issues on the top of Figure 2.1 have negative effects on the seven identity vectors at the bottom of the figure. Patriarchy, sexism against men, gender role stereotypes, restrictive masculinity ideologies, distorted gender role schemas, GRC, and defensiveness all inhibit men from working on the identity vectors. Developing competence and managing emotions are difficult for a young man who experiences a restrictive gender roles and GRC. Autonomy, interdependence, and developing mature relationships are compromised when restrictive gender roles shape attitudes and behaviors during the college experience. Identity development and finding purpose in your life are difficult if you are distorting major gender role schemas and experiencing gender role conflict. Likewise, integrity is difficult to define and embrace if you are a prisoner to your sexist gender role socialization.

Student affairs workers can examine the utility of this paradigm in advancing any call to action for helping men. The costs are high for college men who drop out of school, receive disciplinary actions, or who commit acts of sexual and personal violence, including suicide. Furthermore, the great costs to women as victims need to be fully realized in the context of concepts in Figure 2.1. The paradigm is one way to conceptualize men's problems and potentialities as well as a coherent way to justify expanded programming for college men.

Complexities and Dilemmas with Men's Programming: Gender Role Transitions, Power Loss, Help Seeking, and the Politics of Gender

Any call to action for men's services will encounter complexities, dilemmas and challenges. The first issue is accepting that college men experience gender role transitions when they leave high school and enter college life. Gender role transitions are events in a man's gender role development that alter or challenge his gender role self-assumptions and consequently produce gender role conflict or positive life changes (O'Neil & Egan 1992b). Coming to college is a major gender role transition for most men because they have to adjust to a new campus environment and redefine themselves usually without the full support of close family and friends. One aspect of the transition is experiencing significant losses of power when leaving high school and entering college. Capraro (2000) discusses the paradoxes of masculinity and power loss for college men. He indicates that men are supposed to be powerful, but feel powerless as they cope with the transition from high school to college. Losses in power are experienced because in high school many college bound men have achieved status, success, a sense of pride and accomplishment. Coming to college means losing some of this status and being reduced to a lower male status as a student. This lower status coupled with an unfamiliar campus environment, no established peer group, and distant family support can be unsettling to many young men.

Men's loss of power and control need to be understood in the context of college men's transitional identity problems. Some men may be defensive to their power and control losses experiencing emotional and interpersonal turmoil. The gender related and emotional problems in Table 2.1 and Figure 2.1 are relevant to these transitional and power loss issues. Restrictive masculine norms may be used as a defense to cope with the problems and transitions. This may mean a greater allegiance to traditional gender roles since this is usually what young men have been told brings success and happiness. Freshmen and sophomore students may be particularly vulnerable as they are challenged to recreate themselves in terms of their identity and self-presentation.

The transition dilemma is compounded when men have negative attitudes about seeking help. One of the most consistent findings in the psychology of men is that negative attitudes about help seeking are correlated with masculinity ideology and GRC. Nineteen studies indicate that gender role conflict has been significantly correlated with negative attitudes towards seeking help (O'Neil, 2008a,b). Men have significant problems with transitions and loss but have negative attitudes toward seeking help. Many young men need, help but their restrictive masculine ideology keeps them from seeking it. This makes campus programming complex and challenging. College men's negative attitudes towards help seeking needs to be discussed if programming is to be successful. Providing information, services, and support is one thing, but getting men to use these resources is quite another.

Another potential problem is obtaining support from student affairs staffs for men's services. Administrators may not see the relevance of men's services or have unresolved GRC issues themselves that result in "lukewarm" support of campus programming for men. As mentioned earlier, denial about men's problems or a lack of information can also be significant barriers to funding and comprehensive service delivery for men.

Furthermore, the politics of gender may be a deterrent to comprehensive campus programming. Opposition may come from both feminists and traditionalists because of their respective political ideologies about gender roles. Nonfeminists who support traditional gender roles may reject initiatives for men because it violates their fundamental and essentialist beliefs that traditional gender roles should be retained and not deconstructed. Feminist women may worry that men's services will resurrect and reinforce a sexist system that has devalued women or diminish women's services that have developed over the last four decades. There may be a "knee jerk reaction" against developing services for men. Questions may be asked like: What about the serious problems that women face on campus? Haven't most student services been designed for men by men?

The politics of gender are likely to be stimulated when expanded services for men become a focused and serious possibility. At this point, men's advocates need to use sound theory and research to make their points and focus their arguments. There needs to be full support for services for women and other oppressed groups on campus. The truth is that services for women have helped men define their gender role identities and expanded services for men can do the same for women. Viewing services for men and services for women as separate, unrelated, and unequal is outdated and counter productive. Problems between men and women have a common oppressive source: sexism against people and the oppression of both sexes. These political issues need to be sensitively managed if we are to do better in the next 30 years with our service delivery for both men and women. Whether we can get through these difficult discussions and increase services for both men and women is a true sign of our maturity as a profession. We do not need more divisive gender politics but alliances that will expand services for both genders.

Men's Service Delivery Model for Colleges and Universities: Prevention and Psychoeducation

Based on the theory, research, and the dilemmas mentioned above, we recommend that comprehensive services be developed using prevention concepts (Albee & Gullotta, 1997) and psychoeducation (O'Neil, 2001). Primary and secondary prevention interventions can help men journey with their gender roles (O'Neil & Egan, 1992) by exploring their sexist stereotypes. Primary prevention interventions focus on healthy or vulnerable people at risk and seek to reduce risk factors and increase protective factors. This kind of prevention is ecological, systematic, culturally sensitive, collaborative, and empowering (Conyne, 2004). Given that some men already have problems with sexism and their gender roles, secondary and tertiary prevention interventions may also be relevant to any campus delivery model.

Psychoeducation is a pedagogical approach that uses psychological and learning principles to promote emotional and intellectual development of students (O'Neil, 2001). This approach emphasizes both cognitive and affective processes, meaning that feelings and emotions have equal weight with conceptual and factual knowledge. Psychoeducation uses experiential learning, interactive learning, media, music, and self-disclosures to focus learning on the affective domain. This means that emotions are activated to better internalize course content and promote personal growth. Psychoeducation also focuses on how student resistance and defenses may operate during learning. In the case of campus programming for men, this means dealing with defensiveness as gender roles are examined and deconstructed. Psychoeducation provides unique learning possibilities because the teaching process is designed to raise psychological and emotional issues that prompt personal exploration and growth.

Our call to action includes a systematic model for delivering services for men. The model can serve as a template for developing ongoing, theoretically driven, empirically based programming and services for men. Figure 2.2 depicts a conceptual model for service delivery. At the top of Figure 2.1 is a three-step process that includes: Step 1: Initial Development of the Delivery Model; Step 2: Levels of Delivery Interventions; and Step 3: Maintenance of the Delivery Model. These three steps are described in more detail below.

Step 1—Initial Development of Delivery Model

Assessment of men's need for potential services is the first activity in developing any service delivery model. The purpose of needs assessment is to understand men as a target population in terms of attitudes, problems, potentials, and preferred modes of learning. The data could be gathered at Freshmen Orientation using questionnaires or through focus groups. Data gathered on upper classmen

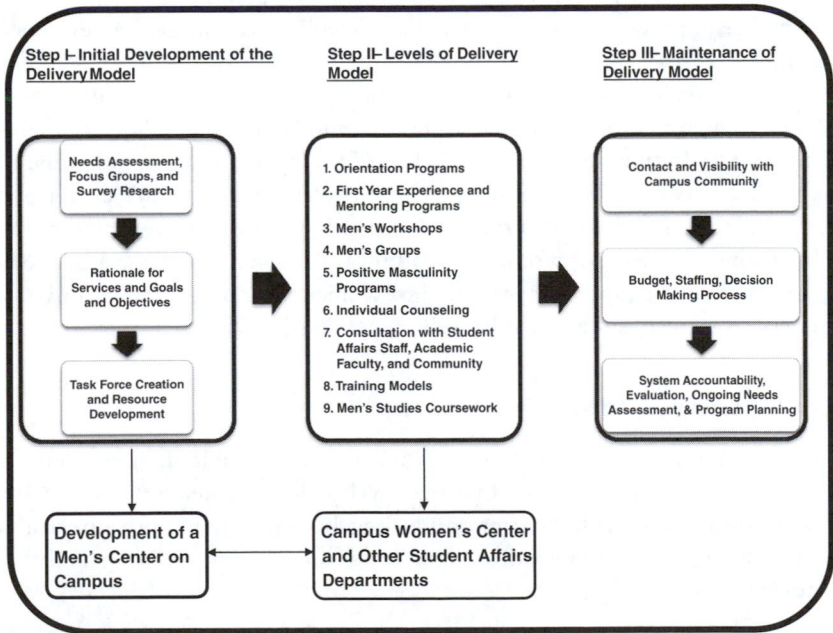

FIGURE 2.2 Men's programming delivery model.

could be gathered by resident assistants or through online surveys. Questions could ask about problem areas, needs, and the kind of programs that interest men. Data needs to be gathered on men from all races, ethnicities, nationalities, sexual orientations, and cultural backgrounds to insure that programs are relevant to the multiple masculinity ideologies present on most campuses. Needs assessment data about men's issues could also be gathered on student affairs staff and faculty. In this way, needs assessment could document the professional training needs of those who provide services for men.

After the needs assessment data is analyzed, a task force on men's services could be convened. Ideally, campus models would be created by a task force or committee on men's services and programming. The task force would work together over a period of years and use the needs assessment data to develop measurable goals and objectives. Goals should be stated in both a short- and long-term ways.

Furthermore, men's resource development needs to be considered. The task force would decide the necessary personnel and educational resources needed to implement the delivery model. Programmers would write cogent rationales and data based proposals that document men's programming needs using both the psychology of men and student development theory. In this chapter we summarized some theory and empirical research using Chickering and Reisser's (1993) identity vectors to justify our call to action. Other theories and paradigms should be developed. Presenting sound theory, research findings, and needs assessment data can help bring a powerful legitimacy to men's programming.

Another important question is whether a men's center should be developed on campus (Davies, Shen-Miller, & Isacco, in press). The justification for a center could be made using the needs assessment data and the theory and research in the psychology of men. A men's center would be a central place to implement services for men described in Step 2 of the delivery model. The line in Figure 2.2 between the proposed men's center and the women's center and student affairs staff implies that the men's center would be directly connected to women's programming and other services in student affairs. Alliances between men's center staff and those committed to women's issues are a critical part of any service delivery system that helps both genders.

Step II—Levels of Delivery Interventions

The second step in the delivery model includes the possible interventions for men's services on campus. The first five levels of service delivery are specific ways to do campus wide programming. Levels 6–9 include both direct and indirect services for men including counseling, consultation, training, and academic coursework.

Men's programming levels and positive-healthy masculinity emphasis. Programs during Freshmen Orientation and the First Year

Experience could help students manage the high school to college transition mentioned earlier. Additionally, organized mentoring programs could include information about being male and the specific problem areas that men experience during the college transition. Men's groups can be developed to critically engage and educate men on the complexities of growing up male. Numerous authors have provided ways to develop groups for men (Andronico, 1995). The challenge is to match men's documented needs to program content that is useful and effective.

Masculine gender roles are sensitive topics for young men and therefore resistance to attending programs is to be expected. As reported earlier, negative attitudes toward help seeking have been significantly correlated with GRC. One strategy to attract college men is offering programs on the positive aspects of being male. Ideas about affirming men and positive masculinity are emerging in the psychology of men (Kiselica, in press; Kiselica & Englar-Carlson, in press; Kiselica, Englar-Carlson, Horne, & Fisher, 2008; O'Neil & Lujan, 2009). Paradigms of positive masculinity that describe men's strengths when transcending sexist stereotypes are needed. Patterns of positive masculinity can help men learn alternatives to sexist attitudes and behaviors that cause gender role conflict. Programming could emphasize what constitutes "healthy masculinity." Men's strengths and potentialities could focus on themes like responsibility, courage, altruism, resiliency, service, social justice, positive fathering, perseverance, generativity, protection of others, and nonviolent problem solving. Positive masculinity transcends what is wrong with men by identifying the qualities that empower males to improve themselves and provide service to other people and the larger society. Programs on healthy masculinity could change the overall perception that the psychology of men is about documenting what is wrong with boys and men.

Suggested Programming Areas. The empirical research and theory reported earlier help focus psychoeducational programming for men on campus. Given the likely resistance to men's programming on campus, we recommend that content areas be labeled "Men's Life Skills" rather than exclusively focusing on masculinity ideology or gender role conflict. The life skills label should not stimulate as much resistance or controversy. The initial programming for freshmen and sophomores should emphasize needed life skills, ways to cope with college, help seeking dilemmas for men, and criteria of positive masculinity including affirmation of men's positive potential. With initial success with these life skills programs, issues related to men's vulnerability with GRC could be introduced in the context of male strengths and empowerment. Both process oriented and outcome evaluations are critical to assess how and whether the programs have positive impact over time.

Table 2.2 lists 30 thematic areas for educational programming for college men. The programming areas are ordered to the degree that gender role issues are emphasized. The programming areas include both life skills topics and information about gender roles. Areas 1–8 could be presented with limited emphasis

TABLE 2.2 Thematic Areas to Implement Psychoeducational Programs for College Men

Thematic Areas for Programming	Description
1. Problem Solving Skills	Knowledge about how to identify problems and the specific steps to resolve them in a positive ways
2. Conflict Management Skills	Knowledge about how to work through disagreements using communication, negotiation, and compromise
3. Decision Making & Goal Setting Skills	Knowledge about the steps in decision making and how to create and achieve goals that can be implemented
4. Career Awareness and Planning	Activities that fosters increased career identity and that lead to career decision making skills
5. Help Seeking Dilemmas For Men	Knowledge about the special problems men face seeking help for their problems because of masculine gender role socialization
6. Personal Health Care	Information about how to stay physically and psychologically healthy
7. Stress Management	Knowledge about how to identify personal stressors and skills to mediate the thoughts and feelings that maintain the stres
8. Service Learning, Altruism, Helping Others	Knowledge about the importance of service and altruism in terms of personal growth and development
9. Positive and Healthy Masculinity	Deriving a personal definition of positive and healthy masculinity
10. Assertiveness Skills	Skills on how to use your personal power positively to protect your rights and roles
11. Self Control and Centering	Skills at being able to control thoughts, feelings, and behaviors and the ability to develop inner solidity inside oneself
12. Empathy Skills	Learning how to sensitively respond to other's feelings, thoughts, and experiences in caring ways
13. Listening Skills	The ability to accurately hear and respond to another's person's thoughts and feelings
14. Competition	Knowledge about how to strive against a rival to win or gain something as well as the potential problems with kind of interaction
15. Courage & Resilience	How to learn to face your fears and bounce back from a failure, loss, or defeat
16. Developing Integrity	How to develop a moral or ethical code of conduct to live your life
17. Sensitivity to Social Justice	Knowledge on how discrimination and oppression operate and how to be involved in eradicating social injustices

Thematic Areas for Programming	Description
18. Emotional Awareness & Expression	Knowledge and experiences on how to label, experience, and express emotions appropriately
19. Power in Relationships	How to understand control, authority, influence, and coercion in relationships
20. Understanding Psychological Abuse	How power, control, and words are used to hurt others emotionally
21. Masculinity Ideology	Knowledge about how men and boys learn assumptions about masculinity and sexist stereotypes that limit human potential
22. Patterns of Gender Role Conflict	Knowledge about how restrictive gender roles can produce negative consequences for boys, men, and others.
23. Relationships With Girls & Women	The critical issues with relationships with girls and women in terms of friendships, dating, co-workers, intimacy, and sexual relationships.
24. Relationships With Boys & Men	The critical issues with relationships with other boys and men in terms of friendships, intimacy, teamwork, competition, and homophobia
25. Homophobia & Hetereosexism	Definitions of homophobia and hetereosexism and how they relate to gender role identity and relationship with other men and oneself
26. Sexuality	The critical issues related to sexuality in terms of masculine identity, and intimacy in human relationships
27. Understanding Parents	Knowledge about how to manage the complex dynamics between sons and parents
28. Dealing With Loss	How to deal with losing something or someone important to you in terms of experiencing grief and recovery
29. Fathers and Becoming One	Exploring the relationship with one's father and thinking about this future role in terms of masculinity identity
30. Body Image	How one feels about their muscularity and overall perception of their body

Adapted with Permission from O'Neil & Lujan, 2009, Wiley-Blackwell, Inc., John Wiley & Sons

on masculinity issues. Areas 9–17 are topics where some masculinity issues could be introduced. Areas 18–30 are thematic areas where masculinity would be central to the programming. The 30 thematic areas need to be assessed for their appropriateness for college men based on cognitive complexity, affective ability, ethnic and racial backgrounds, nationality, and overall maturity. How programs are titled matter since research indicates that program names can affect appeal and resistance to attend (Blazina & Marks, 2001; Robertson & Fitzgerald, 1992; Rochlen, McKelley, & Pituch, 2006). Titles like "Exploring Your Masculine Problems" may be immediately rejected, whereas programs such as "Maximizing Your Potential in Careers and Relationships" could catch a college man's curiosity and attention.

Counseling, consultation, training, and teaching. Counseling services are critical resources for men who need help and a primary service for any college or university. Therapists in the counseling center could be trained in the psychology of men. If already knowledgeable about the psychology of men, the counselors could also serve as trainers of others on campus. Consultation with student affairs staffs and academic faculty are critical to any service delivery system. Consultation may be needed to determine what professional content in the psychology of men is essential for student affairs staff and faculty to know. Specific training programs and curricula need to be created and tested for effectiveness with faculty and student affairs staff. Consultation with academic faculty on developing of men's studies courses could bring the delivery model to the classroom. Teaching the psychology of men has been gaining prominence over the last 10 years (O'Neil, 2001, 2004; O'Neil, Addis, Kilmartin, Mahalik, 2004), but other disciplines like sociology, education, religion, and history are also possible areas where courses on masculinity could be offered.

Step III—Maintenance and Evaluation of the Delivery Model

This step includes important activities to keep any delivery model credible and moving forward. Community visibility on and off campus through disseminated research, brochures, radio interviews, and newspaper articles on men are essential to explain the value of men's services. Furthermore, detailed budgets and requests for resources based on the needs assessment and program evaluation data are critical for any sustained effort to implement a service delivery model. Staffing the men's center and involving resident assistants' and hall directors' in program development may require yearly training. The inclusion of men's and women's programming could become part of residence assistant's and hall director job descriptions. Training upper classmen peers to do programming is another excellent strategy to involve students in service delivery for men.

Conclusions, Omissions, Future Directions, and a Personal Invitation

Our call to action includes a historical context to assess men's programming over the last three decades. Some possible reasons why campus programming for men has been slow to develop were discussed. Conceptual knowledge from the psychology of men was briefly reviewed as a theoretical basis for more expansive programs for men. Our call to action documented that men face legitimate and unique challenges and that these problems are empirically related to men's masculinity ideologies and gender role conflict. A conceptual paradigm was presented that links the psychology of men with accepted student development identity vectors (Chickering & Reisser, 1993). We argued that there is direct and indirect empirical evidence indicating that masculinity problems negatively affect college men's identity development. Furthermore, complexities and dilemmas when implementing campus programming for men were discussed. High school to college transitions, losses of male power, defensiveness, and men's negative attitudes toward help seeking make programming challenging but not impossible for student affairs professionals. A comprehensive service delivery model was presented to stimulate more campus programming. This model recommends data gathering, resource development, program development, and the training of campus professionals to help implement expanded services for men.

In numerous ways our call for action falls short. Specific programming contexts for men from different races, classes, ethnicities, national backgrounds, sexual orientations, and abilities/disabilities are not addressed in our analyses. Future efforts and discussions should be undertaken to consider these intersectional and diversity issues and how to weave them into work with students. There was no discussion of how men with different cognitive abilities (Perry, 1970) or levels of identity may need diverse interventions based on how they think about gender roles. There was no mention of the kind of curricular materials needed to do effective programming with college men. Curricular materials that foster men's gender role journeys need to identified and disseminated widely. Additionally, there was little guidance given on how to develop empirically validated treatments that work with men. Furthermore, critical research questions related to the concepts in Figure 2.1 and 2.2 were not specified but should be developed in the future. Finally, how the psychology of men interacts with college student development theory needs more elaboration and discussion. Future analyzes of how restrictive gender roles negatively affect both men's and women's lives would be very valuable in promoting activism related to issues of sexism and gender roles.

Theory and research indicate that young men are vulnerable to negative consequences of socialized gender roles. The lack of active programming for men is one of the most neglected areas in higher education. The lack of service delivery for men perpetuates serious problems on our campuses which affects all students. Student affairs workers have a long history of educating the whole person. Educating the whole person should now include programming related to men's gender roles. The jury is still out whether student affairs professionals will directly address men's problems. Telling the truth about men will require a paradigm shift and higher consciousness about the effects of sexism on men. Ironically, the profession of student affairs has a long history of commitment to diversity and appreciation of individual differences. C. Gilbert Wrenn as early as 1968 argued that "… women students be given the same academic and vocational consideration as are given to men" (1970 p. 412). He astutely recognized that women had special problems and were discriminated against and therefore needed special consideration. The same is true for men today. The real challenge for the profession is to fully accept that vulnerable college men are a special group that need help and support.

Whether the profession can change its service delivery to help vulnerable men who are negatively affected by socialized sexism is unclear. How many more acts of campus violence, rapes, male suspensions and dropouts, and male suicides will it take for the profession to understand that masculinity ideologies are directly relevant to our work with both men and women? Is our inaction in this vital area part of a backlash against men? When will we fully understand that sexism has negative consequences for everyone? Can we acknowledge this without creating a zero sum game that pits men and women against each other?

More expansive discussions on sexism are needed by student affairs professionals. The cost of silence and inaction is great. We now have theory and research to guide us but we must generate greater empathy and compassion for men to activate more direct services for them. The crisis of being a man in today's society is real and needs proactive attention by the profession of student affairs. Our call to action is an invitation for you to get involved in this important work.

References

Albee, G. W., & Gullotta, T. P. (1997). *Primary prevention works*. Thousand Oaks, CA: Sage.

Andronico, M. (1995). *Men in groups: Insights, interventions, and psychoeducational work*. Washington, DC: APA Books.

Blazina, C., & Marks, I. (2001). College men's affective reactions to individual therapy, psychoeducation workshops, and men's support group brochures: The influence of gender role conflict and power dynamics upon help seeking attitudes. *Psychotherapy, 38*, 297–305.

Blazina, C., Pisecco, S., & O'Neil, J. M. (2005). An adaptation of the Gender Role Conflict Scale for adolescents: Psychometric issues and correlates with psychological distress. *Psychology of Men and Masculinity, 6*, 39–45.

Burk, L. R., Burkhart, B. R., & Sikorski, J. F. (2004). Construction and preliminary validation of the Auburn Differential Masculinity Inventory. *Psychology of Men and Masculinity, 5*, 4–17.

Capraro, R. L. (2000). Why college men drink: Alcohol, adventure, and paradox of masculinity. *Journal of American College Health, 48*, 307–315.

Centers for Disease Control. (2005). Mental health in the United States: Prevalence of diagnosis and medication treatment for attention-deficit hyperactivity disorder – United States, 2003. Atlanta, GA: Author.

Centers for Disease Control (2007a). *Facts at a glance: Youth violence*. Atlanta, GA: Center for Disease Control Center for Disease Control and Prevention.

Centers for Disease Control (2007b). Suicide trends among youth and young adults aged 10–24 – United States 1990-2004, Atlanta, GA: Author.

Chickering, A. W., & Reisser, L. (1993). *Education and identity*. San Francisco: Jossey-Bass.

Chu, J. Y., Porche, M. V., & Tolman, D. L. (2005). The Adolescent Masculinity Ideology in Relationships Scale. *Men and Masculinities, 8*, 93–115.

Conyne, R. K. (2004). *Preventive counseling: Helping people to become empowered in systems and setting* (2nd ed.). New York: Brunner-Routledge.

Davies, J. A., Shen-Miller, D., & Isacco, A. (in press). The men's center approach to addressing the health crisis of college men. *Professional Psychology, Research , and Practice.*

Eisler, R. M. (1995). The relationship between masculine gender role stress and men's health risk: The validation of a construct. In R. F. Levant & W. S. Pollack (Eds.), *The new psychology of men* (pp. 207–225) New York: Basic Books.

Eisler, R. M., Skidmore, J. R., & Ward, C. H. (1988). Masculine gender-role stress: Predictors of anger, anxiety, and health-risk behaviors. *Journal of Personality Assessment, 52,* 133–141.

Fisher, B. S., Cullen, F. T., & Turner, M. G. (2000). *The sexual victimization of college women.* Washington, DC: U.S. Department of Justice, National Institute of Justice.

Garnets, L., & Pleck, J. (1979). Sex role identity, androgyny, and sex role transcendence: A sex role strain analysis. *Psychology of Women Quarterly, 3,* 270–283.

Goldberg, H. (1977). *The hazards of being male.* New York: New American Library.

Harrison, P. M., & Beck, A. J. (2006). Prisioners in 2005. *Bureau of Justice Statistics Bulletin, United States Department of Justice, NCJ 215092.* Washington, DC: U.S. Department of Justice.

Kellom, G. (Ed) (2004). Developing effective programs and services for college men. San Francisco: Jossey Bass.

Kimmel, M. S. (2006). *Manhood in America: A contextual history.* New York: Oxford University Press.

Kiselica, M. S. (in press). Promoting positive masculinity while addressing gender role conflicts: A balanced approach to clinical work with boys and men. In C. Blazina & D. S. Shen-Miller (Eds.), *An international psychology of men: Theoretical advances, case studies, and clinical innovation.* New York: Routledge.

Kiselica, M. S., & Englar-Carlson, M. (in press). The positive psychology/positive masculinity model: A new framework for psychotherapy with boys and men. *Psychotherapy Theory, Research, Practice, Training.*

Kiselica, M. S., Englar-Carlson, M., Horne, A. M., & Fisher, M. (2008). A positive psychology perspective on helping boys. In M. S. Kiselica, M. Englar-Carlson, & A. M. Horne (Eds.), *Counseling troubled boys: A guidebook for practitioners* (pp. 31–48). New York: Routledge.

Koss, M. P., Gidycz, C. A., & Wisniewski, N. (1987). The scope of rape: Incidence and prevalence of sexual aggression and victimization in a national sample of higher education students. *Journal of Consulting and Clinical Psychology, 55,* 162–170.

Levant, R. F. (1995). Toward the reconstruction of masculinity. In R. F. Levant & W. S. Pollack (Eds.), *A new psychology of men* (pp. 229–251). New York: Basic Books.

Levant, R. F., Hirsch, L., Celentano, E., Cozza, T., Hill, S., MacRachorn, M., et al. (1992). The male role: An investigation of contemporary norms. *Journal of Mental Health Counseling, 14,* 325–337.

Lynch, J., & Kilmartin, C. T. (1999). *The pain behind the mask: Overcoming masculine depression.* Binghamton, New York: Haworth.

Mahalik, J. R., Good, G. E., & Englar-Carlson, M. (2003). Masculinity scripts, presenting concerns, and help seeking: Implications for practice and training. *Professional Psychology: Research and Practice, 34,* 123–131.

O'Neil, J. M., Good, G. E., & Holmes, S. (1995). Fifteen years of theory and research on men's gender role conflict: New paradigms for empirical research. In R. Levant & W. Pollack (Eds.), *The new psychology of men* (pp. 164–206). New York: Basic Books.

Mahalik, J. R., Locke, B. D., Ludlow, L. H., Diemer, M. A., Scott, R. P., Gottfried, M., et al. (2003). Development of the Conformity to Masculine Norms Inventory. *Psychology of Men and Masculinity, 4,* 3–25.

Mahalik, J., Morray, E., Coonerty-Femiano, A., Ludlow, L., Slattery, S., & Smiler, A. (2005). Development of the conformity to feminine norms inventory. *Sex Roles, 52,* 417–435.

Mosher, D. L., & Sirkin, M. (1984) Measuring a macho personality constellation. *Journal of Sex Research, 25,* 60–84.

National Center for Education Statistics. (2005). Status and trends in education of American Indians and Alaska natives. Retrieved December 20, 2008, from http://nces.ed.gov/pubs2005/nativetrends/ind-3_2.asp

O'Neil, J. M. (2001) Promoting men's growth and development: Teaching the new psychology of men using psychoeducational philosophy and interventions. In G. Brooks & G. E Good (Eds.), *The new handbook of psychotherapy and counseling with men: A comprehensive guide to settings, problems, and treatment approaches* (Vol. 2, pp. 639–663). San Francisco: Jossey-Bass.

O'Neil, J. M. (2008a). Men's gender conflict: 25 year research summary [Special issue]. *The Counseling Psychologist, 36*, 358–476

O'Neil, J. M. (2008b). Summarizing twenty-five years of research on men's gender role conflict using the Gender Role Conflict Scale: New research paradigms and clinical implications [Special issue]. *The Counseling Psychologist, 36*, 358–445.

O'Neil, J. M. (2010). Is criticism of generic masculinity, essentialism, and positive-healthy-masculinity a problem for the psychology of men? *Psychology of Men and Masculinity, 11*, 98–106.

O'Neil, J. M. (in press). The psychology of men and boys in the year 2010: Theory, research, clinical knowledge, and future directions, In E. Altmaier & J. Hansen (Eds.), *Oxford handbook of counseling psychology.* New York: Oxford University Press.

O'Neil, J. M., Addis, M., Kilmartin, C., Mahalik, J. (2004). Teaching the psychology of men: A potential growth area for psychology and Division 51: A report from the APA Honolulu convention. *SPSMM Bulletin, 10*, 36–47.

O'Neil, J. M., & Egan, J. (1992a). Men's and women's gender role journeys: Metaphor for healing, transition, and transformation. In B. Wainrib (Ed.), *Gender issues across the life cycle* (pp. 107–123). New York: Springer.

O'Neil, J. M., & Egan, J. (1992b). Men's gender role transitions over the life span: Transformations and fears of femininity. *Journal of Mental Health Counseling, 14*, 305–324.

O'Neil, J. M., Helm, B., Gable, R., David, L., & Wrightsman, L. (1986). Gender role conflict scale (GRCS): College men's fears of femininity. *Sex Roles, 14*, 335–350.

O'Neil, J. M., & Lujan, M.L. (2009). Preventing boy's problems in schools through psychoeeducational programming: A call to action. *Psychology in the Schools, 46*, 257–266.

O'Neil, J. M., & Nadeau, R. A. (1999). Men's gender-role conflict, defense mechanism, and self-protective defensive strategies: Explaining men's violence against women from a gender-role socialization perspective. In M. Harway & J. M. O'Neil (Eds.), *What causes men's violence against women?* (pp. 89–116). Thousand Oaks, CA: Sage.

Perry, W. G. (1970). *Forms of intellectual and ethnical development in the college years: A scheme.* Troy, MO: Holt, Rinehart, & Winston.

Pleck, J. (1981). *The myth of masculinity.* Cambridge, MA: MIT Press.

Pleck, J. H. (1995). The gender role strain paradigm: An update. In R. F. Levant & W. S. Pollack (Eds.), *A new psychology of men* (pp. 11–32). New York: Basic Books.

Pleck, J. H., Sonenstein, F. L., & Ku, L. C. (1993). Masculinity ideology and its correlates. In S. Oskamp & M. Costanzo (Eds.), *Gender issues in social psychology* (pp. 85–110). Newbury Park, CA: Sage.

Robertson, J. M., & Fitzgerald, L. F. (1992). Overcoming the masculine mystique: Preferences for alternative forms of assistance among men who avoid counseling. *Journal of Counseling Psychology, 39*, 240–246.

Rochlen, A. B., McKelley, R. A., & Pituch, K. A. (2006). A preliminary examination of the "Real Men. Real Depression" campaign. *Psychology of Men and Masculinity, 7*, 1–13.

Sax, L. J. (2008). *The gender gap in college: Maximizing the developmental potential of women and men.* San Francisco: Jossey-Bass.

Scher, M., Sherrard, P., Canon, H., & O'Neil, J. (1980, April 27–30). *Men's caucus: An open forum for men and their concerns.* Program presented at the American College Personnel Association, Boston, MA.

Thompson, E. H., & Pleck, J. H. (1986). The structure of the male norms. *American Behavioral Scientist, 29*, 531–543.

Thompson, E. H., & Pleck, J. H. (1995). Masculinity ideologies: A review of research instrumentation on men and masculinities. In R. Levant & W. Pollack (Eds.), *A new psychology of men* (pp. 129–163). New York: Basic Books.

United States Census Bureau. (2005). *School enrollment – Social and economic characteristics of students: October, 2003, May 2005.* Washington, DC: Author.

Wade, J. C., & Gelso, C. J. (1998). Reference group identity dependence scale: A measure of male identity. *The Counseling Psychologist, 26,* 384–412.

Wrenn, C. G. (1970). The development of student personnel work in the United State and some guidelines for the future. In L. E. Fitzgerald, W. F Johnson, W. F., & W. Norris (Eds.), *College student personnel: Reading and bibliographies* (pp. 401–414). Boston, MA:, Houghton Mifflin.

3

THE SITUATION OF MEN, AND SITUATING MEN IN HIGHER EDUCATION

A Conversation about Crisis, Myth, and Reality about College Students Who Are Men

Frank Harris III

SAN DIEGO STATE UNIVERSITY

Ryan P. Barone

UNIVERSITY OF CONNECTICUT

Many men find themselves doing extremely well in higher education and beyond. Sexism, patriarchy, and misogyny continue to be oppressive forces which privilege people who identify and pass as men in higher education and beyond. Though mainstream media rhetoric may have us believe that men are in a crisis, currently more men are entering, being retained, and graduating from college than at any other point in history (King, 2006). It's critical to recognize that men are not a monolithic group. Frequently research and scholarship on college men involves homogenous participants due to poorly constructed methodologies. These studies, seemingly as an afterthought, qualify their findings by indicating that sexuality, race, ethnicity, gender identity, ability, socioeconomic status, and religion were unaccounted for and should be studies in future projects. Research that centers on historically marginalized social identities are compared to the "norm"—overserved White men (Liu, 2002).

We therefore construct this chapter holding two assumptions: First, that the lived experiences of college men necessitate our attention and enhanced capacity for better understanding the impacts of hegemonic masculinity on all students. Hegemonic masculinity is the virtually unattainable privileged model of living life as a man. The perpetuation of this as the ultimate way to enact masculinity adversely impacts all of society as individuals knowingly and unknowingly contribute to its potency and are influenced by the sociocultural scripts teaching us how it is performed. Our second assumption is that college men who have gender-based privilege continue to categorically benefit from that privilege. Almost exclusively, White men continue to be overrepresented as CEO's of Fortune 500 companies (Cronin & Fine, 2010) White men from nonworking-class backgrounds are entering college and succeeding at high rates (King, 2006), a gender-based pay gap still exists which facilities men with bachelor's degrees making significantly more money than similarly educated women (U.S. Dept of Labor, 2005), particularly women of color, are grossly underrepresented in the faculty ranks, particularly in math and science related fields (Sax & Harper, 2005).

With these assumptions this chapter will further problematize unqualified discussions and scholarship on college men, reflect on subtle and overt collusion with systems of privilege, and critically overview common misconceptions held by college educators in relation to men and masculinities. We will conclude our analysis arguing for a paradigmatic shift in our engagement efforts grounded in an analysis of hegemony, power and privilege. We will use the terms "men" and "male" intentionally throughout this chapter to reflect an understanding of the elemental difference between gender and sex. Moreover, we recognize that as students are increasingly gender-bending, presenting as androgynous, gender nonconfirming, genderqueer, and identifying somewhere on a transgender spectrum, the gender binary as a tool for social classification is increasingly limited. This acknowledgment causes us dissonance for we still utilize limited gender language in this chapter in an effort to make our writing accessible, though we regret the consequences which include reinforcing a marginalizing binary paradigm.

Even talking and writing about men is problematic. Regardless of how the classification is qualified it implies there is an undifferentiated experience. Moreover, there is much more diversity within a gender category than between the two oft-cited classifications of men and women (Kilmartin, 2001). As a social group, men who conform personally, politically and socially, at least visibly, do have common experiences with gender privilege, though mitigated by other social identities. This privilege functions to push certain groups of people to the margins of institutional discourse (Adams, Bell & Griffin, 2007; hooks, 1984). We have seen, and at times contributed to this phenomenon, within the growing field of "masculinities" where men with [dis]abilities, men who are gay/queer, people who are transgender, men of color, and men who are working class, largely seem to be an afterthought. Calls for studying masculinities as a "cultural competency" may perpetuate the notion that employable generalizations can be drawn to inform work with "all men" (Liu, 2005). We must therefore question research on "college men" which inadequately examines men who are already overserved in our institutions and society writ large.

While it is true that many of the issues and topics discussed in this chapter and this volume are related to hegemonic masculinity, all people contribute to this constructed narrative. "Hegemony is lived out a thousand times a day in our intimate behaviors, glances, body postures, in the fleeting calculations we make on how to look at and speak to each other, and in the continuous microdecisions that coalesce into a life" (Brookfield, 2005, pp. 96–97). Therefore issues and concerns that are framed as problems with men, or with masculinities, are in fact societal and systemic in nature. For example, focusing on why men abuse alcohol must be analyzed with a critical understanding of hegemony. Furthermore, taking this approach will also mean we must negotiate how presenting alcohol abuse by men as a "men's issue" serves to further privilege a narrative of masculinity that marginalizes people often already underserved.

As a result, work on men and masculinities must be conducted with a focus on the multiple intersections of identities as the primary lens through which issues and interventions are viewed. Challenging the compartmentalization of identity-related issues on campus will necessitate an increased commitment to professional capacity building on privilege and social justice, and it will allow us to better understand the complexities of identity-related work (Adams, Bell, & Griffin, 2007; Landreman, Edwards, Balon, & Anderson, 2008). "By encouraging a differentiated look at the variety of identities, a campus is in a better position to engage diversity pluralistically and with greater equity and inclusiveness" (Smith, 2009, p. 63). When students hear patriarchy, they often assume it is a synonym for men (Johnson, 2005). Through engaging diversity pluralistically we can move beyond individual people and their specific identities and look to the myriad identities operating in a system where oppressive forces such as patriarchy impacts everyone. If we can address issues related to men and masculinities from a system level, we can help people understand that the problem is not men, it is the systems though which we are all socialized that contributes to oppressive forces serving to confine everyone's creativity and common humanity.

A model for social justice engagement around issues related to men and masculinities may be found in the emerging field of Universal Design (UD) and University Instructional Design (UID) in higher education. UID is "an adaptation of the architectural concept of UD ... a relatively new model for providing access to higher education for students with disabilities. Through UD and UID, staff and faculty create more welcoming spaces for all students by rethinking professional practices to develop curricula and programs that are inclusive for all learners" (Higbee & Goff, 2008, p. 486). Using UD and UID as a framework, we could approach work with men and masculinities privileging those who are often an afterthought. For example, an ongoing dialog series discussing how racism and homophobia and gender conformity impact retention and success in higher education will create a space where examining intersecting social identities are foundational to the discourse. Much like feminist scholar bell hooks' (1984) call to center the experiences of people at the margins of society and the academy, re-thinking who our scholarship and interventions center may allow for a maturation of engagement which is inclusive for all students.

With an increased focus on college students who identify as men engaging in harming or counter-productive behaviors on campus, a critical examination of how positive behavior is reinforced is instructive. Instead of dealing punitively with poor behavior, the "bad dog" phenomena described by Laker (2003), educators should strive to create systems and influence cultural shifts that move beyond reward and expect positive, contributing, individual and community behaviors. These behaviors should be role-modeled by staff and faculty with the understanding that modeling comes with the responsibility of acknowledging faults, setting up systems of accountability, and acknowledging mistakes.

Beyond role modeling, we must also scrutinize our positive behavior re-enforcement and examine if our expectations for behavior are too low. Should it be extraordinary behavior if a student who identifies as male and as a man attends a Take Back the Night program? Or might cultural change necessitate a more holistic shift in behavior modification and enforcement? Our expectations of students, colleagues, and staff might then shift to *expect* authentic engagement across campus in programs and interventions which positively contribute to a validating and welcoming community for all people. If we can contribute to positive peer behavior and reinforce positive behavioral supports, we can make longer-term change.

For example, using Harper's (2006) important finding that African American men's academic success is encouraged and embraced in African American peer circles, we can seek out the positive contributing aspects of peer support. If Harper's finding is a surprise, we must examine why this is the case, and re-learn how our ill-informed low expectations impact service delivery. Again using Harper's study, a program designed for African American men at a predominantly White institution focusing on increasing peer support for academic success may be redundant and unnecessary. However, knowledge that peer support for academic success is likely to already exist, a more successful series may be one supporting and refining this already existing asset.

When our expectations are reduced to students refraining from damaging property and binge drinking, we are contributing to expectations of mediocrity and will continue to perpetuate a non-transformative status quo where forces such as patriarchy and racism persevere unchallenged. At times administrators and educators subtly and overtly encourage and socialize students who identify as men that having a null impact on their environment is in fact positive given the negative impact often assigned certain groups of men (thereby problematically ascribed to all men). As we focus most of our time and energy on the 10% of men who hold executive positions in student organizations, and the 10% who cause "problems" for us, the middle 80% receive messages that as long as they are not in the latter 10% we are content. In this sense a limited understanding and commitment to fostering who men can be limits their potentiality.

As the field of men and masculinities grows, it is important to look at the body of work being created and identify limitations and opportunities in that scholarship. Anecdotally, increasingly more programs with "men" or "male" in the titles have been observed at the American College Personnel Association (ACPA) and National Association of Student Personnel Administrators (NASPA) conferences. What are the implications for this shift? What is the primary content of these programs? Men and Masculinities courses are gradually more common on campuses, and programming around "men's issues," is no longer aberrant. What are the pedagogical and paradigmatic assumptions of these courses and programs? How is success evaluated? In our research and practice it is essential that we pay particular attention to the feminist, Women's studies, and Queer studies scholars who have been studying gender, femininities, and masculinities for decades. More poignantly, if a Men and Masculinities syllabus has more men than women scholars cited, it is a problem because it does not appropriately acknowledge the intellectual foundation upon which current masculinities scholarship rests. Discussions encouraging the establishment of "Men's Centers" are also increasingly common. What deficit do such centers aim to remedy? What partnerships are created and maintained through these centers? Regardless of a value judgment about these changes, it is productive to look at who is contributing to this shift. What identities do the people behind this scholarship and these programs share, and how might privilege, power, and oppression impact the work? A recent joint meeting of members from the ACPA Standing Committee for Men and NASPA Men and Masculinities Knowledge Community was attended by approximately one dozen White men ranging in age from 22 to 45. If these homogenous demographics are representative of the majority of scholar-practitioners advancing this growing field, the programs, courses, and centers connected with this work will be limited in scope and understanding. When socialized sexism, racism, and other oppressions inevitably emerge in these meetings, it may flourish unchecked and unchallenged thereby retarding the productive aspects of the scholarship and practice. "We should always be conscious of who is not there and that we are not hearing those perspectives" (Gilfus et al., 1999, p. 1207). Therefore homogenous groups must work diligently at self-monitoring while simultaneously asking themselves (and colleagues) why a particular grouping is not as diverse as desired.

In times of increasingly limited resources, we must not assume that programming and research is a zero-sum endeavor. We encourage moving past either/or thinking to a both/and paradigm where we are advocating for all social justice engagement, including certain programs centering discussion of gender and masculinities (Harper & Harris, 2010). For success, we must be able to create meaningful spaces where multiple identities are examined and we resist the temptation to isolate. We can therefore avoid the tendency to tokenize people and engage the multiplicity of identities acknowledging asymmetry and acknowledging all people in meaningful ways (Smith, 2009). If a program designed to examine gender role socialization for men is grounded in an understanding of privilege and a commitment to fostering the implementation of bystander intervention strategies, it is likely all constituencies will support this endeavor. Examples include programs that at inception incorporate multiple voices in the design, implementation and evaluation processes. Ongoing dialog series with specific learning outcomes, social justice leadership retreats, and some sexual assault prevention groups designed at engaging men provide models (e.g., see Barone, Wolgemuth, & Linder, 2007). However, programs and interventions singularly aimed at engaging men, without an analysis of social justice activism and/or race, class, sexuality, and other social identities, may be met with resistance from a zero-sum perspective. One-time programs focusing on men's gender role conflict awareness, men's co-curricular engagement, or men in the conduct processes may re-enforce a gender binary and perpetuate generalizations or stereotyping. Dichotomous thinking and programming occurring without accountability and diverse groups of decision-makers will limit our potential for coalition building and collective action.

The proceeding reflection should serve as a framework for conceptual, theoretical, and pedagogical dialogues about our engagement with men and masculinities. We now shift to focus on some common misconceptions about college men that we have found diminish the efficacy of campus-based efforts to ensure their achievement of successful academic and developmental outcomes. We will attempt to dispel these misconceptions and offer suggestions for what institutions and educators should do to effectively address these issues and help support college men in their development and success.

Myths and Misconceptions about College Students Who Are Men

Having offered a conceptual framework to shape our thinking about college students who are men, in this section we present and challenge some common myths and misconceptions that are held by college educators about them. While our list of myths and misconceptions is not meant to be exhaustive, the prevalence of those presented herein are likely to garner agreement among scholars and educators who study and work with college students who are men.

Men Are 'Disappearing' from Higher Education

On the surface, this argument has some merit (King, 2006). However, two questions should always be considered in this discussion: Which men are we talking about? and In which educational settings are men disappearing? Women currently outnumber men in college enrollment and degree attainment.

However, this trend has persisted for more than 30 years. In 1976, men accounted for slightly more than half (52%) of U.S. undergraduates and less than half (47.7%) by 1980 (U.S. Department of Education, 2009). A similar pattern has persisted in degree attainment over the past 30 years. Women were awarded 46% of bachelor's degrees in 1977, approximately half of the bachelor's degrees awarded in 1981, and 57% of the bachelor's degrees awarded in 2000 (King, 2010).

Attention to the gender gap is often misplaced and overlooks men among whom the gaps are most pronounced, notably African American, Latino, and low-income men, as well as important areas where men are overrepresented. For example, 33% of men who began postsecondary education between 1995 and 1996 and 2001 entered Science, Technology, Engineering, and Mathematics (STEM) fields, which was more than two times the percentage of women (14%) who entered these fields (U.S. Department of Education 2009). Men are also equitably represented at the country's most selective universities. Among *U.S. News and World Report*'s (n.d.) top five national universities, only Harvard enrolled more undergraduate women (51%) than men (49%) in 2009.

Equally problematic is the fact that gaps between White men and men of color are rarely discussed. Data highlighted in Mikyung's 2009 report on minorities in higher education revealed that White men represented 62% of all men enrolled in higher education in 2006, compared to 10% for Black men, 10% for Hispanic men, and 6% for Asian American men. Also reported were the number and percentage of bachelor's degrees that were awarded to men in 2006, of which 69% were to White men. In comparison, Black, Hispanic, and Asian American men represented 7%, 6%, and 7% of 2006 bachelor's degrees awarded to men, respectively. It is also important to note that the percentage of 18- to 24-year-old men who were enrolled in college has also increased more significantly for White men (10%) than it has for their Black (5%) and Hispanic (3%) peers during this same time frame.

Our intention is not to undermine or diminish concerns about the declining presence of men in higher education. Instead we compel educators to be critical and intentional in their exploration of the gender gap and recognize how this trends plays out for key groups of men.

Supporting College Men Derails Efforts to Achieve Gender Equity for Women

Because men have historically been the beneficiaries of years of unearned privilege that has resulted in a host of advantageous outcomes they have experienced in higher education, women have rightfully been the focus of policies and programs that aim to bring about gender equity. Also, despite ongoing efforts to achieve gender equity, men are still afforded significant privilege in society that can be directly attributed to their gender and status as men. As we noted earlier in this chapter, men overwhelming occupy positions of power and influence, such as corporate executives, college and university faculty, and university presidents to name a few. Given that gender equity has yet to be fully achieved in higher education some, scholars, educators, and advocates wisely question the recent attention and efforts to support the achievement and success of men in higher education. We share our colleagues' concerns about the extent to which the emerging emphasis on college men may reduce the efficacy of efforts to bring about gender equity for women. However, we believe "either/or" propositions regarding support for men and women in higher education presents a false dichotomy—that institutions can only be responsive to the gender-related needs of one group at a time. We also concur with Harper and Harris III's (2010) assertion: "because gender is relational, the status of women cannot be improved without a corresponding emphasis on tending to the social forces that misshape men's attitudes and behaviors and helping them develop productive masculinities" (p. 5). While, sexism, academic segregation, and concerns about body image are issues that disproportionately impact women, men are challenged by a different set of concerns. We contend that institutions of higher education possess the intellectual capital and administrative expertise necessary to simultaneously address the problems and issues that threaten the success of college men while also ensuring the equitable treatment and outcomes for women. At most institutions, the type of supports that are enacted toward men and women will likely be different, but need not be less robust for one group than they are for others.

Boys Will Be Boys

Educators often rely on "boys will be boys" reasoning to make sense of young men's tendencies to engage in risky and objectionable behavior. However, scholars who study the social construction of masculinity have argued rather convincingly that men's misbehavior is directly related to internalized scripts about how men are *supposed* to behave and what men must do in order to be perceived as "masculine" and avoid suspicions about their sexual orientations. Thus, it should come as no surprise that on many campuses college men are well represented among the students who are most often cited and punished for violations of campus judicial policy. Men who participate in exclusive communities of men, such as fraternities, athletic teams, and single-sex living communities are especially susceptible to pressures and gender conflicts that lead to men's misbehavior. James O'Neil, who proposed the concept of male gender role conflict, theorized that when men are unable to express their masculinities according to socially-prescribed and stereotypical expectations, conflict and anxiety often ensue (1981). Gender role conflict is directly related to hegemonic masculinity and men's fears of being perceived by others as feminine or unmanly and often engenders a host of destructive behaviors that are frequently observed among college men including binge drinking, homophobia, risky sex, and in extreme cases, physical violence and sexual assault. Some men misbehave to express themselves as men because that is what they are taught to do. Others do so out of anger, fear, and frustration with their inability to attain the status and attributes they believe are necessary to fulfill the masculine ideal. In both respects, we do not suggest condoning this misbehavior, but rather suggest it must be understood as a consequential outcome of hegemonic masculinity and traditional patterns of men's gender socialization. Therefore, it is important for college educators to not brush off men's misbehavior and assume it to be expected. Instead, educators must constantly seek insight into the local contextual influences that motivate and reward men who break the rules.

Men Are Not Responsive to Gender-Related Outreach and Support

Some educators assume that men are not responsive to campus-based efforts that have a gender focus because men are socialized to distance themselves from exploring and expressing gender beyond the narrow range of attitudes and behaviors they are socialized to embrace. In contrast, we have found that men are very responsive to gender-related outreach and, in fact, desire this type of support. However, we qualify this statement with several conditions that must be in place to effectively engage men in gender-based interventions. First, interventions must be facilitated by educators who the men trust and who are transparent about the challenges they have faced with respect to gender. Second, the intervention cannot be perceived by men as simply a program that amplifies their flaws and shortcomings. Instead, they need to be affirmed as men while also challenging and offering the support necessary for their growth and maturity. Third and perhaps most important, the intervention must provide a safe space where men can connect with other men and feel compelled to share deep-seeded fears and concerns about their masculinities. Learning from peers who are men and struggle with similar gender-related challenges, and hearing first-hand that they too are not completely secure with who they are as men, can be an incredibly powerful and transformative experience for many young men. Davis and Laker (2004) and Harris (2010) reported that contrary to prevailing assumptions about college men, they do desire meaningful and bonding relationships with other men. However, men often assume they must engage in sexism, homophobia, and abuse alcohol in order to establish and maintain these relationships with each other. Men need guidance for bonding and connecting with other men without relying on destructive acts and attitudes that reinforce hegemonic masculinity.

We've Learned All There is to Know about Men

In higher education and student affairs graduate programs across the country, students learn that most models and theories of human and student development (Chickering, 1969; Erikson 1968; Marcia, 1980) were grounded in the experiences of a small subset of men—most of whom were White and affluent. Therefore, some scholars and educators question the extent to which further inquiry into the gender-related experiences of contemporary college men is warranted. In response, we offer three compelling reasons why we must continue to interrogate masculinities in college contexts. First, as Edwards and Jones (2009), Davis and Laker (2004), and other scholars have argued, these models were indeed based exclusively on samples of men, however, the construct of gender was not purposefully explored in these studies. Therefore, they offer very little insight into the ways gender identity development is influenced by men's participation in higher education. Moreover, beyond Harper's (2004) study of conceptualizations of masculinities among high-achieving African American college men, we know even less about the nexus between men's gender identity development and their achievement of successful and measurable outcomes in college. Second, in his 2008 book *Guyland: The Perilous World Where Boys Become Men*, sociologist Michael Kimmel noted that today's college students, men in particular, are very different from the men who attended college decades earlier. The social movements and cultural shifts that have taken place over the past 50 years, when many of the prevailing models of human development emerged, have substantially altered the way that today's cohorts of undergraduate men experience college. Finally, as we alluded to in the introduction of this chapter, the experiences of men who represent certain backgrounds and identities are not fully accounted for in the past and recently published research on college men and masculinities. For example, men who return to college as adults, men from low-income backgrounds, men with [dis]abilities, men who are gay or bisexual, and transgendered people are only minimally represented in the published literature and discussions on college men and masculinities. These gaps in the discourse can easily lead educators to erroneously conclude that college men are a monolithic group and experience campus contexts in similar ways. Given these reasons, much remains to be studied and learned about college men and masculinities.

What's Right with College Men?

At this point, we have spent the majority of our time in this chapter problematizing the troubled status of men in higher education. Consequently, some readers may logically conclude that *all* men are disengaged, violent, homophobic, sexist, and racist underachievers who rely exclusively on destructive strategies to express their gender identities. To our own admission, we have allowed the pervasive fascination with the handful of men who engage in destructive and disruptive behaviors to command our attention. Perhaps a more productive way to invest our efforts is to learn how men who transcend hegemonic masculinity and make the most of their college experience (in the face of social forces and pressures that encourage them to do otherwise) are able to do so, and what elements of their approach could be shared with and encouraged among their peers. We desperately need models and proven strategies to identify characteristics of masculinities that can be leveraged by all students, regardless of their gender identities and expressions.

Shaun Harper's anti-deficit framework offered a new paradigm for studying African American men's college achievement (Harper 2004, 2006). In response to decades of research motivated by scholars' preoccupation with the two-thirds of African American men who do not complete college and, consequently, reinforce deficit perspectives of these students, Harper focused his inquiries on high-achieving African American men. As a result, college educators now have a rich body of scholarship to inform their efforts in helping African American men achieve academic excellence. While Harper's framework was developed to study the experiences of African American men, it also has implications for studying the collective experiences of college men and masculinities. What new and important lessons might we learn from men who excel academically; consume alcohol legally and responsibly; never express and always challenge homophobia, sexism, and racism; refrain from aggression and violence when resolving conflicts; enjoy relationships with peers that are grounded in authenticity, love, and respect; and invest their time selflessly in campus activities and community service? Surely these men are present on every college campus. However, rarely are their experiences and perspectives the exclusive focus of studies of college men. Nor are they used as benchmarks in interventions that supposedly aim to produce productive masculinities in college settings. Until we reframe our narrow focus on conflicted masculinities and seek a broader understanding of what it means to be a man in today's college context, we should expect little beyond the negative trends and narratives that have dominated the discourse surrounding men on college campuses for decades.

Conclusion

As we continue to engage men programmatically and though research on masculinities, thereby becoming better prepared to respond to popular myths and misconceptions, it is essential to critically analyze and understand the paradigms which inform our work. "Student affairs practitioners and scholars have a responsibility to know from which paradigm(s) they are working and to consider how their practice may be impacting those they serve" (Guido, Chávez, & Lincoln, 2010, p. 16). Once we identify our paradigmatic focus (Positivist, Cultural, Blended, etc.) and subsequent values, our work will more easily be evaluated, adapted, and implemented more comprehensively. "If a primary purpose of scholarship and practice is an understanding of the phenomenon around us and an ability to respond to its complexity, it makes sense to encourage a variety of research paradigms, disciplines, and methods to gain richer understanding of our students and institutions in this complex world" (p. 16). Embracing these multiple paradigms, and therefore a richer sociological understanding of the institutions which contribute to stifling socialization and stereotyping, will help our current programs and research evolve.

We must also conduct empirical research and practice to better inform our work highlighting outcomes of interventions and programs (Harris III & Edwards, 2010). One-time programming will likely have a limited impact on college students, so our efforts must be ongoing, systemic, and multi-pronged. A substantial commitment to examining intersections of identities and a dedication to understanding men and masculinities from a social justice framework will allow us to do the transformative work that our institutions, students, and specifically college men, deserve. This commitment will allow us to comprehensively respond to ill-informed cries of a "crisis" in terms of college men, and focus on the populations of men who are often pushed to the margins of institutional discourse.

References

Adams, A., Bell, L. A., & Griffin, P. (Eds.). (2007). *Teaching for diversity and social justice* (2nd ed.). New York: Routledge.

Barone, R. P., Wolgemuth, J. R., & Linder, C. (2007). Preventing sexual assault through engaging college men. *Journal of College Student Development, 48,* 585–594.

Brookfield, S. D. (2005). *The power of critical theory: Liberating adult learning and teaching.* San Francisco: Jossey-Bass.

Chickering, A. W. (1969). *Education and identity.* San Francisco: Jossey-Bass.

Cronin, L., & Fine, H. (2010). *Damned if she does, damned if she doesn't: Rethinking the rules of the game that keep women from succeeding.* Amherst, NY: Prometheus.

Davis, T., & Laker, J. A. (2004). Connecting men to academic and student affairs programs and services. *Developing effective programs and services for college men: New directions for student services* (Vol. 107, pp. 47–57). San Francisco, Jossey-Bass.

Edwards, K. E., & Jones, S. R. (2009). "Putting my man face on": A grounded theory of college men's gender identity development. *Journal of College Student Development, 50*(2), 210–228.

Erikson, E. (1968). *Identity: Youth and crisis.* New York: Norton.

Gilfus, M. E., Fineran, S., Cohan, D. J., Jensen, S. A., Hartwick, L., & Spath, R. (1999). Research on violence against women: Creating survivor-informed collaborations. *Violence Against Women, 5*(10), 1194–1212.

Guido, F. M., Chávez, A. F., & Lincoln, Y. S. (2010). Underlying paradigms in student affairs research and practice. *Journal of Student Affairs Research and Practice, 47*(1), 1–22.

Harper, S. R. (2004). The measure of a man: Conceptualizations of masculinity among high-achieving African American male college students. *Berkeley Journal of Sociology, 48*(1), 89–107.

Harper, S. R. (2006). Peer support for African American men: Racial identity, male role norms, gender role conflict, and prejudicial attitudes. *Journal of Men's Studies, 3,* 107–118.

Harper, S. R., & Harris III, F. (Eds.). (2010). *College men and masculinities: Theory, research and implications for practice.* San Francisco: Jossey-Bass.

Harris III, F. (2010). College men's conceptualizations of masculinities and contextual influences: Toward a conceptual model. *Journal of College Student Development, 51*(3), 297–318.

Harris III, F., & Edwards, K. E. (2010). College men's experiences as men: Findings and implications from two grounded theory studies. *Journal of Student Affairs Research and Practice*, *47*(1), 43–62.

Higbee J. L., & Goff, E. (2008). *Pedagogy and student services for institutional transformation: Implementing universal design in higher education*. Minneapolis: Regents of the University of Minnesota.

hooks, b. (1984). *Feminist theory: From the margin to center*. Cambridge, MA: South End Press.

Johnson, A. G. (2005). *The gender knot: Unraveling our patriarchal legacy*. Philadelphia: Temple University Press.

Kilmartin, C. (2001). *Sexual assault in context: Teaching college men about gender*. Holmes Beach, FL: Learning Publications.

Kimmel, M. S. (2008). *Guyland: The perilous world where boys become men*. New York: HarperCollins.

King, J. (2006). *Gender equity in higher education: 2006*. Washington DC: American Council on Education.

King, J. E. (2010). *Gender equity in higher education: 2010*. Washington DC: American Council on Education.

Laker, J. (2003). Bad dogs: Rethinking our engagement of male students. In P. Brown (Ed.), *Men on campus series*. Washington DC: Standing Committee for Men, American College Personnel Association.

Landreman, L., Edwards, K. E., Balon, D. G., & Anderson, G. (2008, September). Wait! It takes time to develop rich and relevant social justice curriculum. *About Campus*, 2–10. Retrieved June 29, 2009, from http://www.keithedwards.us/SJEC%20About%20Campus.pdf

Liu, W. M. (2005). The study of men and masculinity as an important multicultural competency consideration. *Journal of Clinical Psychology, 61*(6), 685–697.

Liu, W. M. (2002). Exploring the lives of Asian American men: Racial identity, male role norms, gender role conflict, and prejudicial attitudes. *Psychology of Men and Masculinity, 3,* 107–118.

Marcia, J. E. (1980). Identity in adolescence. In J. Adelson (Ed.), *Handbook of adolescent psychology* (pp. 159–187). New York: Wiley.

Mikyung, R. (2009). *Minorities in education, 23rd annual status report, 2009 supplement*. Washington DC: American Council on Education.

O'Neil, J. M. (1981). Patterns of gender role conflict and strain: Sexism and fear of femininity in men's lives. *Personnel and Guidance Journal, 60,* 203–210.

Sax, L. J., & Harper, C, E. (2005, May). *Origins of the gender gap: Pre-college and college influences on differences between men and women*. Paper presented at the Annual Meeting of the Association for Institutional Research, San Diego, CA.

Smith, D. G. (2009). *Diversity's promise for higher education: Making it work*. Baltimore: Jossey-Bass.

U.S. Department of Education. (2009). Digest of education statistics, 2008. Washington DC: Institute of Education Sciences, National Center for Education Statistics.

U.S. Department of Labor. U.S. Bureau of Statistics (2005). Highlights of women's earnings in 2005 (Report 995). Washington, DC: U.S. Government Printing Office. Retrieved May 17, 2010, from http://www.bls.gov/cps/cpswom2005.pdf

U.S. News and World Report. (n.d.) 2011 best colleges. Retrieved from http://colleges.usnews.rankingsandreviews.com/best-colleges/national-universities-rankings

4

INVITING AND INSPIRING MEN TO LEARN

Gendered Pedagogical Considerations for Undergraduate Teaching and Learning Environments

Jason Laker

SAN JOSÉ STATE UNIVERSITY

There has been much discussion and debate, in this text and elsewhere, about whether and how boys and men may be in crisis with regard to their participation in K–16 education. Most of the discussion begins with statistical information about the relative percentages of boys and girls or men and women enrolled in, and/or graduating from schools and colleges. More recent scholarship disaggregates this data in order to highlight the particular situation of various subpopulations of boys and men.

These are important issues, and they require sophisticated analysis and strategies for resolution. In addition, the subject seems also to stimulate a debate regarding the benefits and consequences of feminist movements and feminism in general. Typically, those debating either argue that girls' and women's educational advances have harmed boys and men, or that boys' and men's difficulties in education are not directly related to those earlier reforms.

In contrast to popular either/or thinking, I believe that girls' and women's advances have actually taught us that gendered analysis and interventions can be highly effective, and we should therefore apply what has been learned about supporting girls and women to the current situation of boys and men. I join with the authors of this text in asserting that this is not a zero-sum game, and that we can effectively improve the engagement and success of boys and men generally, and those of particular subpopulations of men, by considering gender socialization's influences on boys' and men's notions of education, men's motivation to participate in and complete educational programs, and how faculty and staff can use these analyses to positively design effective interventions and educational processes.

I confess from the outset that I have virtually no background in biology or genetics. As such, I cannot make an assertion about whether and to what extent genetic variation may influence boys' and men's interest or efficacy with regard to their education. Are boys and men hard-wired to need action-oriented and physical approaches to education? Some have suggested this is the case. As a teacher and professional, I find it difficult to distinguish between the learning and engagement benefits of inquiry-based and experiential pedagogies for students generally versus those enjoyed by boys and men in particular. As the old adage goes, "people support what they help to create." Is this truer for men than for women? I would argue that it is not. But, I would suggest that the approach to *inviting* students to co-construct their learning experience, and the extent to which they will accept, are mitigated by gender. As such, I will offer some examples and suggestions for making effective invitations later in this chapter.

In this chapter, I will provide the reader with some context and history vis-à-vis men's issues and engagement in college settings, because it is important for establishing an understanding of the present state of college men. From there, I will turn attention to the question of how to effectively promote male students' development and success. In my view, the responsibility for this falls primarily on the teacher/practitioner more so than on the student. So much of the literature speaks of "boys/men's engagement." Obviously students have a level of responsibility for their commitments, especially at the collegiate level. However, we need to be critically reflecting on how and to what extent we practitioners and teachers are engaging. This semantic nuance is critical, because we are placing more blame on our male students than I believe they deserve. I have argued in other venues that the student affairs (SA) field in particular (not to suggest this problem does not manifest in faculty culture) socializes practitioners into a professional ethos that displays (overtly and implicitly), frankly, a distaste for male students—particularly those who exhibit traditional masculine gender performance. I have coined the term, "Bad Dog" (both noun and verb; 1995) to describe the diminishing and non-developmental approach often taken by practitioners and teachers in responding to male students, especially when responding to inappropriate behavior such as in disciplinary settings. I will elaborate on this later in this chapter as well. For now, I invite you, the reader, to take a moment to authentically reflect on a few questions before continuing: When you think about male students, what comes to mind? Do you like and enjoy your male students? Do you genuinely wish to inspire or invite them to learn? If so, under what conditions, and with what pre-conditions? Please keep these questions in mind as you continue reading, and perhaps in general to inform your practice.

I will now turn my attention to the ways in which male students pose challenges to college faculty and staff. I will also ask you to forgive them and to transform that forgiveness into a powerful renaissance in your professional work with male students. I will not ask you to overlook or justify inappropriate behavior, but rather to understand what is potentially behind it, and to be developmental and committed to ethical educational principles as you respond. In short, my aspiration is to invite you to learn about men and apply any insights to your developmental work with students generally and male students in particular.

A Little History

Over the last 60 years, the numbers of women arriving at and completing college have steadily risen and have eclipsed those of men (Mortenson, 1999). In fact, the numbers of bachelor's degrees awarded to men by state has declined between 8.1 and 22.3% (depending on state) during this time. As it pertains to the shifting percentages in gender makeup of college campuses, researchers such as Mortenson (2002, cited in Kirk) explain this widening gap in terms of three perspectives. First, much of the problem begins before boys reach college age. Boys are disproportionately failing in the K–12 system (Pollack, 1999), which undermines the ability of higher education to reverse the decline in male enrollments (except, perhaps, through outreach to younger prospective students). Second, this issue is exacerbated by shifts in the racial and ethnic makeup of the U.S. population. In particular, the racial makeup of the United States will continue to significantly increase in the percentage of people belonging to races other than Caucasian (Bureau of the Census, 2000). The structural barriers that affect the persistence of students of color in high school and also college-bound trends will thus further exacerbate the gender disparity since boys of color persist in smaller numbers than girls of color (Tierney, 2000). Third, shifts in business and industry are causing an increase in jobs that utilize skills traditionally generally viewed as stronger in women (e.g., communication, human capital analysis, teaching/training) and a decrease in jobs that emphasize physical labor, which are generally seen as skills held by men. Related to the third issue is the increase in women's presence within traditionally male-dominated fields such as medicine and law (Mortenson, 1999).

A focus on trends in the K–12 school system is generally outside the scope of this chapter, but suffice it to say that as a policy issue, higher education has a vested interest in partnering with K–12 institutions, industry, government, and communities to address the issues which will preclude having a strong pool of male applicants in the future.

In any event, once on campus, students generally and men in particular navigate a campus defined by its culture. Theorists such as Tinto (1993), Pascarella and Terenzini (1991), and Kuh, Schuh, and Whitt (1991), among others, point to the importance of this interaction. Tierney (2000) indicts the functional nature of the discourse on departure. In addition to affirming earlier points about population and enrollment trends, he asserts the need to reframe "dropping out," which inherently looks at an individual, and shift our analysis to the culture in which the behavior called "dropping out" happened, with a focus on groups, power, and oppression.

Critiques of campus cultures relative to diversity and identity issues, particularly by SA scholars and practitioners, often focus on the term "patriarchy." However, much like Tierney's analysis of "dropping out," there is a focus on how individual men are privileged in society and on campus. And, like Tierney's concern, there is an inordinate focus on individual men (who do not tend to feel powerful, particularly at 18–22 years of age) and not enough focus on how the campus climate not only marginalizes people of color; women; gay, lesbian, bisexual, and trans-gendered (GLBT) people; etc., but indeed it perpetuates the rigid gender scripts that men receive in their socialization (Johnson, 2001).

> The important fact of men's lives is not that they are biological males, but that they become men. Our sex may be male, but our identity as men is developed through a complex process of interaction with the culture in which we both learn the gender scripts appropriate to our culture and attempt to modify those scripts to make them more palatable.
>
> (Kimmel & Messner, 1998, p. xx)

These words provide an articulate conception of the developmental journey men undertake in search of a salient masculine identity. College attendance and completion is one of the few formal rites of passage available to men as they reach adulthood.

As one of the few rites of passage existing for young adults, college attainment, retention, and completion trends suggest an emerging crisis of identity for American men. One of the fundamental missions of SA staff is to facilitate the developmental transition of students from adolescence to adulthood. Since fewer men are coming to college, this removes an additional opportunity for men's guidance through maturity.

College faculty and staff have a limited role in addressing whether adolescent males actually attend college. It is therefore incumbent upon us to be purposeful in working with the men who actually do enroll at postsecondary institutions. Student affairs staff have an especially significant role to play in the retention and psychosocial development of male students. Yet, I contend that this responsibility and opportunity is being underutilized, if not squandered. This is curious to me, since questions about SA's efficacy with male students have been asked for at least the last 20 years, and questions about male gender identity development for nearly 40. For instance, in their landmark book, *Changing Roles for Men on Campus*, May and Scher (1988) engaged these issues and questions as they pertain to male college students. They refer to an even earlier notion that men live "in harness" (Goldberg, 1976, p. 13) and call upon higher education and student affairs practitioners to help them to struggle free from this confining experience.

Instead of seeing an increase in the discourse about male identity development within the field, with the exception of a select few instances there has been a stunning absence of public and meaningful dialogue in the associations and graduate programs. This relative lack of needed attention will only be exacerbated given the population shifts discussed earlier. The politics of this issue are delicate. I distance myself from those who argue that men as a sex are "oppressed" and root their calls for attention to men in this idea. Rather, I am arguing that we have a professional and ethical responsibility to educate all students, and to develop our pedagogy in a sophisticated and informed manner. I believe that more clearly understanding the underlying influences on men's development will offer the best potential for achieving learning and developmental goals, and reducing instances of some men's negative or harmful gendered behavior.

Men Behaving Badly

Students, staff, and faculty arrive on college campuses with particular purposes in mind, and the expectation that they will be able to achieve these aims without interference. However, incidents of sexual harassment and assault, violence, alcohol and drug abuse, and other community disruptions can quickly undermine opportunities to achieve academic or personal goals on campus. Male students cause these community disturbances with disproportionate and alarming frequency (Berk, 1990; Downey & Stage, 1999; Herek & Berrill, 1992; Levin & McDevitt, 1993).

Specifically, researchers have shown that compared to female students, college men exhibit significantly greater rape myth acceptance and propensity to rape (Quackenbush, 1991); and men are more likely to blame women for being sexually harassed, believe that sexual harassment issues have been exaggerated by the media, and are far less inclined to see certain behaviors (e.g., sexual remarks and propositions) as sexual harassment (Dietz-Uhler & Murrell, 1992). Further, fraternity members engage in the "heaviest, most frequent, and most problematic drinking in college" (Kuh & Arnold, 1993, p. 327) and they exhibit lower capacity for moral reasoning than non-Greek-affiliates (Sanders, 1990). Finally, male students exhibit far more racist and homophobic attitudes and perpetrate significantly more hate-motivated assaults than do women (Qualls, Cox, & Scher, 1992; D'Augelli, 1991).

Such behaviors often result in forcing both perpetrator and victim out of school. Further, perceived lack of safety on campus can interfere with enrollments of new students, as well as undermine the persistence of students who are on the border of a decision to stay or leave.

The Role of Student Affairs

As SA administrators (especially those at the entry-level) interact with students to facilitate individual development, they are in an ideal position to address this problem and the underlying developmental issues. A central focus of SA professionals is to promote students' psychosocial development, and indeed the field claims expertise in this area. It is therefore incongruous for SA staff to have such little impact on the behaviors described earlier. Either the SA field must concede an inability to address male student development (which would necessarily have implications pertaining to its efficacy with other students), or it needs to confront a vacuum in the knowledge about male identity development. Neither the graduate preparation programs nor the workplaces of new SA professionals are filling this knowledge gap.

Let me illustrate the problem using a case example such as would occur in a residence hall or other social space on a college campus. It is not uncommon for young male students to use the term "gay" or "fag." These terms are certainly offensive and hurtful. It has been my experience that some young men will use these terms in two general ways. First, something that is said or done by a peer whom a male student finds to be "stupid" may result in the phrase, "That's so gay." Second, when a male peer acts in a manner that makes the first male uncomfortable (almost invariably through behavior perceived as feminine, such as being sensitive), he may be called a "fag." It has been my experience that a hall director or other SA practitioner will respond by saying something to the effect of, "that is homophobic and completely unacceptable," or hold forth on how the student needs to "get in touch with his privilege." I refer to these responses as "Bad Dog" approaches to male students because they are behavioral and sharp rebukes, and/or shaming, depending on the language used and the context. I think it is important to point out that I do not condone homophobic, racist, sexist, or other denigrating language or behavior, nor do I believe it should be tolerated. However, the responses not only fail to invite (my first preference before using challenge) the young man to excavate the meanings of the phrases/words and why he said them, but they also alienate him from the practitioner. I contend that the student learns only one thing in such a dynamic, which is simply not to say such things in front of that one practitioner. If we are to promote psychosocial development, we must channel personal offense strategically and create engaging spaces for young men to explore their socialized paradigms. Remember that the male student in this case example is using language that has been encouraged and accepted by his peers (among others). More particularly, his use of such phrasing is often a triggered response to transgressive gendered expressions, meaning that someone has "violated" the socialized norms of masculinity, such as by being vulnerable or expressive. This is threatening in that it interferes with the socialized order. The homophobic or sexist language, in turn, is intended (though perhaps unconsciously) to discipline the other man into compliance with the hegemonic standard. For us to be shocked, in many ways is analogous to being surprised that performers on a stage are actually following their script. Being offended and wanting to say so is understandable, but approaching it so directly does not engage students in a learning process—at least not a sustainable one. An alternative response to a male student who uses the phrases/words mentioned earlier might be, "have you noticed that you call guys 'fags' when they open up? What's that about? Are guys necessarily gay if they talk about their feelings?" The part about the word "fag" being offensive and perhaps hate-speech is relevant, but the student who uses that word may be initially unprepared to understand that. By starting with a means of grappling with the underlying assumptions, the practitioner can bridge a connection that can eventually transform the student. If we snap at the student, he may go to a readily accessible peer group that affirms this language and perspective rather than engage in critical thinking. The "Bad Dog" approach, therefore, makes practitioners complicit with bad behavior-because we could have intervened in an effective way, but instead allowed our own agenda (which can include investment in a particular style just as it could refer to a philosophical position) to construct a barrier for the student. As such, we become implicated in the next situation in which he repeats the behavior.

As a boy and adolescent, I recall feelings of being diminished by male peers who were closer to the traditional masculine standard than I. This came in the form of name-calling or even occasional physical intimidation. I am fortunate that unlike many other males, I was never subject to direct violence as so many others have been. I now realize that as a younger professional I projected many of those experiences onto male students who themselves were struggling with the difficulties of developing into a young adult man. Again, I feel inclined to repeat that I do not justify any of the offensive or inappropriate behavior some of them exhibited, nor does this change that it hurt at the time. In fairness, my social contract with my peers was not an educational one, and so either indignation or reciprocity were among the reasonable strategies. But as I began my career in higher education and student affairs, I do not believe I was taught to effectively and developmentally respond, and I regret this because it undermined my own early development as a practitioner. Had I better understood how male role socialization so powerfully influences male (and female for that matter) behavior and development (including my own), perhaps I could have been more effective. Mercifully, I do believe I had my good moments with students. In any case, I am reminded of a story, a form of which I shared in my dissertation (Laker, 2005), that illustrates this struggle.

Boys' Career Day

About seven years ago I was working as a dean of students at one of the few remaining all-male universities—a small, private, religiously affiliated, liberal arts institution. One day, I was contacted by a male colleague who had received a call from a woman working for the local school district. The district was planning a boys' career day and wanted to know if he knew of someone who could speak to a group of boys between the ages of 11and 13 about what it means to be a man today. When the woman contacted him, he said that he immediately thought of me and wondered if I would do it. I was struck by the strange irony associated with a woman calling a man for this purpose, and his referring her to another man. What is it about being a man today that is so mystifying that a person living that experience would defer to another?

The event, which was organized by the public school district, took place in the community room of a church, which had been sectioned off into smaller rooms by moveable walls, and which had a very large cross and Bible verses posted on its walls. I remember wondering why an organization that owns so many buildings (which were not in session that day due to teacher in-service training) would choose such a venue. After I checked in and affixed my name tag, I was directed to an area of the main section where the boys were making crafts and playing games. Several of the speakers were either setting up displays or mingling. One man was setting up a display about the financial services industry, and another was a military recruiter who was preparing to show a video about being a soldier. Still another man was preparing to discuss being a mechanic.

I poured myself some coffee and went over to a couple of men who were standing quietly in a corner. One of them was a tall, beefy guy with a jacket embossed with the name of a gym where he was employed. I introduced myself and asked him what he was speaking about, to which he replied, "the health and wellness services field." I found myself puzzled by this. I couldn't help but wonder how those words could be represented by the large musculature of his frame and the ways in which similar images have been used to create a stereotypical male ideal. "Healthy" and "well" just didn't fit for me as authentic descriptors for this kind of masculinity. The other man was employed by the local community college, and he was there to talk about their vocational and technical programs.

It has been my experience that when I meet a man, the first thing I get asked after my name is "what do you do?" This, of course, is an inquiry about my employment, but it is also a tool to determine my place in a hierarchy that can be felt but is rarely discussed. I generally make it a point to avoid the question, change the subject, or to give a vague answer. I also try not to ask other people (regardless of gender) this question, since I do not want to be complicit in legitimizing this sizing up process. When the health and wellness guy asked me the question, I simply told him that I worked at the particular university. He pressed further, "Oh, what do you do there?" I told him that I work with student housing and discipline, and that I do a little teaching there and at the public university in that city (at which I was an adjunct professor). He asked what I teach, and I said mainly women's studies courses. He got a conspiratorial look on his face, with one eyebrow arched, leaned in slightly, and, with a little snicker said, "I went to [that school], and I took a women's studies class, but it didn't turn out to be what I thought it was." Then, proud of his joke, he stood back up straight. In this "joke," he was basically suggesting that he thought women's studies courses would be a great place to pick up chicks, so to speak, but it had not worked out that way. More deeply, he was announcing his heterosexuality, asserting and re-inscribing his dominance within a patriarchal hierarchy, denigrating women, and denouncing men (including me) who did not fit within the hegemonic masculine paradigm—not too shabby an accomplishment this early in the morning. He was, of course, not consciously aware that he had done all of this with one "little" comment. I suspect, though, that he was viscerally aware.

As the time approached to begin the event, I was directed to a large, round table where I would have my "life station." There were laser-printed signs above the different tables with brief descriptors of the topics, "A Military Career," or "Financial Services," etc. My table didn't have a sign, which was an apparent oversight, but I thought apt since one is not supposed to examine what it means to be a man. This reminded me very much of the movie, *Fight Club* (1999), in which the narrator, Jack, played by Ed Norton, and his flamboyant alter ego, Tyler Durden, played by Brad Pitt, establish an underground organization that encourages men to beat each other up, and whose first two rules are "You do not talk about Fight Club." Nonetheless, after inquiring about this, a woman hastily prepared a handwritten sign with a pen and note paper which read, "What does it mean to be a man today?"

Groups of 8 to 10 adolescent boys would soon arrive at each table for a 25-minute presentation, and this would happen twice before speakers were free to go. The sociological complexity of the phenomenon of being asked to tell these boys what it means to be a man in 25-minutes cannot be overstated. In any event, I had decided that instead of ME telling THEM, I would instead ask THEM to tell ME.

So it was that little boys with awkward confusion on their faces shuffled through, looking for their life station. Soon I had eight of them sitting at my table. As they didn't all know each other, we did brief introductions. As we began, I asked them why they chose this particular table, and determined that they were, in fact, all assigned to it because their first choices were full. Pressing on, I asked them, "What do you think it means to be a man today?" Sheepishly, one of the boys said, "provider," and like dominoes, several of the others chimed in, "good job," "wife," "have kids," "make a lot of money," "strong," and variations on these themes. I then read the entire list back to them and asked how they felt about doing all the items on the list, and one pudgy little boy said, "overwhelmed," and then immediately looked embarrassed at having been the only one to say anything—perhaps especially at revealing a vulnerability. But, several boys nodded in agreement. I asked them what they thought about the fact that they had all given similar responses for the list—how did they think that happened? In our conversation, several of the boys talked about how different sources such as TV, friends, parents, school, church, and others each gave them a little bit of this list. I then inquired whether any of them had ever been picked on for not being manly in the way their list described. All of them raised their hands. I asked one of them to say more, and he told a brief story of being teased by another boy because he was hanging around with a particular girl—and so the other boys called her his girlfriend and made fun of him. (Here is an instructive story about how boys and men are encouraged or even coerced into proving their heterosexual masculinity by having sexual relations with women, and at the same time being ashamed of, and hostile toward anything and anyone who is deemed feminine.).Several of the boys shared similar stories of teasing, except for one very attractive blonde-haired and blue-eyed boy wearing fashionable clothes and a sterling silver chain on his neck. He said this kind of thing hadn't happened much to him in recent memory. I suspected that he was quite popular. He was the tallest, and he carried himself with more confidence than the assortment of boys with shorter, and/or fatter bodies and less pristine skin sitting around the table.

I then shared a personal story about how I felt similarly (with the exception of the one boy who I just described) to them as a boy. I told them that they should not forget the reasons why they had similar items to put on the list, that there is a script we are not usually aware of, but that forces us to act in ways that don't feel real. And, I reminded them that the things each of them shared shows that they are not alone in their experience and it's just that we are taught not to talk about it, so it doesn't change. I asked them if they would be willing to not tease other boys about not being manly enough. They said they would agree to that. I asked if they could remember to try to do what their heart says, they should instead of trying to fit someone else's script. They said they would try to do that. Finally, I asked how many of them had ever had a conversation like this, and none of them had. Then, it was time for them to go.

The next group was the same.

I wonder what these boys will be like if and when they get to college. I wonder if anyone else will take 25 minutes to find out.

At this point I return to the questions posed earlier. When you think about male students, what comes to mind? Do you like and enjoy your male students? Do you genuinely wish to inspire or invite them to learn? If so, under what conditions, and with what pre-conditions?

Implications

The hegemony described in my story about boys' career day, the untenable contemporary situation regarding boys and men described in the "Men

Behaving Badly" section, and our central roles and responsibilities as educators and developmental professionals call for important shifts in our practice. In this section, I will discuss five strategies intended to improve professional practice and effectiveness with male students.

Strategy #1: Develop a Foundation of Reflection and Awareness

My graduate degree is in Community Counseling, and particularly preparation for service as a therapist. In my graduate training, I was taught to recognize when a client is eliciting a potentially dysfunctional or at least distracting reaction. In the case of the triggering personality described earlier, the risk is that I would project old experiences on him, when, in fact, he wasn't even born when those situations occurred. The first strategy is to weave critical reflection into your professional practice. This involves asking yourself questions such as those I posed earlier, and remaining present and in touch with the reactions and assumptions that arise when encountering male students (perhaps even male colleagues). To what extent does some of your own unfinished business flow into your work with students? For instance, I find that working with young men in disciplinary processes can inadvertently situate the practitioner as the deliverer of retribution rather than developmental facilitation. We may rationalize a rebuking response as supporting our notion of social justice. That is, we may presume that we are acting on behalf of a marginalized group, under the banner of ally, as we require a written essay about what he has learned from his choices. These types of situations represent a set-up that, absent mindful awareness, may cause us to be complicit in the reifying the status quo. There are additional specific strategies one can employ, but the first step is to highlight the risk and strategies for raising consciousness.

Strategy #2: Engage the "Middle 60"

I use the phrase "Middle 60" to conceptually refer to those male students who are neither involved in student conduct situations in the residence halls or on campus nor among the most involved student leaders. One of the difficulties we face as practitioners is that we are so consumed by the students (overwhelmingly male) who are "in trouble," and so easily drawn to those men who participate in organized campus leadership, that we forget or perhaps are too busy to seek out the rank and file male students who are getting about their educational business below our radars. This is not to suggest they are doing well, but suffice it to say they are not eliciting university attention. I would contend that spending purposeful time engaging these men could help to redefine the social norms which underpin the decision making of the men in trouble, and grow the population of male students who are pro-socially active on campus.

These men can be found on residence hall floors, studying in the library, eating in campus dining commons, among other places. They may be involved in a team or fraternity, but as the name suggests, they may be the less engaged or visible members. The friendly practitioner would have little trouble striking up a conversation, followed by inviting these men to participate in or assist with programs on campus or in the community. One of the most striking things I have encountered when working on this strategy is that so many of these students have simply never been directly asked to participate. When I talk with groups of student leaders, I find they often bring up "student apathy" as a difficulty in their work. I challenge them by asking how many of them came into their current leadership roles by seeking it out, which tends to elicit the majority of raised hands. Then I ask how many of them were invited, and these are rare indeed. The "Middle 60" are ripe for the picking in this regard.

Strategy #3: Gender-Informed Pedagogies

As discussed in other chapters, men's gender identity development is shaped by hegemonic messages promoting eminence, independence, efficacy, career orientation, and the like. For this reason, I believe questions of genetics and brain structures are less important than ones of how to contend with male students who have been scripted to orient in such a manner. As a teaching faculty member and administrator, I have found it productive to keep this in mind as I design my pedagogy.

This also resonates well with current literature about good teaching practice in general. For instance, the learning outcomes movement has called us to be explicit about the goals we have for our teaching, and to align our approach, assignments, and grading schemes to these goals. It is critical to be explicit with students about the purpose for an assignment or lecture. I have sometimes invoked a co-conspiratorial tenor when doing this. For instance, I might say, "I know this essay might be a pain in the behind, but it's ideal to develop your analytical tools to be on top of the bigger research project later this term. And for those of you interested in management or consulting, you're going to see a connection between working with a conceptual framework and problem solving in organizations." This acknowledges that the students are busy, that you value their time, and that you took care in putting together an assignment that will given the a "leg up" on later assignments and in their career. This is what I mean by weaving it into the pedagogy. Further, if possible it should be okay or even encouraged for students to propose alternative approaches to an assignment. If that counter-proposal would reasonably attend to the learning goals, then perhaps it should be agreeable—and sharing the idea in a complimentary fashion with the class or group adds value in terms of validating the students and motivating them to remain engaged in co-constructing their learning.

Strategy #4: Invoke, Invite, and Inspire Utilizing Masculine Script Narratives

This strategy relates to interacting with men individually or in groups, where your interest is to inspire or effect behavior change. For instance, in disciplinary meetings, I use a rhetorical device which has been effective. I will usually begin the meeting by welcoming the students and thanking them for coming (even if they were mandated to do so), and indicating that I realize we have some business to do but since we don't know each other, let's take a few minutes to fix that. Note that I used the term "fix," to call upon the efficacy script, and to convert the adversarial dynamic into a collaborative one (e.g., we will be fixing or working on things together).

From there, I will spend some time just asking basic introductory questions about a student's hometown, major, interests and involvements. This serves two functions. First, it gives me insight into his personality. Second, it helps me to understand how he makes meaning of his college experience and eventually the incident being discussed. After several minutes I usually say, "Well, as you know we have some business to do, so let's take a look at that." Again, I am using language which is consistent with the scripts, even as I plan to interrogate those scripts later in the meeting. I will read the incident out loud, and often it is a story of a guy who was intoxicated and exhibited abusive, sexist, and/or homophobic language. From here I will pause, and have a confused look on my face. I'll say something to the effect that I am confused by something and would it be okay if I ask him a question. The student will usually agree to this, and I will further ask if I may be blunt? Again, this willingness to be trust him with candor fits the script. Then I will say something like, "Well, to be honest, the guy in this report sounds like a jerk, and I'm surprised because even though we don't know each other well, my few minutes with you so far suggest you are a pretty level-headed and decent guy, so help me understand the gap between the guy sitting here with me and the guy in this report."

I can honestly say that some of the most powerful conversations I've ever had followed after this moment. Note that I used a "straw man" in "that guy," even though it's really this guy. By doing this, he can be critically reflective without feeling immediately shamed. Often his answer will be, "I was just being stupid." I will then say, "No, I don't accept that—you aren't stupid, so what's really behind this." We will typically discuss themes relating to perceived social norms and his desire to fit in. Sometimes I have had male students say they are usually pretty quiet, but when they drink their peers think they are funny, to which I respond by asking when they decided they had nothing worth saying or weren't worthy company when sober … and this has often elicited tears. Our space here is limited, but one caveat is that it is essential to be authentic and sincere when using this approach. Even though a part of it is scripted, it is coming from a genuine interest in the student and is a tool for that purpose.

You will need to find your own style for utilizing it authentically. I will usually conclude this part of our meeting by talking about the scripts we are given as men—a woman can be equally effective here. The point is to build a bridge with the student. By making the unspoken rules of manhood explicit, one can then discuss the question of whether this man is ready, now that he is in college, to "be the captain of his life," and to stop following other people's scripts—people who will not live his life or take the consequences of his decisions on his behalf. Virtually every time I have had this conversation, it has been effective in getting the student to be willing to make right what had occurred, and to change his patterns. Sometimes it doesn't work, and the incident is of a severity or things escalate to suspension or expulsion, but those circumstances are exceptions to the norm.

When speaking with groups, like a team or fraternity, about a hazing incident, I often use concentric circles in which the outer group of men must sit in silence, with explicit rules against giggling or making ridiculing faces. I'll have a similar conversation with the internal circle, periodically switching inner and outer participants until all or most have participated. It is riskier to do this with a group, and one should be quite experienced and perhaps have a co-facilitator before attempting it.

Strategy #5: Model Authenticity, Vulnerability, and Empathy for the Struggle

I briefly alluded to this in Strategy #4, when I suggested speaking about gender scripts given to us as men or women, with a view to making these more transparent and thus negotiable. That was, however, episodic. This strategy involves weaving it into daily practice, much like a ministry. By this I mean that the practitioner or teacher is courageous enough to appropriately share quite human vulnerabilities and struggles. For instance, in presentations about sexual health and decision-making, I have started to talk about situations I encountered in college which were embarrassing, but nonetheless effective illustrations of the difficulties we might face privately and which result in shame. I am referring to stories about having opportunities to engage in sexual activity which one may or may not have pursued, and for what reasons, and the reflections on those moments. In particular, stories about feeling a pressure to demonstrate sexual prowess and yet privately being scared resonate strongly with the dilemmas of enacting the masculine scripts.

In the professional culture of student affairs, there is a hegemony of our own which mediates our conversations about identity, privilege, power, and the like. For instance, it may be politically transgressive to acknowledge that it is difficult to be a man—because it is difficult to be a human, and not immediately get into the business of comparing who has it worse. Interestingly, I have found female students to be very sympathetic to their male counterparts, even as they struggle with their own challenges, many of which implicate or involve men. A willingness to sit with male students in their humanity as a normal daily practice, and to make explicit references to the specific dimensions of the male script, can be very effective as a precursor to support or challenge them to take responsibility for exploring the full range of human expression, and to reject in whole or part the voices telling them to tow the hegemonic line.

In this chapter I have raised questions and concerns about the present state of our understanding and work with male students, and offered suggestions for use in practice. However, I recognize that the issues are more complex than there is room here to address. For instance, student affairs is a field predominately comprised of women practitioners. Given that many women are sometimes subject to diminishing sexist encounters or dynamics with male students, there are ethical dilemmas inherent in questioning their practice with men. While I certainly do not believe that male faculty and practitioners are more qualified as a group to be effective with male students, perhaps it is fair to ask them to carry more of the responsibility. The balance between self-care and protection, and being authentic and present is a delicate one—for women and also for men. Regardless, I stand by the assertion that entry into an educational field, as a practitioner, teacher or both, is certainly an employment contract, but it is also a social one. Each and every practitioner and teacher should bring their best capabilities to each and every student. We have a great deal more learning and work to do in order to be able to say we have done this for our male students.

References

Berk, R. A. (1990). Thinking about hate-motivated crimes. *Journal of Interpersonal Violence, 5,* 334–349.

D'Augelli, A. (1991). Gay men in college: Identity processes and adaptations. *Journal of College Student Development, 32,* 140–146.

Dietz-Uhler, B., & Murrell, A. (1992). College students' perceptions of sexual harassment: Are gender differences decreasing? *Journal of College Student Development, 33,* 540–546.

Downey, J., & Stage, F. (1999). Hate crimes and violence on college and university campuses. *Journal of College Student Development, 40*(1), 3–9.

Fincher, D. (Director). (1999). *Fight club* [Motion picture]. USA: 20th Century Fox.

Goldberg, H. (1976). *The hazards of being male: Surviving the myth of masculine privilege.* New York; Signet.

Herek, G. M., & Berrill, K. T. (1992). *Hate crimes: Confronting violence against lesbians and gay men.* Newbury Park, CA: Sage.

Johnson, A. (2001). *The gender knot: Unraveling our patriarchal legacy.* Philadelphia: Temple University Press.

Kimmel, M., & Messner, M. (Eds.). (1998). *Men's lives* (4th ed.). Boston: Allyn and Bacon.

Kirk, L. M. (2002, January 15). Where the boys are. *The Providence Journal,* p. G1.

Kuh, G.. & Arnold, J. (1993). Liquid bonding: A cultural analysis of the role of alcohol in fraternity pledgeship. *Journal of College Student Development, 34,* 327–334.

Kuh, G. D., Schuh, J. H., Whitt, E. J., Andreas, R. E.. Lyons, J. W., Strange, C. C., et al. (1991). *Involving colleges.* San Francisco: Jossey-Bass.

Laker, J. (2005). *Beyond bad dogs: Toward a pedagogy of engagement of male students.* (Unpublished doctoral dissertation). University of Arizona, Tucson.

Levin, J., & McDevitt, J. (1993). *Hate crimes: The rising tide of bigotry and bloodshed.* New York: Plenum.

May, R., & Scher, M. (Eds.). (1988). *Changing roles of men on campus.* San Francisco: Jossey-Bass.

Mortenson, T. G. (1999, November). *The changing gender balance: An overview.* Paper presented at Fewer Men on Campus–A Puzzle for Liberal Arts Colleges and Universities, Baltimore, MD.

Pascarella, E., & Terenzini, P. (1991). *How college affects students.* San Francisco: Jossey-Bass.

Pollack, W. S. (1999, Winter). The sacrifice of Isaac: Toward a new psychology of boys and men. *The Society for the Psychological Study of Men & Masculinity Bulletin, 4*(1), 7–14.

Quackenbush, R. (1991). Attitudes of college men toward women and rape. *Journal of College Student Development, 32,* 376–377.

Qualls, R., Cox, M., & Scher (1992). Racial attitudes on campus: Are there gender differences? *Journal of College Student Development, 33,* 524–530.

Sanders, C. (1990). Moral reasoning of male freshmen. *Journal of College Student Development, 31,* 5–8.

Tierney, W. G. (2000). Power, identity, and the dilemma of college student departure. In J. Braxton (Ed.). *Reworking the student departure puzzle* (pp. 213–234). Nashville, TN: Vanderbilt University Press.

Tinto, V. (1993). *Leaving college: Rethinking the causes and cures of student attrition* (2nd ed.). Chicago: University of Chicago Press.

U.S. Census Bureau. (2000). *USA quickfacts: People quickfacts.* Retrieved July 6, 2010, from http://quickfacts.census.gov

SECTION B

Identity Intersections with Masculinities

Section Editor, Tracy Davis

5

MAN OF MULTIPLE IDENTITIES

Complex Individuality and Identity Intersectionality among College Men

Shaun R. Harper

UNIVERSITY OF PENNSYLVANIA

Cameron C. Wardell

UNIVERSITY OF NORTH CAROLINA AT CHAPEL HILL

Keon M. McGuire

UNIVERSITY OF PENNSYLVANIA

> A man who graduates from college without having benefitted from a well-guided exploration of his gender identity is likely to find himself stranded on a destructive pathway of confusion and self-doubt... Those who work at colleges and universities have a professional responsibility to aid women and men alike in productively resolving identity conflicts and transitioning into a version of adulthood where patriarchy, sexism, homophobia, misogyny, misandry, sexual harassment, and all forms of abuse and oppression ends with them.
>
> (Harper & Harris, 2010, p. 10)

In their book, *College Men and Masculinities*, Shaun R. Harper and Frank Harris III (2010) challenge educators and administrators to respond more purposefully to the developmental and educational challenges faced by undergraduate men. Doing so requires moving beyond what they have termed "the model gender majority myth"—a common misconception that all men similarly benefit from the power and privilege historically and contemporarily conferred to men because of their gender. Also necessary, Harper and Harris argue, is a more complete understanding of college men as men with gender-specific needs and often unresolved identity issues. Other scholars have noted the various ways in which young men experience conflict around gendered norms regarding the performance of their masculinities in college environments (Davis, 2002; Edwards & Jones, 2009; Harper, Harris, & Mmeje, 2005; Harris & Harper, 2008; O'Neil, Helms, Gable, David, & Wrightsman, 1986).

On its own, Male Gender Role Conflict (MGRC) is extremely complex and multifaceted. However, an erroneous assumption could be made that healthy identities are achieved once men resolve the various aspects of gender role conflict that have been described in the literature. But what about those who are simultaneously experiencing dissonance concerning their class and racial identities alongside fear of femininity, restrictive emotionality, and other behavioral manifestations of MGRC? The point here is that men are not just gendered beings with unidimensional needs and patterns of identity development. Several students experience additional conflict, subordination, stereotyping, and differential treatment on college campuses because they are not White, middle class, strictly heterosexual, and so on.

In an attempt to more accurately capture the complexity of identity development, Judith Butler (2004) illustrates how gender is performative. She notes that there are numerous socially constructed expectations concerning how women and men act, how they talk, what they do, and the intimacy with which they interact that compel them to think and behave in certain manners. The same could be said about the social construction of race—Blacks, for example, are often stereotyped and expected to behave in particular ways that often wrongly renders them a homogeneous group (Harper & Nichols, 2008; Smith & Moore, 2000; White, 1998). Those who decide to concurrently perform race and gender in unanticipated ways rarely do so without conflict or consequence. College students, therefore, must negotiate the multiple dimensions of their identities; some of them are men.

Recent higher education and student affairs literature on identity intersectionality has focused mostly on women (e.g., Abes, Jones, & McEwen, 2007; Abes & Kasch, 2007; Jones & McEwen, 2003; Patton & Simmons, 2009; Robinson & Howard-Hamilton, 2000). With a few notable exceptions (e.g., Edwards & Jones, 2009; Harris & Harper, 2008), comparatively less has been written about the complex convergence of masculinities with other aspects of men's social identities. Harris and Harper considered gender plus one other dimension of identity (e.g., plus class identity, plus sexual identity) among four male students attending community colleges. Their "two-at-a-time" approach, while in some ways helpful, neglected to consider more complex identity intersections (e.g., masculine plus gay, Native American, low-income, and deeply spiritual, all at the same time). Evans, Forney, Guido, Patton, and Renn (2010) offer an example of a gay male student who is also Jewish. Concerning the intersection of his gender, sexual orientation, and religious identities, the authors maintain "he cannot separate these [three] interlocking identities, but worries he may be forced to live an incongruent life separating and hiding his identities at different times" (p. 247).

Ways in which masculinity intersects with other dimensions of identity are explored and discussed in this chapter. Our major argument is that college students are complex *individuals*. Thus, understanding the complexities of individuality is essential for those who aim to construct educational environments and conditions that foster productive developmental change in students. Because so little has been written about identity intersectionality among college men, we use this as an occasion to juxtapose existing research with an example of a real-life college student. In the next section we review some of the published literature on undergraduate students and multiple dimensions of identity. We then introduce Tyson, an actual undergraduate student with a multilayered identity, as a case example. Although a pseudonym is used in lieu of Tyson's real name, nothing described in his case is fictitious. The chapter concludes with implications for postsecondary educators and administrators.

Multiple Dimensions of Identity among College Students

Much foundational literature and many developmental theories concerning various components of students' social identities (e.g., sexual orientation and gender) focus on individual aspects of personhood. Rather than seeking to understand how students simultaneously make sense of themselves as raced, gendered, or classed individuals, identity development theorists tend to concentrate on only one dimension at a time (Torres, Howard–Hamilton, & Cooper, 2003). Researchers have recently incorporated Feminist, postmodern, and queer theories into studies of college student development, and employed concepts such as intersectionality, performitivty, and liminality to represent students as they see themselves (Abes & Jones, 2004; Abes et al., 2007; Abes & Kasch, 2007; Jones & McEwen, 2003; Patton & Simmons, 2008; Renn, 2007; Renn & Bilodeau, 2005; Reynolds & Pope, 1991; Robinson & Howard–Hamilton, 2000; Stewart, 2008, 2009; Stewart & Lozano, 2009; Torres & Hernandez, 2007; Torres, Jones, & Renn, 2009).

Emphasizing the ways in which identities intersect and intrasect complicates static or essentialized perceptions that educators may hold about students. By considering multiple dimensions of an individual's identity, researchers are explicitly acknowledging the fluid and context-specific nature of how students view themselves and make sense of their own development. Moreover, challenged by postmodern queer conceptualizations of identity, scholars continue to explore the balance between core selves and other distinguishable dimensions (e.g., sexual orientation and class) and the reality that there are no clear boundaries for demarcation (Abes et al., 2007).

Two models and one concept that are particularly informative for framing the case we later present in this chapter are: The original and reconceptualized versions of the *Model of Multiple Dimensions of Identity* (MMDI) (Jones & McEwen, 2000; Abes et al., 2007); Wijeyesinghe's (2001) *Factor Model of Multiracial Identity* (FMMI); and Abes and Kasch's (2007) *Developmental Concept of Queer-Authorship*. Susan R. Jones and Marylu K. McEwen's original MMDI reflects a student's constructed identity at a particular time and in a particular context. The individual is visually represented (through the model) as both a core self and a set of external identities. The external identities are those that are socially constructed (e.g., race, gender, and class), while the core is said to consist of personal attributes, values, and characteristics. The model considers how important each external identity is to the individual. Thus, the closer to the core, the greater saliency the external identity holds. As contexts (or college environments) change, so too can the saliency of particular external identities, and as such, the model captures the fluid and constantly changing nature of students' identities.

The Abes et al. (2007) reconceptualized MMDI includes meaning-making as essential in representing ways in which students filter social contexts to inform how they perceive themselves. Accordingly, complex meaning-making filters enable researchers and others to more carefully parse contextual factors and perceptions of identity. Consistent with the original MMDI, an internal core self (a set of personal characteristics, values, and attributes) and external identities (socially constructed identities, such as religion) are represented. Thus, in adding the filter, Abes et al. recognize how and to what degree students' identities are shaped by contextual influences.

Wijeyesinghe's (2001) FMMI is also useful in explaining the case example presented later in this chapter. Based on a qualitative study of African American/ European American adults who self-identified in different ways (e.g., White, Multiracial), the FMMI consists of eight factors that affect choice of racial identity by multiracial persons: racial ancestry, cultural attachment, early experience and socialization, political awareness and orientation, spirituality, other social identities, social and historical context, and physical appearance. A multiracial person may choose her or his identity based on a combination of these factors, but typically not all. Although Wijeyesinghe presents these factors as distinct, she states that many are interrelated. For example, physical appearance is often directly linked to racial ancestry. Hence, any attempt to understand who multiracial students are must take into account the factors that shape their identities. The same could be said for students who bring with them to college a varied combination of identities.

Last, Abes and Kasch's (2007) concept of queer-authorship provides substantive content for understanding how a gay, multiracial, male student like Tyson may construct his identity in resistance to heteronormative social structures. Abes and Kasch describe queer-authorship as "the necessary deconstruction of heteronormativity that enables lesbian students to change the dominant social order in order to redefine the meaning of their multiple identities and the contexts in which their lives are situated" (p. 630). This idea employs a form of self-authorship that includes a social change component; meaning the individual is *influenced by* and *influences* her or his environment. As such, students are given greater agency in not only determining to what extent they will filter contextual factors, but also complicating and disrupting perceivably rigid notions of gender, race, spirituality, class, and other social identities.

As these frameworks demonstrate, researchers and educators must take more seriously the complexities of individuality, as many students come to college with multilayered identities and prior socialization experiences that compel them to rank order certain dimensions of identity above others. Exclusively accounting for one single dimension of identity, without responding to other aspects, can potentially lead to misguided programming and counseling approaches. The following case is illustrative of the nuanced process of identity development among an individual college student whom we have named Tyson.

Identity Intersections: The Case of Tyson

In this section we introduce Tyson, a biracial, gay, male student with salient academic and spiritual identities who straddles two socioeconomic statuses. Described herein are his prior racial socialization experiences, conflicts that ensue because of the duality of his socioeconomic backgrounds, as well as strategies he employs to negotiate friendships in a heteronormative college fraternity house. Tyson, an actual 20-year-old undergraduate student at the University of North Carolina at Chapel Hill (UNC), represents the multilayered individuality with which many students enter colleges and universities. We conclude this section by explaining what is problematic about expecting a student like Tyson to rank order the multiple dimensions of his identity.

Developing a Biracial Identity

Growing up in a family with an African American father and a Caucasian mother, the concept of race was explicitly introduced and discussed with Tyson. From an early age, he was aware that he was biracial and often took pride in proclaiming his multiracial heritage, following his older sister's example. Since race was often talked about in his home, Tyson does not recollect any specific experiences of feeling unaware that he was biracial or primarily identifying with one single race over the other.

Tyson's first realization of his unique racial identity came at the early age of 5 years old. Having attended elementary schools in Puerto Rico, Missouri, and Maryland, he had the opportunity to witness three drastically different schooling environments. In Puerto Rico, he noticed that many of his peers were similar in racial appearance (in that they were light-skinned), but there were very few White or Black students. In Missouri, he was the only non-White student in his entire grade. His classes in Maryland were almost racially balanced between Black and White students, and there Tyson met several other biracial kids. His involvement in Boys Scouts, church, and soccer opened the door to friendships that were predicated on similar interests, not racial similarity, a trend that would influence his future peer relationships.

Middle school was the first time Tyson began to receive criticism from peers regarding his racial identity. He was enrolled in advanced-level courses, participated in student government, and played on the club soccer team; all activities lacking Black student representation. Consequently, he was deemed *more* White than Black by his peers. Tyson would often laugh off these remarks, yet he felt compelled to intentionally befriend more Black students and date Black girls in an effort to "balance" how he was perceived racially by his schoolmates. Although he never actually viewed himself to be either more Black or White, Tyson became keenly aware of the stereotypes and stigmas associated with both races in terms of academic achievement and extracurricular participation.

Having attended one of the largest public high schools in the state of Maryland, Tyson cultivated numerous friendships with individuals from various races. Although there was an abundance of racial diversity, common areas of the school such as the cafeteria were racially divided. The segregation prompted him to avoid these spaces because he did not feel it necessary to associate with one race over the other. Academically, Tyson was on the Advanced Placement (AP) track; he was the only African American male student in each of his 14 AP classes. On the whole, these classes, at most, had only four non-White students. Having maintained straight As in these courses, Tyson's scholastic success was often deemed surprising and unexpected by his White peers, which bothered him immensely. As the only African American student on the soccer team and on the Superintendent's Student Advisory Board often affirmed his peers' perception that he was not "really" Black. Regardless of these assumptions, Tyson never truly felt bothered, but instead used them to fuel his focus and attention towards receiving admission into a prestigious university. Near the end of high school, he no longer felt that he needed to intentionally hang out with more Blacks, as he was comfortable with his racial identity and core group of friends.

Prior to his arrival at UNC, Tyson harbored some feelings of caution when contemplating how his racial makeup would be received at an institution in the South. Growing up in a very diverse and progressive community in suburban Baltimore, he had taken for granted his exposure to a wide array of races and ethnicities (beyond Black and White) throughout his childhood. While the university heralded their claim at being one of the most "diverse" institutions in the country, Tyson noticed during his campus visit that there were numerous locations in which there was explicit racial separation—the dining halls, the gym, fraternity row, and the student union, to name a few.

Throughout his undergraduate tenure, Tyson experienced only one situation that engendered racial conflict. UNC offers incoming first-year students from underrepresented populations (namely, African Americans, Native Americans, and Latino Americans) the opportunity to have a Minority Advisor. This mentoring program affords new students various benefits such as tutoring from peers who have taken the same classes and companionship during the transition from high school to college. Rather than asking if he would like to participate in this program, Tyson was automatically assigned a Minority Advisor. Although he appreciated the positive and endearing invitations from his assigned mentor, Tyson was quite comfortable during his college transition, and thus did not feel the need to take advantage of this program. For the first semester of college, he harbored feelings of angst and disappointment because it was presumed he was African American and therefore *needed* and *wanted* to participate in this program.

Duality of Class Identity

Tyson's parents divorced when he was 3 years old and custody of him and his older sister was given to his biological mother. Having lived with his mother until he was 7 years old, he believed she was more financially stable than his father because she was taking care of him. At the time, his mother worked two jobs. Although they did not have much, Tyson understood and appreciated how hard his mother worked for their family. Despite this realization, he remained unaware of how poor his living conditions actually were.

Midway through his second-grade year, Tyson moved to Maryland to live with his father and stepmom due to his mother's financial hardships. The transition from Kansas City to suburban Baltimore was quite difficult. Rather than living in a one-bedroom apartment, Tyson now resided in a four-bedroom house. Instead of arriving home alone, his stepmom and older sister now picked him up from the bus stop each day. And as opposed to aimlessly lounging around the house, he now had daily chores and responsibilities. As a result of this new lifestyle, Tyson slowly began to notice himself straddled between two disparate socioeconomic statuses.

The summer heading into his eighth-grade year, Tyson's father and stepmother earned promotions that drastically increased their salaries. Subsequently, their family moved into an upscale neighborhood that was fundamentally different from any other environment Tyson had previously experienced. This transition marked the first time he felt unsure of his class identity. On one hand, he was proud of his parents' hard work and success, but on the other hand, he felt uncomfortable with the stigma of "being rich," as denoted by his peers and others.

Throughout high school, Tyson struggled to make sense of his class identity. While he lived comfortably with his father and stepmom, he never associated or felt comfortable with his affluent neighborhood peers. He was the only teenager in his neighborhood who worked throughout high school, something that caused him to actually identify more with his lower-income mother. Although Tyson never embraced being "middle class," he also did not feel comfortable disclosing his mother's financial hardships. He knew his mother proudly worked at Wal-Mart where she earned minimum wage, but would often lie about her employment to prevent his friends from knowing she was low-income. When Tyson lied about his mother's job, he often felt ashamed of himself, thus exacerbating his struggles with the duality of his class identity—it seemed as if he actually preferred the (mis)perception that he was at all times middle class.

As a financially independent college student, Tyson feels more comfortable negotiating situations that drastically differ along socioeconomic lines. Because he is solely responsible for paying tuition and his own college expenses, Tyson no longer feels it is necessary to identify financially with one side of his family more so than the other. Being active in an almost exclusively White social fraternity, he is constantly surrounded by students who come from wealthy families. Of his 60 fraternity brothers, Tyson is one of only four men who are solely responsible for paying their own fraternities dues. Though Tyson sometimes feels frustrated with how privileged most of his brothers are, he is simultaneously proud of his ability to pay for this experience. Because of Tyson's financial situation, he also is one of only three brothers in his chapter with jobs. Due to his work schedule, he sometimes has to forego participation in certain fraternity events and other campus activities, something that was initially disappointing.

Looking to the future, Tyson plans to earn a Ph.D. in education from a prestigious university. While this career path would predictably secure his position in the middle class, Tyson does not feel he will ever shed his low-income identity. He appreciates this aspect of his identity because he values and respects the work ethic and perseverance of certain low-income individuals, particularly his mother. Regardless of Tyson's future financial standing, he feels he will always have a bifurcated class identity because of the socially constructed stigmas associated with being rich or poor.

Juxtaposing Masculine and Gay Identities

Tyson has lived in his college fraternity house for 2 years. During the rush and pledging process, he had no intentions of disclosing his sexual orientation to any of his brothers until after graduation. While Tyson never feared that his brothers would alienate or ostracize him for being gay, he was hesitant in revealing his sexual identity, as he did not want to jeopardize the reputation of his fraternity. During the pledging process, he deliberately sought to befriend each individual fraternity brother in an attempt to establish relationships predicated on similar interests, character, and personality. Therefore, if he were to ever disclose his sexuality, the friendships would be cemented in substantive prior experiences and interactions.

The summer leading into his junior year, Tyson came out to his family and five of his closest fraternity brothers. After revealing his sexual orientation, his brothers were very open, accepting, and curious about why he had not told them sooner. Although they had some speculation, these men were proud that he felt at ease enough to share something so taboo in fraternity culture. Living in a house with 28 guys and sharing communal showers, Tyson never feels worried. However, the thought of bringing potential romantic interests to the house continues to incite anxiety for him. His chapter brothers welcomed and have even encouraged him to do so, yet Tyson continues to feel uncomfortable having his same-sex dates come to such a heteronormative space.

Tyson's room is typically filled with chapter brothers and friends from outside the organization, including women and men. As a strategic move, he usually keeps his door open with music playing to facilitate a comfortable and inviting environment. He accurately predicted that his maintenance of a clean, open, and fun room would ease any feelings of discomfort or resistance that may have been felt by his heterosexual brothers. Because Tyson did not come out until his junior year, he feels that he was able to foster meaningful friendships predicated on his character and personality rather than his sexual orientation. Among his fraternity brothers, Tyson is known for coordinating pickup basketball games, holding leadership in numerous campus organizations, and always being willing to help out anyone in need. As a result of his positive reputation in the chapter, he was elected to his fraternity's executive board for 2 consecutive years.

Beyond his extracurricular involvement and seemingly masculine hobbies, Tyson believes his heterosexual brothers feel comfortable with him because he does not perform stereotypes that are commonly ascribed to gay men. Because he plays sports and hangs out mostly with heterosexual women and men (as opposed to other queer students), many of Tyson's fraternity brothers have joked that he "is not really gay." They believe "normal" gay men are usually into fashion, romantic movies, and doing non-romantic feminine things with women. Although Tyson finds satisfaction in being "one of the guys," he hopes to reach a level of comfort where he can actively and publicly date men, while more aggressively disrupting universal misperceptions of who gay men are and what they do. Tyson realizes that his situation is unique because he performs a version of masculinity that is perceivably atypical. He recognizes that if the behavioral manifestation of his masculine and sexual identity convergence were different, so too would be his experiences in a heteronormative residential fraternity environment.

Academic and Spiritual Dimensions of Identity

In addition to being biracial, masculine, gay, and situated within two socio-economic statuses, Tyson also possesses what he would characterize pervasive academic and spiritual identities. In any given semester, it is customary for him to devote 16 hours or more each day to his job, academics, campus activities, and assorted leadership roles. He has accepted the reality that for him to be satisfied with his performance at UNC, he may only get up to 5 hours of sleep per night. Claiming to be a "night owl," Tyson usually works in the library five nights a week until at least 3:00 a.m. Since early adolescence, being an achiever has been a salient aspect of his identity. Whether it was success through sports, academics, or other forms of recognition, he has long felt that achievement would supersede any particular labeling of his individual identities. Tyson especially values exemplary academic performance because he is a first-generation college student; his grandparents and parents experience college vicariously through him. Furthermore, Tyson believes his scholastic success carries much significance in the eyes of his younger siblings. Hence, studying hard and making good grades are as a much of who he is as his race, sexual orientation, and other dimensions of his identity.

Also important to Tyson are his faith and spiritual identity. He was very active in his neighborhood church throughout high school. While his upbringing was not firmly rooted in Christian practices, he made a commitment to seek religion through the church in high school, a decision that was not accepted by his parents or siblings. During this period of deep and routine religious engagement, Tyson began to develop a spiritual identity. Although he cherished his involvement with a church youth group in high school, he has strayed away from the church since enrolling at UNC. With most local churches denouncing homosexuality, he does not feel comfortable nor sees the importance of attending. Notwithstanding, spirituality (as opposed to religiosity) remains critical to him. Tyson embraces Christianity, but feels it is a profoundly personal dimension of his identity. He experiences the presence of the Holy Spirit and believes in the power of God. He also engages in regular prayer and devotions, which he feels necessarily sustains a connection that enables him to be successful.

Problematizing Identity Ranking

In each social environment in which Tyson is immersed, he faces pressure to prioritize and value some identities over the others. Consistent with his high school experiences, simply being a successful undergraduate student at UNC often warrants speculation that he must be "more White than Black." Also, being an out-of-state student often compels people to presume that Tyson is more rich than poor. Furthermore, being an active member in a social fraternity who acts in stereotypically masculine ways typically leads people to conclude, by default, that he is heterosexual instead of gay. These are all misconceptions that he thinks about almost every day alongside the expectation that he privilege some aspects of identity over others. For example, Black students expect him to be more Black than gay; LGBT students expect him to be more aligned with their identity groups; and his fraternity brothers sometimes expect him to relax his academic identity in exchange for social activities that facilitate homosocial bonding.

Because Tyson has encountered these pressures from his peers and family members for most of his life, he commonly employs two response strategies. First, he unabashedly acknowledges the various intersections of his identity. Tyson feels no shame with his multifarious self and often takes pride in the fact that he can relate to so many different populations. He openly celebrates and makes known his complex individuality. The second response involves what Tyson calls "playing to situational expectations," a technique he started using in high school. This entails performing the identity that he believes an individual person or social group expects of him at a given time and in a particular context. He developed this approach as a response to individuals who wish to ascribe to him a dominant or one-dimensional identity. Tyson knows that simply playing to their expectations sometimes helps reinforce negative or widely accepted stereotypes. Although these assumptions disturb him and he does not understand why one identity has to be more salient than the others, Tyson recognizes the importance our society places on identity categorization. He is often left with the task of reflecting on and performing all his identities to his own satisfaction, while also managing the performative expectations of others he encounters. Clearly, this is a lot for a 20-year-old college student to manage by himself.

Implications for Educational Practice

At the beginning of this chapter, we offered an overview of research and theoretical/conceptual models that have been developed to explore the multiple dimensions of college students' identities. Offered in this section are what we hope are thought-provoking implications for faculty and administrators who endeavor to respond effectively to students with multilayered identities, as well as colleagues who are specifically charged with developing gender-specific programs for college men. We begin to frame our discussion with a pair of quotes from Kimberlé Williams Crenshaw (1989), an acclaimed critical race theorist who has written much about identity intersectionality, particularly among Black women:

> Black women sometimes experience discrimination in ways similar to White women's experiences; sometimes they share very similar experiences with Black men. Yet often they experience double discrimination—the combined effects of practices which discriminate on the basis of race, and on the basis of sex. And sometimes, they experience discrimination as Black women—not the sum of race and sex discrimination, but as Black women.

(p. 149)

Neither Black liberationalist politics nor feminist theory can ignore the intersectional experiences of those whom the movements claim as their respective constituents. In order to include Black women, both movements must distance themselves from earlier approaches in which experiences are only relevant when they are related to certain identifiable causes.

(p. 166)

Although this chapter is about identity intersectionality among men in college, much about Crenshaw's perspectives on Black women is relevant. For example, students with intersecting identities sometimes experience college environments (classrooms, social settings, residence halls, etc.) in ways that engender situational feelings of marginalization. That is, being the only man in an elementary education major may bring about alienation because of gender underrepresentation, whereas being the only Latino student on a residence hall floor may evoke similar feelings—this Latino male elementary education major who lives in Wiley Hall could be the same person who experiences these settings differently because of the multiplicity of his identities. Or sometimes he could encounter racist stereotypes (e.g., assumptions that he might be dangerous or was previously in a gang) because he is a Latino man.

Crenshaw's point about feminist and Black liberationalist movements can also be used to critique the "one-identity-at-a-time" approach employed by most college and university administrators, especially those who work in student affairs and multicultural affairs. Black culture centers, many of which emerged from civil rights era activism, have done much to make campuses more welcoming for Black students and to affirm their Black identities (Patton, 2006, 2010). Likewise, there has been a recent call for increased gender-specific programming for male undergraduates, such as men's centers and men's health campaigns (see Kellom, 2004; Harper & Harris, 2010). Jason A. Laker, Tracy L. Davis, Chuck Eberly, Rachel Wagner, Frank Harris III, Brian D. Reed, Ryan Barone, Keith Edwards, Shaun R. Harper, and a few others have worked collaboratively over the past several years on a movement to bring men's studies to student affairs. So far, their efforts have led to two national conferences, several publications and presentations, and the initiation of several men's programs and centers on campuses across the United States and Canada. Problematic, though, is the compartmentalization of race- and gender-specific programming and services that typically occurs at postsecondary institutions. Where would a student like Tyson go for support and the simultaneous exploration of his multiple identities? In most places, he would have to go to the Black culture center for matters pertaining to his Blackness, to a discussion series for men to explore his masculine identity, to the LGBT Center to connect with other non-heterosexual students, and so on. In this way, most institutions of higher education are ill-structured and thus underprepared to meet the developmental needs of students whose identities are as complex as Tyson's.

Any Black liberationalist-type movement on a campus would be insufficient if it failed to include an emphasis on the particular gendered realities of women and men, Black heterosexuals and LGBT persons, multiracial students whose ethnic identities are variably Black, and those who come from myriad socioeconomic backgrounds (from deeply impoverished to filthy rich). Likewise, a movement intended to improve men's educational outcomes must be inclusive of all men and simultaneously responsive to their masculinities and other dimensions of identity. There are undergraduates like Tyson who are left to negotiate the complexities of self without effective support from educators who supposedly specialize in student development. We deem this bad educational practice.

Conversely, good practice rests upon an understanding of what we have termed in this chapter *complex individuality*. Individuals and the nuanced aspects of their identities are often lost when student activities offices, for example, attempt to sponsor as many programs as possible that will appeal to the masses. Or when a professor endeavors to treat all students the same, despite developmental differences among them. Complex individuality entails understanding who individual students are, where they are developmentally, and what they need to resolve identity conflicts, amass portfolios of desired educational experiences and outcomes, and transition into productive lives and careers after college. Tyson, for sure, is a complex individual, but he is not alone; there are thousands, if not millions, of others like him who are men and many other things all at the same time.

Scholars, particularly Kristen A. Renn (2000, 2003, 2004, 2008), have written much in recent years about the complex identities of multiracial college students. Tyson is an example of a student who is not only biracial, but also concurrently possesses and performs numerous other social identities. Postsecondary educators, even at large universities like UNC, must reorganize their work in ways that enable them to spend more time with individual students to understand their complex individuality. Consistent with participants in Renn's research, Tyson continues to encounter expectations that he choose sides in his racial identification. Would it not be helpful for him to have routine interactions with educators and administrators who not only understand the complexities of being biracial, but are also able to process with him the duality of his socioeconomic status and other dimensions of his identity? What we are advocating here is counterbalancing wide-sweeping educational interventions with increased attention to students as individuals.

Understandably, being responsive to complex individuality is extremely difficult in most educational contexts—the larger the institution, the more unrealistic it may seem. However, large-scale programming could be reconceptualized to include an emphasis on intersecting identities; educators could commit themselves to using time they already spend with students to more deeply explore identities that may be less obvious than their gender or race; and classrooms could be used as sites where readings, discussions, and assignments focus more on multiple dimensions of identity (e.g., a men's studies class that includes a discussion on lower-income gay men of color). Patton and Harper (2009) make a persuasive case for using theory to guide educational practice. Among the examples they offer is a director of an LGBT center who reads Jones and McEwen (2000), Abes et al. (2007), and Stewart (2008, 2009) to better understand why racial minority students might feel the center insufficiently meets their needs. Efforts such as this are necessary for making offices, programs, and curricula more responsive to the complexities that individual students bring to college environments.

Conclusion

Patrick G. Love and his colleagues (Love, Bock, Jannarone, & Richardson, 2005) conducted a study that explored the intersections of sexual and religious identities among seven lesbian and five gay male undergraduate students. The authors concluded:

> For most of them, these stories involved sharing pain, struggle, and frustration. For some of them, the struggles have resulted in significant growth and a reconciliation of their sexual and spiritual identities. Most continue to struggle. Each of their stories reinforces the complexity of the issue of identity interaction in general and the additional complexity of the interaction between spirituality and sexuality.

> (p. 208)

Similarly, Tyson's story is one mostly of reconciliation and effective strategy. That is, he has learned how to negotiate the complexities of his identities in a range of social contexts and situations at UNC. On the one hand, his case is effective for illustrating our concept of complex individuality. But on the other hand, we doubt that every college student would be as successful as Tyson in negotiating the multiple dimensions of her or his identity, or willing to perform those identities in the same ways Tyson does. Thus, as educators and administrators begin to necessarily offer gender-specific programs, resources, and curricula focused on college men, there must also be much consideration for the intersection of masculinity with race, class, religious, and sexual identities.

References

Abes, E. S., & Jones, S. R. (2004). Meaning-making capacity and the dynamics of lesbian college students' multiple dimensions of identity. *Journal of College Student Development, 45*(6), 612–632.

Abes, E. S., Jones, S. R., & McEwen, M. K. (2007). Reconceptualizing the model of multiple dimensions of identity: The role of meaning-making capacity in the construction of multiple identities. *Journal of College Student Development, 48*(1), 1–22.

Abes, E. S., & Kasch, D. (2007). Using queer theory to explore lesbian college students' multiple dimensions of identity. *Journal of College Student Development, 48*(6), 619–636.

Butler, J. (2004). *Undoing gender.* New York: Routledge.

Crenshaw, K. W. (1989). Demarginalizing the intersection of race and sex: A black feminist critique of antidiscrimination doctrine, feminist theory and antiracist politics. *The University of Chicago Legal Forum, 1989,* 139–167.

Davis, T. L. (2002). Voices of gender role conflict: The social construction of college men's identity. *Journal of College Student Development, 43,* 508–521.

Edwards, K. E., & Jones, S. R. (2009). "Putting my man face on": A grounded theory of college men's gender identity development. *Journal of College Student Development, 50*(2), 210–228.

Evans, N. J., Forney, D. S., Guido, F. M., Patton, L. D., & Renn, K. A. (2010). *Student development in college: Theory, research, and practice* (2nd ed.). San Francisco: Jossey-Bass.

Harper, S. R., & Harris III, F. (Eds.). (2010). *College men and masculinities: Theory, research, and implications for practice.* San Francisco: Jossey-Bass.

Harper, S. R., Harris III, F., & Mmeje, K. (2005). A theoretical model to explain the overrepresentation of college men among campus judicial offenders: Implications for campus administrators. *NASPA Journal, 42*(4), 565–588.

Harper, S. R., & Nichols, A. H. (2008). Are they not all the same? Racial heterogeneity among Black male undergraduates. *Journal of College Student Development, 49*(3), 199–214.

Harris III, F., & Harper, S. R. (2008). Masculinities go to community college: Understanding male identity socialization and gender role conflict. In J. Lester (Ed.), *Gendered perspectives on community colleges. New Directions for Community Colleges* (No. 142, pp. 25–35). San Francisco: Jossey-Bass.

Jones, S. R., & McEwen, M. K. (2000). A conceptual model of multiple dimensions of identity. *Journal of College Student Development, 41*(4), 405–414.

Kellom, G. E. (Ed.). (2004). *Developing effective programs and services for college men. New Directions for Student Services* (No. 107). San Francisco: Jossey-Bass.

Love, P. G., Bock, M., Jannarone, A., & Richardson, P. (2005). Identity interaction: Exploring the spiritual experiences of lesbian and gay college students. *Journal of College Student Development, 46*(2), 193–209.

O'Neil, J. M., Helms, B. J., Gable, R. K., David, L., & Wrightsman, L. S. (1986). Gender role conflict scale: College men's fear of femininity. *Sex Roles, 14*(5/6), 335–350.

Patton, L. D. (2006). The voice of reason: A qualitative examination of Black student perceptions of their Black culture center. *Journal of College Student Development, 47*(6), 628–646.

Patton, L. D. (Ed.). (2010). *Culture centers in higher education: Perspectives on identity, theory, and practice.* Sterling, VA: Stylus.

Patton, L. D., & Harper, S. R. (2009). Using reflection to reframe theory-to-practice in student affairs. In G. McClellan & J. Stringer (Eds), *Handbook of student affairs administration* (3rd ed., pp. 234–260). San Francisco: Jossey-Bass.

Patton, L. D., & Simmons, S. L. (2009). Exploring complexities of multiple identities of lesbians in a Black college environment. *The Negro Educational Review, 59*(3), 197–215.

Renn, K. A. (2000). Patterns of situational identity among biracial and multiracial college students. *The Review of Higher Education, 23*(4), 399–420.

Renn, K. A. (2003). Understanding the identities of mixed race college students through a developmental ecology lens. *Journal of College Student Development, 44*(3), 383–403.

Renn, K. A. (2004). *Mixed race college students: The ecology of identity, race, and community on campus.* Albany: State University of New York Press.

Renn, K. A. (2007). LGBT student leaders and queer activists: Identities of lesbian, gay, bisexual, transgender, and queer-identified college student leaders and activists. *Journal of College Student Development, 48*(3), 311–330.

Renn, K. A. (2008). Research on biracial and multiracial identity development: Overview and synthesis. In K. A. Renn & P. Shang (Eds.), *Biracial and multiracial college students: Theory, research, and best practices in student affairs. New Directions for Student Services* (No. 123, pp. 13–21). San Francisco: Jossey-Bass.

Renn, K. A., & Bilodeau, B. L. (2005). Queer student leaders: An exploratory case study of identity development and LGBT student involvement at a Midwestern research university. *Journal of Gay and Lesbian Issues in Education, 2*(4), 49–71.

Reynolds, A. L., & Pope, R. L. (1991). The complexities of diversity: Exploring multiple oppressions. *Journal of Counseling and Development, 70*(1), 174–180.

Robinson, T. L., & Howard-Hamilton, M. F. (2000). *The convergence of race, ethnicity, and gender: Multiple identities in counseling.* Upper Saddle River, NJ: Merrill/Prentice Hall.

Smith, S. S., & Moore, M. R. (2000). Intraracial diversity and relations among African Americans: Closeness among Black students at a predominantly white university. *American Journal of Sociology, 106*(1), 1–39.

Stewart, D. L. (2008). Being all of me: Black students negotiating multiple identities. *The Journal of Higher Education, 79*(2), 183–207.

Stewart, D. L. (2009). Perceptions of multiple identities among Black college students. *Journal of College Student Development, 50*(3), 253–270.

Stewart, D. L., & Lozano, A. (2009). Difficult dialogues at the intersections of race, culture, and religion. In S. K. Watt, E. E. Fairchild, & K. M. Goodman (Eds.), *Intersections of religious privilege: Difficult dialogues and student affairs practice. New Directions for Student Services* (No. 125, pp. 23–31). San Francisco: Jossey-Bass.

Torres, V., & Hernandez, E. (2007). The influence of ethnic identity on self-authorship: A longitudinal study of Latino/a college students. *Journal of College Student Development, 48*(5), 558–573.

Torres, V., Howard-Hamilton, M. F., & Cooper, D. L. (2003). Identity development of diverse populations: Implications for teaching and administration in higher education. *ASHE-ERIC Higher Education Report* (Vol. 29, No. 6). San Francisco: Jossey-Bass.

Torres, V., Jones, S. R., & Renn, K. A. (2009). Identity development theories in student affairs: Origins, current status, and new approaches. *Journal of College Student Development, 50*(6), 577–596.

White, L. S. (1998) "Am I Black enuf fo ya?" Black student diversity, issues of identity and community. In K. Freeman (Ed.), *African American culture and heritage in higher education research and practice* (pp. 91–119). Westport, CT: Praeger.

Wijeyesinghe, C. L. (2001). Racial identity in multiracial people: An alternative paradigm. In C. L. Wijeyesinghe & B. W. Jackson III (Eds.), *New perspectives on racial identity development: A theoretical and practical anthology* (pp. 129–152). New York: New York University Press.

6

QUEER MASCULINITIES IN HIGHER EDUCATION

Beth Berila

ST. CLOUD STATE UNIVERSITY

Shifting Masculinities

Both queer and women's studies disciplines have analyzed the relationship between gender and sexual identity. This chapter will examine how those fields trouble hegemonic masculinities to enable more complex analyses of the diversity of gender found in lesbian, gay, bisexual, and transgender communities. Drawing on research in queer, gender, and women's studies, I will analyze the unique circumstances facing queer men in college. While this chapter will focus on men, I do not see gender as a static or given category. Indeed, I recognize that other members of the queer community perform masculinity. For this group of marginalized students, hegemonic masculinity can be just as oppressive to men as it is to women, and even more so for individuals who do not conform to either half the gender binary. Instead, many queer men perform variations of masculinity as a form of empowerment and resistance to heteronormative culture. Such performances become complicated if the campus climate is unwelcoming to LGBT students, which can be severely alienating for all queer students, including queer men of color. This chapter will examine the insights that queer, gender, and women's studies theories of men and masculinities offer higher education professionals.

Women's studies as a discipline was historically created to foreground the experiences, oppressions, and resistance of women throughout society. It has long argued that gender is a social construction. Gendered norms are learned behaviors that result in inequitable power dynamics. Those behaviors that are rendered feminine are typically devalued, while those that are considered masculine are valorized and granted more social power. For example, qualities such as passivity, submissiveness, emotionality, nurturance, and caretaking, which are typically considered feminine, are given much less power and status than are assertiveness, independence, rationality, and strength, which tend to be seen as masculine. While feminine behaviors have long been projected upon women and masculine ones upon men, feminism has noted that these behaviors are socialized from a very young age and perpetually reinforced by social institutions such as the family, the schools, the media, the military, and the law.

Gender and queer studies have honed this understanding even further to recognize that femininity and masculinity are not neatly attached to women and men's bodies, respectively. Both fields have helped us see that if gender is a social construction, then men's behavior is as shaped by sociopolitical contexts as is women's (Kimmel, 2007). If gender is learned, then we must carefully study what kinds of behavior men learn to perform, where they learn it, and what the social consequences are for those behaviors. As a White, lesbian, feminist who comes to women's studies in part through my location in the queer community, I cannot position masculinity as singular or as wholly problematic. I instead understand masculinities as multiple and as codes of behavior that take on different meanings when performed by different people in different contexts. When gay men, for instance, perform masculinity, it is often an expression of both their gender identity and their sexual identity. It may or may not reflect the more oppressive elements of hegemonic masculinity. For young college men, in particular, who may just be coming out and claiming their own sense of gay male identity, their performance of masculinity may be an important site of self-expression and pride for them. It may also mark them as targets for discrimination on campus, a point which I will discuss later in this chapter.

While it is not always clear where the boundaries between these disciplines are, together they provide valuable insights into masculinities in higher education. These intersections offer practical considerations in working with students at the university level. As the editors of this volume have stated, hegemonic masculinity refers to "the meta-narrative of an essential masculinity, which shapes our socialization and lived experiences, and the ways in which we construct knowledge, ways of knowing, and bureaucratic structures such as colleges and universities" (Laker & Davis, this volume). Hegemonic masculinity makes certain practices normative, both at the individual and institutional levels (Connell & Messerschmidt, 2010). Certain forms of masculinity, then, remain dominant, often privileging rationality, independence, authoritativeness, toughness, and patriarchal power relations. This hegemonic masculinity tends to be upheld by the very structure of higher education in the West, with its emphasis on linear, rational thought and its compartmentalization of disciplines. Scholars Connell and Messerschmidt (2010) note that hegemonic masculinity "embodie[s] the currently most honored way of being a man, [and] it require[s] all other men to position themselves in relation to it" (p. 218).

So while certain forms of masculinity reflect the dominant norm, other forms not only exist but also trouble that hegemony. Queer studies has theorized the interplay between gender and sexual identity. It has helped us better understand why, when someone does not neatly perform the femininity or masculinity traditionally attached to their gender, they are often presumed to be gay: gender and sexual identity are deeply intertwined. While hegemonic masculinity upholds not only patriarchy but also the norm of heterosexuality, alternative forms of masculinity trouble both meta-narratives. The prominent feminist, queer scholar Judith Butler (2006) has theorized how gender is a performance, noting that gender does not preexist our performances of it. According to Butler, there is no essential man or woman; rather, we create our sense of male and female by performing a series of acts. Gender, then, is a performance that is an ongoing process of repetitive acts, which allows for an interruption and redefinition of the gendering process. This influential theory has opened the way for understanding the myriad of masculinities and femininities that exist, as well as the fact that they do not need to conform to the woman/feminine, man/masculine binaries. In fact, as the queer scholar Judith Halberstam (1998) notes, masculinity becomes understandable when it leaves men's bodies. For example, transgender theorists have theorized the ways that masculinity takes on different meanings when it is performed by transgender individuals who are often targets of oppression (Rubin, 2003). Even performances of "hegemonic masculinity" do not protect them.

The point here is that masculinities are a set of behaviors that take on different meanings when they are embodied by different people. When lesbian women perform masculinity, the very same behaviors that would be oppressive when performed by the dominant social group (White, straight men, for instance) take on a more socially resistant, transgressive edge. Women are taught to be meek, passive, submissive, dainty, and, above all, heterosexual, so lesbian women who perform masculinity challenge socialized gender norms on fundamental levels. They therefore deal a blow to hegemonic masculinity by creating the cultural dissonance that results when we see women performing qualities we expect in men. Similar complexities and possibilities occur for gay men in college. But it will first be helpful to examine the processes through which traditionally aged college students experience their queerness, before then talking about how college campuses can better support them.

LGBT Identity Development

Scholars of college student development have theorized identity trajectories for LGBT students, who face unique issues apart from the standard adjustment to university life. While several models exist, the one that best addresses the sociopolitical complexities of race, class, gender, and sexuality comes from Anthony R. D'Augelli (1994). He posits several elements of the identity development process: exiting heterosexual identity; developing a personal LGB identity status; developing a LGB social identity; becoming an LGB offspring;

developing an LGB intimacy status; and entering a LGB community. D'Augelli sees these as fluid, life-long processes, in which an individual may be working on multiple levels at one time, and may circle back to part of the process more than once. This model is productive in a discussion of masculinities because it recognizes that a person's identity is shaped by environmental and sociopolitical factors and recognizes that no two people's trajectory is identical (D'Augelli, 1994; Bilodeau & Renn, 2005).

Because of the complexities of queer students' identity development, it is worth briefly talking about each element of D'Augelli's (1994) model, before also discussing issues of transgender identity development. One of the first elements involves an individual becoming aware of their physical, emotional, and spiritual attraction to others of the same sex and, by extension, their difference from the dominant heternormative ideology. This realization often includes periods of denial and internalized homophobia, both of which can be detrimental to a student's queer identity. Because mainstream U.S. culture presumes and privileges heterosexual identity and often stereotypes and pathologizes queer sexuality, LGB individuals often internalize those negative perceptions and turn it upon themselves. The feminist scholar Beverly Tatum (2008) describes racism with a metaphor that is useful here: it is like breathing in smog, ingesting the negative perceptions because they are so prevalent. Not only is the same process at work for internalized homophobia, but it can be compounded for LGB individuals of color who also have to struggle with the oppression of internalized racism. Eventually, LGB students often accept their queer identity but may still struggle with internalized homophobia throughout their lives. This makes it even more crucial for universities to provide accurate education on LGB issues and to create queer-friendly spaces.

The second element in D'Augelli's (1994) model involves developing a personal LGB identity status, in which the student forms a more accepting and stable sense of their LGB identity. This can only happen if s/he is educated about gay stereotypes and understands the insidious process of internalized homophobia. If students can name it, they can better see how it is working in their own lives; otherwise, they may just presume that their experience is a personal one (rather than a cultural one) and take the negative self-perceptions to heart, a process which is both unhealthy and dangerous. We know that many queer youth struggle because they have nowhere to go with their questions and do not have support to work against the deleterious effects of a homophobic culture, so it is incumbent upon college campuses to combat that pattern.

The next aspect of the D'Augelli (1994) model includes becoming an LGB offspring, in which individuals "come out" to their family support structure. Some students will experience severe tension with family members and even loss of relationships when they disclose their sexuality, which adds great distress that can affect their emotional health and their college performance. In addition, they may be placed in the odd position of having to educate their families about LGB sexuality at a time when they are just learning it themselves, a situation which can be either empowering or disempowering, depending on the receptivity of their family and their own awareness level. While this stage can add a great deal of stress to their lives, so can the choice to remain in the closet. The D'Augelli model recognizes that people choose to come out to their families at different times in their lives (and sometimes not at all). Some students might be hiding their identity from their families, which adds a different kind of stress to their emotional health.

In the fifth aspect of the model, students develop an LGB intimacy status with a person of the same sex. When students embark on their first queer relationships, it can be both an exciting and a fearful time. They will feel the same excitement and passion of any new relationship, but they will often lack role models for healthy relationships because of the relative absence of queer sexuality in mainstream culture. Depending on their access and familiarity with a healthy and active queer community, they may have to forge relationship models on their own, which may or may not result in healthy relationships, and they will have to combat heteronormative cultural discrimination. This can again lead to undue stress. If a campus climate is not queer friendly, students may not feel safe disclosing their relationship, which can compound internalized homophobia. Moreover, since every individual works this identity development model in different ways, each party in a relationship may be at a different place with their own internalized homophobia. It can add stress to a queer relationship if one person is very out in every realm of his/her life while the other is closeted. These are added layers of relationship negotiations that queer college students may have to deal with, and if college counselors and other mentors are not familiar with these issues, the students may get very little support with their problems. In addition, when the first few relationships break up, queer students may have a resurgence of internalized homophobia, as they take on the heteronormative discriminatory messages and wonder if their sexual identity is the problem rather than seeing the break up as a normal process of early relationships. Alternatively, students may begin to experiment a lot when they develop their LGB intimacy status, and if they are not well informed about sexual safety, that may result in unhealthy and risky sexual behavior.

Some of these issues can be addressed by the type of LGB community with which they get involved (the sixth element of the D'Augelli model). If students can find a healthy, informed, and politically active LGBT community on campus, they have a place to forge healthy relationships, find mentors, and learn about LGBT issues and history. This can help a great deal in counteracting some of the more detrimental situations they may face in the other aspects of the model, but it is not inevitable. It has to be cultivated. D'Augelli (1994) notes that not all LGB folks ever pursue this aspect, and some may find themselves at risk for losing their jobs or housing if they end up in a homophobic environment, before, during, or after college. Nevertheless, cultivating a strong LGB community in college will provide students with a crucial foundation that they can build on for the rest of their lives. With the right kind of campus support, LGB college students often find an exciting empowerment through offices such as LGBT student centers, women's centers, multicultural student centers, women's studies programs, gender studies programs, and ethnic studies programs. Of course, they also run the danger of feeling pressure to compartmentalize their identities. If these campus units are not adequately aware of the importance of intersecting identities, students may experience oppression in unexpected places; they might, for instance, feel racial and cultural support from multicultural student services but experience homophobia there, while they might feel queer support from LGBT offices but experience racism there. It is crucial that the various campus offices and personnel be well-educated about intersections of oppression, so that they can, in turn, help educate students about those issues and teach them how to be effective allies.

D'Augelli's (1994) model speaks mostly to LGB students, though some of the aspects also explain the identity development of transgender individuals. Though few studies have been done on transgender students, the few that do exist suggest that they follow a similar trajectory to D'Augilli's identity development model (Renn & Bilodeau, 2005; Bilodeau, 2005). Gender identity refers to a person's internal sense of being male, female, or some other gender identity, particularly if that internal sense does not neatly match up with the biological sex of male/female. "The term transgender focuses on individuals whose gender identity conflicts with biological sex assignment or societal expectations for gender expression as male or female" (Bilodeau & Renn, 2005, p. 29). Gender identity issues may or may not result in sexual identity issues; that is, a transgender individual may identify as lesbian, gay, bisexual, or heterosexual. While changing cultural patterns have produced better understandings of LGB issues in recent years, transgender issues continue to be severely misunderstood. Transgender students, then, experience compounded discrimination and invisibility. They may have no language to explain the internal gender dissonance they experience, and they may only be "out" in certain contexts, while feeling the need to hide in others.

While transgender students face unique issues of discrimination, well-educated campus officials can help university students, faculty, and staff understand the gender issues that face everyone. Queer theorists such as Kate Bornstein (1994), Judith Butler (2006), Leslie Feinberg (1998), Judith Halberstam (1998), and Riki Ann Wilchins (1997) have all noted how transgender issues destabilize the false gender binary of male/female. This destabilization helps us recognize the ways that we all learn to "perform" gender, often by conforming to socially constructed gender expectations. As Bilodeau and Renn (2005) suggest, "beyond normalizing support of transgender identities, a number of feminist, postmodern, and queer theorists suggest that all individuals may benefit from the dismantling of dual gender systems, promoting greater freedom from rigid gender roles" (p. 32). We learn what is acceptable for a woman or man to do, and what is not acceptable. Queer theorists have troubled the idea that masculinity is always and only attached to men's bodies, that femininity is always and only attached to women's bodies, and that gender and sexual identity are the same. In doing so, they have taken the feminist idea that gender is socially constructed even further to note that gender can be fluid, learned, and unlearned. Thus, when campus officials understands transgender issues enough to create safe spaces for transgender students, a productive byproduct is that they can also help all students understand the implications of the gender they perform.

Being Queer and Male in College

So what does all this mean for our study of masculinities? For gay college men, socialized gendered norms may or may not fit them appropriately. The dominant forms of masculinity that receive the most attention in traditional women's studies often fail to adequately address the variety of masculinities that queer students might be exploring. Indeed, gay, bisexual, and transgender men often receive conflicting messages about masculinities. Many of them grow up bombarded with the same hegemonic masculinities as everyone else. We live in a heteronormative culture, so most children are pressured to conform to them throughout childhood and adolescence. If youth are not in a gay-friendly environment, which is the case for many youth, they often do not know what is happening when they feel dissonance when the social expectations of hegemonic masculinities and heterosexuality do not fit them. Many queer youth struggle with how to make sense of this dissonance and where to go for help. They often try to conform to social expectations, but feel empty and disconnected because they cannot. Often, the pressure to be heterosexual or to "prove" one's heterosexuality is intertwined with the pressure to perform a particular kind of masculinity. These are the students who enter our colleges, and as university faculty, staff, and administrators, we need to be cognizant that these students will bring this history with them to their new college community.

Many young college men are newly exploring their queer identity. Students are increasingly coming to college campuses already out as queer to themselves and/or to others, but many go through the coming out process after arriving at college. As U.S. population becomes better versed in LGBT issues, there is increasingly cultural discourse and resources about gay issues for youth to turn to, but this wider discourse may not make it much easier for youth from more isolated, rural areas. Students might be scared, confused, empowered, and/or enthralled with their developing sense of queer identity. They might experiment with types of masculinities as they locate themselves within the queer community, try to accept themselves, and cultivate a sense of belonging. The identity development model in higher education needs to be inflected with the journey of coming out. As higher education professionals, depending on where we teach, we may be working with students with this kind of past. Of course, gay men are not the only ones who may feel this dissonance; heterosexual men may not feel comfortable with hegemonic masculinities either. This is one way in which queer studies can teach us, as higher education professionals, something about how to trouble hegemonic masculinities and open up a wider array of options.

This vexed relationship to hegemonic masculinity weaves itself through a students' coming out process as well. Some students have come out early in life and are quite confident in who they are by the time they get to college. Others may be very early in their coming out process, or may even discover their queer sexuality in college, and will be exploring their sexual and gender identity as they navigate their place in the campus community. We are, therefore, often working with people at a range of stages in their identity development: not just in college student development, but also in their coming out process. That process, as many scholars have noted, is often imbued with internalized homophobia, which can manifest in students' relationship with themselves and with others. It can also shape students' relationships to both their sexual identity and their masculinity.

Performances of diverse masculinities are often part of students' identity development as queer students. As students explore their sexual identity, they may also be experimenting with different codes of masculinity. Sometimes, performing more "stereotypical" gay masculinity is a part of how newly out people feel connected to the queer community. Similarly, some transgender individuals try to pass by conforming to socially prescribed feminine or masculine behaviors. In doing so, they are not trying to reinforce hegemonic masculinity, they are trying to "fit in" and finally feel comfortable in their own body. Sometimes, this performance changes as they come to terms with their gay and/or transgender identity, at which point they might decide to conform less and to instead perform some combination of feminine and masculine behaviors. But this attempt to "fit in" needs to be understood as a part of their coming out process, not as an attempt to reproduce oppressive power dynamics. In a society that assumes a clear and limiting binary between man/woman, masculine/feminine, these performances that might resemble traditional masculinities actually have very different meanings when they are combined with the marginalized identity of gay, bisexual, or transgender. These forms of masculinity, far from being hegemonic, are often expressed as a form of belonging to queer communities and as a form of resistance to homophobic oppression.

Campus communities bring together large numbers of students from different backgrounds, though the degree of racial, ethnic, sexual, gender, economic, and cultural diversity will vary by campus. Students' understanding of sociopolitical power dynamics and diversity issues will also vary, and, indeed, it is part of the mission of most higher education institutions to help students learn about those issues. But as they do so, issues of discrimination often arise, which can be particularly tricky for students early in their coming out process. Students' sense of safe space and of community support might shift dramatically from moment to moment on campus. Depending on how accepting and informed about LGBT issues the specific college campus is, queer male students might experience both a sense of welcomed and long-overdue belonging to a queer community but also sudden and dramatic shifts of safe space. For queer students, safety can dissolve instantaneously as an uninformed student enters the classroom or a professor makes a homophobic joke. In addition, queer students might lose family and friends when they come out, which can increase their sense of isolation and the difficulty of transitioning.

These issues might translate into performances of masculinities and need to be addressed if students are to be successful in college. For instance, one gay, Black, male student of mine heightened his performance of hyper-gay masculinity when he felt out of place. When I first had him in class, he would always be at the front of class, in front of my desk, when I entered the room, engaging other students in banter. He would interrupt me during my talks during class to ask whether students really had to do the papers or tease about class being cancelled. These were not intended to be direct challenges to my authority or to disrupt class. They were heightened performances of gay male banter that I see in many LGBT communities, but they were inappropriately timed and amplified to the point of disruption. Early in the semester, I could see new students averting their eyes, putting on false smiles, or other signs of discomfort as this student engaged in these public displays, particularly when he was at the front of the room before I entered the classroom. I myself, admittedly, became frustrated with his need to step into the spotlight and engage the entire class in a banter that only really works when all the participants play along. In LGBT communities, this banter is common among friends, but it is not appropriate in a college classroom to the degree to which he was trying to create it.

Of course, I could have shut it down immediately, but I was also aware that something else was going on here. As a gay, Black, male who had just transferred to our predominantly White, midwestern university from a much more urban environment, I sensed that some of this performance of masculinity was about navigating the shift in climate. I teach at a four year state school that often struggles with diversity issues. Though there are many excellent efforts at anti-racist, feminist, and queer-friendly education, the dominant climate is not conducive to a student such as this one feeling comfortable and safe, especially so soon after transferring to the college. I thought carefully how to handle the situation without silencing him, and often resorted to redirecting or not engaging the banter until I became more familiar with his situation. After a while, his contributions to class discussions became less gay male banter and more issue related. His comments reflected a solid feminist analysis about issues of oppression and about his own outsider position on our campus. At one point, he even acknowledged that when his discomfort and lack of safety became heightened, he used his humor to try to fit in. Over time, his performance became more muted, and he forged meaningful relationships with his classmates, who joked with him, inquired after him, and stayed after class to talk with him. My point here is that had this student merely be seen as a class disruption and shut down, his lack of safely and alienation from our campus would have been heightened. While there are many productive ways to handle such a situation, it is important to see his masculinity performance as a manifestation of his positionality on campus as a gay, Black, male.

Other students I have worked with have performed similar variations of gay masculinity as they forge their identity. As an out lesbian faculty member, I have worked with several students from the LGBT community. Some students "try on" different variations of masculinity throughout their college career. Some relish the freedom of finally fitting in but are still developing a more integrated identity. This process may mean that, like the student I just described, they perform more informal and community-based masculinity to a degree that is not appropriate in a more formal or professional context. That is, they feel so free and delighted with their newfound outness or their new queer community that they perform that playful, heightened masculinity not just with their friends but also in the classroom and job experience.

I want to be clear that I am not saying such performances are inherently or always problematic. In many ways, they help challenge the heteronormative climate of most college campuses and assert the presence of queer identity in ways that can productively alter that climate. Assumptions about what constitutes appropriate behavior in the college classroom or in professional arenas are shaped by heteronormative and cultural ideologies, which these performances can help challenge, so that it is not the students who need to change their behaviors but rather the ideological norms of public spaces.

Helping Students Navigate Integrated Identities

It is crucial to mentor students as they navigate a more integrated out identity. There is a difference between acceptable behaviors with friends and those that for more public, formal spaces, and it is in the students' best interest to help them identify ways to be "out and proud" while also being professional. That can be done in a way that creates room in the larger climate for gay identities. Such mentoring is one of the ways that those of us in student services and faculty positions can help students succeed in college.

Effective mentoring of LGBT students requires an understanding of their complex positionalities on campus. Depending on the climate of the university, students' intersections of race, class, gender, and sexual identity can result in issues that shape their college experiences in both positive and negative ways. They may finally feel they can be who they are, and they may face discrimination that can affect their college success. Higher education professionals need to better understand these dynamics in order to effectively support and mentor queer students. While student services professionals often understand student development issues, they may not be well-versed in the unique experiences of LGBT students. Faculty, on the other hand, may not consider identity development issues at all nor see it as their purview. This false divide between academics and student development needs to be bridged if we are to successfully support queer students.

Given the detrimental effects of internalized homophobia, college personnel need to take a proactive strategy to combat it. LGBT and allied students need to be educated about how homophobia and internalized homophobia operates and given specific tools with which to combat such oppression. Campuses need to provide numerous positive role models and educate students about the history of LGBT social movements in order to help queer students understand their cultural contributions. These positive images can help counter the negative stereotypes of the gay community. More importantly, the history of LGBT social movements helps students develop a politicized lens through which to understand their own identity and the cultural discrimination they may experience. In other words, a critical analysis is crucial to a healthy and self-aware identity development. College faculty and staff need to educate themselves before they can educate students. As they do so, it is important to address intersections of oppression. Studying how race, class, gender, and sexual identity intersect in complex ways and play out differently between rural and urban universities can provide a valuable foundation from which to successfully support students.

The model of women's studies departments and women's centers and of ethnic studies departments and multicultural student centers offers a productive one for integrating the two realms of the college experience. Women's studies and ethnic studies departments educate students, faculty, and staff about oppression which can gradually help create a campus climate free from discrimination. Such fields also provide students from marginalized groups an understanding of the history of their groups and the social movements they have forged, which can be extremely empowering for youth who are claiming their marginalized identity. Moreover, women's studies and ethnic studies departments have long worked closely with their counterparts in student development, women's centers and multicultural resource centers, to support and empower students. Their partnerships have integrated student identity development with academic learning to provide mentoring and education both inside and outside the classroom. Such models are critical for the success of marginalized students.

Most campuses have LGBT centers, which often end up working with women's studies and ethnic studies departments because of the lack of LGBT studies academic units. Most campuses do not have such established LGBT or queer studies programs to do the equivalent types of education about homophobia and the gay and lesbian movement. Such academic units are slowly emerging, but most of that education ends up being housed in women's studies departments. The growth of gender studies or gender and sexuality studies departments attests to the increasing awareness of the links between feminist issues and LGBT rights, as well as the range of masculinities and femininities that exist. Universities need to more fully support these academic units in their growth because they play a crucial role in educating all campus participants in how to create a diverse and empowering community.

One of the key places where such support can be particularly effective is in the residence halls. Research has shown that residence halls are often unwelcoming to LGBT students (Evans, 2001). A study by D'Augelli and Rose (1990) found that many first–year, White, heterosexual students held negative views of homosexuality. This harsh environment is particularly damaging because residence halls are often the first places where students experience independence while moving away from home. As such, they provide a place to forge community and explore their (sometimes) newly discovered queer identity. Issues of homophobia can emerge as gay students date or when gay students room with heterosexual ones. If their "home" life away from classes is fraught with psychological oppression, it will dramatically affect their emotional health and academic success. Residence hall directors and staff can foster a supportive environment by educating their residents and taking a positive, proactive stance when LGB students are present. Gay-friendly educational programming can be really effective. In addition, as Evans points out, college staff should proactively try to place out queer students with queer friendly roommates and to hire openly queer residence hall staff to serve as role models. If there is a large enough group of incoming LGBT and allied students, a learning community could be a really effective way of helping them forge community and learn about the specific identity development issues that are unique to queer students. Of course, such a learning program should also be diverse in terms of race and gender as well, so those issues would also need to be covered in the curriculum. Such a visible and active cohort on campus would increase LGBT visibility on campus, thereby countering the invisibility that many LGBT students feel on the one hand, and provide the diversity education to counter the hyper visibility they may experience on the other.

Such learning communities could be an effective way to complement the widespread existence of safe space trainings. Many college campuses have safe space programs, which serve as a useful foundation for learning about heterosexism and homophobia. However, such training also has its limits.

They can imply that there are "safe spaces" wherever such stickers exist, but many LGBT students know that a space can turn unsafe surprisingly quickly. Moreover, if the trainings do not effectively address intersections of race, gender, and sexuality, then a queer student of color may unexpectedly face racial discrimination in a space that s/he expects to be safe. The psychological exhaustion of constantly having one's guard up, or letting it down and then experiencing unexpected oppression, can take its toll. This is not to say that safe space trainings do not have their value, but they should be complemented by other types of trainings as well.

One useful strategy might be to do widespread gender performance education on campuses. For instance, I teach a gender and the body course in which I have a guest performance studies professor facilitate gender-based exercises with the students. She divides the students by gender (after noting the problematic male/female binary) and has students engage in several everyday activities. Whoever is not doing the exercise watches the other group, and then performs what they saw back to them. So, for example, the men are asked to pretend they are walking in late to a class or catching someone's attention at the airport, and then the women, after watching them, imitate what they saw the men do. In one class, the gender differences were striking. The men were very vocal, shouting, whistling, and waving as they performed their tasks. But even when the women imitated what they saw, *none* of the women vocalized. We were then able to talk about the gendered nature of who felt authorized to take up more space and why the women remained silent *even* when they were asked to mimic very vocal men. These types of activities make it very evident that we all perform gender in socially constructed ways, and that different power dynamics are attached to the ways that men and women perform. The discussions that result help us examine shifting masculinities and femininities, and help students see that everyone—not just LGBT students—can benefit from creating a wider range of acceptable gender performances.

These types of initiatives can be cultivated more intentionally so that queer students have more support on campus. Part of that support needs to include the understanding that there are multiple forms of masculinity that change meaning in different contexts. Such shifts in meaning, when combined with the education that women's, gender, and queer Studies offers, opens possibilities for new ways of relating to masculinity. As queer students perform shifting modes of gender, they help us realize that all gender is fluid and performed, albeit with real material consequences. As we learn to understand their gender performances in context, we can help then better succeed in college. And as we understand all masculinities to have vexed relations to hegemonic ideals, we can open possibilities for all men, queer and heterosexual, to rethink the consequences of the masculinity them perform.

References

Bilodeau, B., & Renn, K. A. (2005). Analysis of LGBT identity development models and implications for practice. *New Directions for Student Services,* 111, 25–39.

Bilodeau, B. (2005). Beyond the gender binary: A case study of transgender college students development at a midwestern university. *Journal of Gay and Lesbian Issues in Education, 3*(1), 29–44.

Bornstein, K. (1994). *Gender outlaw: On men, women, and the rest of us.* New York, NY: Routledge.

Butler, J. (2006). *Gender trouble: Feminism and the subversion of identity.* New York, NY: Routledge.

Connell, R. W., & J. W. Messerschmidt. (2010). Hegemonic masculinity. In J. Lorber (Ed.), *Gender inequality: Feminist theory and politics* (pp. 218–225). New York, NY: Oxford University Press.

D'Augelli, A. R. (1994). Identity development and sexual orientation: Toward a model of lesbian, gay, and bisexual development. In E. J. Trickett, R. J. Watts, & D. Birman (Eds.), *Human diversity: Perspectives on people in context* (pp. 312–333). San Francisco, CA: Jossey-Bass.

D'Augelli, A. R., & Rose, M. L. (1990). Homophobia in a university community: Attitudes and experience of white heterosexual freshmen. *Journal of College Student Development, 31*, 484–491.

Evans, N. J. (2001). The experiences of lesbian, gay, and bisexual youths in university communities. In A. R. D'Augelli, & C. J. Patterson (Eds.), *Lesbian, gay, and bisexual identities and youth: Psychological perspectives* (pp. 181–198). New York, NY: Oxford University Press.

Feinberg, L. (1998). *Trans liberation: Beyond pink and blue.* Boston, MA: Beacon Press.

Halberstam, J. (1998). *Female masculinity.* Durham, NC: Duke University Press.

Kimmel, M. (2007). *The gendered society* (3rd ed.). New York, NY: Oxford University Press.

Renn, K. A., & Bilodeau, B. (2005). Queer student leaders: An exploratory case study of identity development and lesbian, gay, bisexual, and transgender students involvement at a Midwestern research university. *Journal of Gay and Lesbian Issues in Education, 3*(1), 49–71.

Rubin, H. (2003). *Self-made men: Identity and embodiment among transsexual men.* Nashville, TN: Vanderbilt University Press.

Tatum, B. (2008). Defining racism. In A. Kesselman, L. D. McNair, & N. Schniedewind (Eds.), *Women images and realities: A multicultural anthology* (4th ed., pp. 380–385). New York, NY: McGraw Hill.

Wilchins, R. A. (1997). *Read my lips: Sexual subversion and the end of gender.* New York, NY: Firebrand Books.

7

SOCIO-ECONOMIC AND WORK IDENTITY INTERSECTIONS WITH MASCULINITY AND COLLEGE SUCCESS

Brian D. Reed

UNIVERSITY OF VIRGINIA

Recent research suggests that many qualified students do not participate or succeed in postsecondary education for reasons other than ability (Astin & Osegeura, 2004; Carter, 2006; King, 2000, 2006; Sax, 2008; Tinto; 2007; Titus, 2006). Though postsecondary participation and success[1] across all demographics has increased in varying degrees over the past four decades (Engle & Tinto, 2008; Wellman et al., 2009), low–SES students and low–SES males in particular continue to be underrepresented among postsecondary enrollees and graduates (King, 2006). While these educational disparities have been well documented in recent years (Bowen, Chingos, & McPherson, 2009; King, 2000; Titus, 2006; Walpole 2003, 2007), a gap remains in the literature regarding the role that gender plays in perpetuating these disparities, especially for men from low–SES backgrounds and their efforts to succeed in college.

This chapter summarizes the literature on low–SES student success with a specific focus on low–SES males and low–SES White males particularly, offers theoretical considerations that may help us understand their underrepresentation in college graduating cohorts, and provides recommendations for practice. The goal of this chapter is to make college administrators aware of the current disparities in low–SES male's postsecondary success and how the construction, performance, and negotiation of a low–SES masculine identity may mediate their opportunities and chances of success in college. While any study of student success should avoid what Reason (2009) terms "conceptual isolation" by focusing on the multi-theoretical traditions affecting student success, this particular chapter focuses specifically on the socio-cultural formations of gender identity, specifically masculinity, provided the limited availability of literature on low–SES male masculine identity and postsecondary outcomes.

Thus, this chapter should be read as part of the larger theoretical project examining persistence-to-graduation.

Why Focus on College Success?

As recent ACT (Lotkowski, Robbins, & Noeth, 2004) and College Board (2008) reports attest, national and individual success is increasingly reliant on postsecondary education. If the United States hopes to increase or even maintain its global educational and economic edge, the nation will need an increasingly more educated and skilled workforce. As the ACT report notes, currently 60% of U.S. jobs require some type of postsecondary training or education. This need will increase precipitously in the coming years according to the U.S. Department of Labor (2000) as jobs requiring advanced skills will double compared to those requiring only basic skills. For those industries still reliant on lower skilled labor, those jobs are being increasingly moved to countries with cheaper labor or are being automated (U.S. Department of Education, 2002). Simply put, the face of U.S. labor is changing from one of rote tasks to one of flexibility, adaptability, and ongoing skill development. This does not mean that the United States will have fewer jobs but simply different jobs requiring increasingly greater levels of education. Consequently, this also means that the quality of life disparities (e.g., earnings and health) between those with additional education and those without are also sure to grow (Gladieux & Swail, 1999).

Postsecondary education is arguably the most important element in social mobility and breaking the cycle of intergenerational poverty. Irrespective of race/ethnicity, age and gender, the more education one has, the greater annual earnings one can expect (Bill & Melinda Gates Foundation, 2009). Specifically, the Gates Foundation report on Postsecondary Success notes that compared to their non-college enrolling peers, persons with some college but no degree earn 18% more annually, while those with an associate's degree earn 29% more, and those with a bachelor's degree earn 62% more. Over a lifetime, the earnings gap between college graduates and non-college graduates is in excess of $1,000,000 (U.S .Department of Education, 2003). What is more, bachelor's degree recipients can expect an average annual unemployment rate of only 6% while those with a high school diploma or less have an annual unemployment rate of 14% (Lotkowski et al., 2004). Clearly, not only is postsecondary education significant in developing the nation's human capital and ultimately its economic, social, and political capital, but also provides a significantly better life for individuals.

The Situation for Low-SES Students

Despite the documented benefits of postsecondary participation and success, Goldrick-Rab (2006) states that one of the most troubling features of the

American education system is the significant and widening SES gap in postsecondary achievement. Specifically, Haveman and Smeeding (2006) note that while 51% of the highest SES quartile eight graders in 1988 reported having attained a bachelor's degree 12 years later only 7% of students from the lowest SES quartile reported the same. Unfortunately, it appears as if the postsecondary education success gaps of low-SES students will become only more pressing in the years to come as the population of children growing up in low-SES households continues to burgeon (Postsecondary Education Opportunity [PEO], 2008). Specifically, between 1989 and 2006 the number of K–12 students receiving free lunch has increased to just over 45%, up from 31.4%, while the number of children living above the poverty line has decreased from 68.6% to 54.9% (PEO, 2008). This is especially prevalent in states located in the Southwest (e.g., Arizona and New Mexico) and Central Appalachia (e.g., Kentucky and West Virginia) that currently comprise the bottom quarter of college participation and educational attainment rates among students from low-SES households (PEO, 2008).

As it stands, a low-SES student's chances of postsecondary success are disproportionately uncertain. Currently, of the nation's 4.5 million low-SES undergraduates, 26% will leave college following their first year compared to only 7% of high-SES students (Engle & Tinto, 2008). Moreover, after 6 years Engle and Tinto find that only 11% of low-SES students will have earned a bachelor's degree compared to 55% of their more affluent peers. For those students from modest backgrounds who begin their studies at 2-year institutions success is equally if not more elusive. In a recent Education Trust report, Engle and Lynch (2009) find that less than one-third of all entering 2-year students attain a certificate, associate's degree, or transfer. While troubling in its own right, this statistic is even more disconcerting provided that students from the most modest financial backgrounds are overrepresented in 2-year institutions (Engle & Lynch). Moreover, Bailey, Jenkins, and Lienbach (2005) note that while roughly 30% of students who begin at community colleges transferred to a 4-year institution, only 10% actually earned a bachelor's degree. While these aggregate trends of low-SES student success are both persistent and troubling, they also hide disparities across gender.

Gender Disparities in Postsecondary Success

In the latter 1970s, women began to outpace men in both college enrollment and persistence-to-graduation (Mortenson, 2003). Before this time, males held a distinct advantage in both categories, with a specific spike in degree attainment coming for men in the late 1960s and early 1970s as a result of the Vietnam war (King, 2006). Since that time however, women have steadily outpaced men in persistence-to-graduation, and in 1992–1993 specifically, disparities between women and men across races/ethnicities became more pronounced. Specifically, while White males' college completion rates dipped between 1992 and 1998 (39% to 33%), White females' rates of graduation remained steady at 44% to 45% of all bachelor's degrees conferred (Sax, 2008). Also, racial/ethnic minority women's college success rates steadily increased while their male peers' success rates remained relatively flat. Currently, though all gender and racial demographics have experienced increases in persistence-to-graduation, the increases experienced by males across race/ethnicity has not been significant enough to close the gaps in their success compared to that experienced by their female peers (Sax, 2008). What is more, these gender gaps remain most prevalent in the lowest-SES quartiles (King, 2006).

In response to the growing popular and scholarly concerns about males in postsecondary education, King (2000, 2006) explored the access and success gaps across gender. Sponsored by the American Council on Education (ACE), King examined the educational achievement of men and women in the United States. Specifically, King (2006) disaggregated national data by race/ethnicity, age, and income in an effort to verify whether a gender gap indeed existed, where the gap was most prevalent, and what concerns about the gender gap were real or misguided. Since her initial report in 2000, King notes in 2006 that several changes in gender equity within postsecondary education have occurred. The most profound shift, King asserts, is the widening gender access and achievement gap among White and Hispanic traditional-age undergraduates as a result of the larger shares of enrolling and graduating low-income White females and low- and middle-income Hispanic females. King notes that this shift resulted in a smaller percentage of traditional-age males in higher education, from 48% to 45% of the national postsecondary cohort, between 1996 and 2004.

Further analyses by King (2006) shows that women who enter college with the aim of attaining a bachelor's degree are more likely (35%) to do so within 5 years as compared to their male peers (28%). In addition, despite aggregate research suggesting that all college men are struggling to succeed in college (Mortenson, 2003), King (2000) counters, "there is not a generalized educational crisis among men, but there are pockets of real problems. In particular, African-American, Hispanic, and low-income males lag behind their female peers in terms of educational attainment" (p. 1).

Concerning access, a condition for success, King's (2006) analysis reveals that as a share of dependent undergraduates in the lowest income quartile, low-SES White males declined by 4% (48% to 44%) between 1996 and 2004, while low-SES Hispanics males representation in postsecondary education also dipped (46% to 43%) during this period. Low-SES African American and Asian American males saw only modest gains during this time, 1% and 2%, respectively. Conversely, high-SES White males (50% to 51%), high-SES African American (41% to 54%), and high-SES Hispanic (47% to 51%) males all increased during this same time period. Thus, King's research reveals that SES greatly influences male access and success in postsecondary education and that overall, the much-discussed gender gap in enrollment and persistence-to-graduation, when examined more closely, is largely influenced by SES.

Explaining the overall gender gap among economically disadvantaged students, King (2006) suggests that the low wages consistently paid to women with high school diplomas provides a special incentive for women to pursue postsecondary study, while the income paid and health benefits afforded to men with high school diplomas, though modest, is enough to create a similarly powerful inverse incentive.[2] While King (2006) and Sax (2008) assert that both low-SES males and females are negatively affected by the nation's current economic and educational structures, national data, as presented by Mortenson (2003) shows that low-SES males of all races/ethnicities appear particularly disadvantaged in terms of postsecondary education success. In summary, King's (2006) research reveals that while male shares of postsecondary enrollees and bachelor's recipients have not lost considerable ground in the aggregate, particular low-SES male shares have actually declined in both areas.

In an equally comprehensive examination of the gender gap in postsecondary education, Sax (2008) states that in the aggregate, women's increasing representation among college enrollees and graduates does not fully explain the diversity of the gender gap and the overall complexities of gender once students are enrolled. Using nationally representative data, Sax (2008) engaged in a comprehensive review of the differential effects of college on women and men. Like King (2000, 2006), Sax's research suggest that the gender gap in postsecondary education is largely related to race/ethnicity and SES, with the largest gender disparities befalling low-SES males and African-American and Latino males.

While not specific to low-SES males, Sax (2008) finds that in the year prior to college enrollment, college males, compared to their female classmates, reported that they were less likely to engage in educationally and personally enriching activities consistent with postsecondary persistence-to-graduation. Conversely, these males were more likely to engage in behaviors that were actually detrimental to their success, habits that we can assume some, if not many, will carry with them to college. Particularly, Sax finds that only 27% of the males in her sample studied 6 hours or more per week compared to 38% of females. In addition to having lower rates of interaction with faculty outside of class and lower rates of participation in school clubs and groups, 43% of males reported being bored in class, and 62% noted that they came late to class. Males also reported higher rates of video game play (22% of college males dedicate 6 hours or more per week to this activity) as well as higher rates of alcohol consumption than women.

Though current research (King, 2006) has done well to acknowledge college experience and outcome disparities across biological sex, with females from low-SES backgrounds enrolling in and completing college in greater numbers than males, there has been insufficient discussion concerning how the formation, negotiation, and performance of gendered identities influence post-secondary outcomes once low-SES males enroll. Though discouraging economic realities negatively influence the success of low-SES women as well, what might the formation of low-SES men's gendered identities comparatively tell us about their lower success rates (Mead, 2006; Sax, 2008)? This is not to suggest that low-SES females are particularly advantaged, but that there remain unanswered questions regarding the formation of social class and masculine identities among low-SES males that influence the supposition of college as a non-viable opportunity, before and even after they matriculate.

Similar to the work of Archer, Pratt, and Phillips (2001), this chapter is written in line with research theorizing masculinity in terms of hegemony and multiple representations of masculinity, paying particular mind to the complex intersectionality of social class and gender. That is, masculine identities are constructed, negotiated, and performed in a multitude of ways and are differentially positioned in regards to stratifications of dominance and subordination (Connell 2005; Kimmel & Messner, 2004). This stratification is based on the unequal distribution of social, economic, and political resources that provide some discourses of masculinity greater legitimacy and influence over others (Messerschmidt, 1993). As Archer et al. (2001) state, hegemonic masculinity is often defined and organized around the discursive subordination of classed, raced, and sexually oriented others. To this end, the struggle to control the meaning of masculinity is central to power struggle of other social groupings (class, race, etc.) (Edley & Wetherell, 1995).

According to Connell (2005), the hegemony of masculinity means that at any point a single form of masculinity will be exalted over all others, and in the case of classed masculinities, it is theorized that as a result of their class marginalization low-SES males will construct and perform masculinities that are quite different from that of men from higher social classes. While to speak of masculinity in such narrow terms risks what Connell (2005) notes is a collapsing "character typology" of masculinity, for the purposes of examining low-SES males' college persistence, it may prove useful to cautiously restrict our analysis given the growing class segregation of US culture and the growing gaps in low-SES males' college completion (p. 76).

Research related to socio-economic status, gender, and higher education clearly reveals that low-SES males are not enrolling and graduating at rates similar to their low-SES female and high-SES male peers. In addition, men overall are participating in fewer educationally purposeful activities associated with persistence-to-graduation and increasing their time spent on activities that actually impede their chances of success. While popular reports focus on the gender gap, bemoaning the aggregate decline of men in higher education, SES in combination with gender appears to have the most significant influence on male student postsecondary success.

Low-SES men continue to lag behind their female peers in college success statistics is the result of several factors, largely related to the socio-cultural conditions of gender and gender identity formation, negotiation, and performance. While several scholars of low-SES student postsecondary access and success focus on the structural disparities associated with academic preparedness, finance/economics (Paulsen & St. John, 2002) college information (Perna, 2000), and within college organizational/environmental dynamics (Titus, 2006) the ways in which gender and gender identity formation affect college success have been relatively unexamined. Specifically, while much of the literature on low-SES males' exclusion from higher education has suggested that these men struggle to reconcile their class and masculine loyalties within compulsory education (Lehmann, 2007; Quinn et al., 2006), there is scant research (Archer et al., 2001 as the exception) connecting these complex gender and class locations to low-SES male persistence-to-graduation once they matriculate into postsecondary education. While Connell (1989) and others have employed discussions of gender power relations and multiple masculinities to address the educational disparities of low-SES males, Bourdieu's (1987) notion of habitus, I propose, is an additionally salient concept for addressing the classed and gendered subjectivities of low-SES males and their marginal college success. In addition, habitus might also provided college administrators with a fresh lens through which to theorize and enact low-SES male drop-out interventions.

Habitus

Largely employed in the discipline of sociology, habitus, as defined by Bourdieu (1987), is the collection of perceptions, aspirations, and actions shared by persons of a similar social class. Habitus reflects the ways in which the individual internalizes personal possibilities in response to structural limitations and constraints (Cooper, 2006; Paulsen & St. John, 2002) and the ways in which people derive their understanding of social rules and their place within the social order (Horvat, 2001). Habitus can be thought of as the tacit understandings that shape student behaviors and choices, specifically the choice to persist to graduation. Applied to the examination of low-SES male college completion, it is theorized that these students experience a disconnect between their low-SES masculine habitus and the perceived effeminate middle class culture and aims of postsecondary education. That is, low-SES males over-identify with work, specifically manual labor, as a means to compensate for the lack of social and material capital that they feel should be afforded them as male, but yet they do not have as a result of their specific class location. As a result, education is often interpreted in two ways by low-SES males. As I will detail, either education is the dividing characteristic between men who engage in physical labor, or real work, and those who take-up positions of power and order giving in labor (Pyke, 1996; Willis, 1977), or is interpreted as too difficult and financially risky with no guarantee on its return (MacLeod, 2009; Weis, 1990, 2004). Each interpretation results in what Pyke (1996) suggests is low-SES males unwitting obscuring and justifying of "macrostructural inequalities and microlevel power relations" (p. 528).

Habitus, then, is helpful in understanding why and how the marginalized accept and even contribute to their low status in society (Bourdieu (1987), and for the purpose of this chapter, explains how low-SES males may have their college success derailed by the long-standing dispositions created by the marginalization and subordination of their particular form of masculinity.

For the purposes of this chapter, the complex relationship between low-SES males' class, race, and gender are understood as the principal contexts shaping their unique and particular habitus. For low-SES students and their aspirations for postsecondary success, Walpole (2007) states that aspects of low-SES student habitus lead to lowered educational aspirations and the acceptance of their marginalized place in society. As is suggested, the limited exposure that these low-SES students have to postsecondary role models in their immediate environs, especially within the family, serve to level their postsecondary aspirations (Cooper, 2006). This is most readily illustrated in Paulsen and St. John's (2002) research, which finds that despite earning "A" grades in postsecondary education, low-SES students in their study were the least likely group to have high educational aspirations (e.g., to attain a bachelor's degree). In higher education, Lehmann (2007) states that as a result of long standing class dispositions low-SES students "retreat to a more intense identification with their working-class roots" rather than conform to the middle-class norms of postsecondary education (p. 100).

Based on his study, MacLeod (2009) suggests that once low-SES males realize that they are unlikely to assume professional or managerial positions within the labor market, they resign themselves to the fact they will likely take on low-wage jobs similar to those of their parents or persons of similar class location. This resignation is exacerbated by within school structures such as curriculum tracking and the expectation of failure by school personnel (Archer et al., 2001). These students, according to MacLeod, eventually come to believe that their own deficiencies are the source of their school challenges. Similarly, Willis' (1977) working-class "lads" also realized that their chances for success in school and eventually in the labor market were remote. As Willis further notes, the lads saw no immediate or future benefit to conforming to school standards; even if they did, they were not convinced that such conformism could take them beyond where they currently were in the social class hierarchy. While such attitudes are cited as largely affecting patterns of enrollment, they too can influence success if and when low-SES males decide to enroll in higher education.

As research suggests, parents are instrumental in the development of the student's postsecondary aspirations (Hossler, Schmidt, & Vesper, 1999;

McDonough, 1997; Perna, 2000). Unlike their high–SES peers whose parents define success in terms of a postsecondary degree, low–SES students' parents, as a result of long-standing class habitus, are more likely to view a high school diploma and full-time employment following high school as the standards of success for their children (Walpole, 2003). Hsiao (1992) notes that while college may be a rite of passage for many high–SES students, for those from low–SES backgrounds, attending college can seem like a great separation from the people and culture with which they are familiar. In fact, Dimaria (2006) suggests that many low–SES families may actually discourage postsecondary participation out of financial necessity or fear that their student will be changed by the middle-class values inherent in higher education. While McDonough (1997) notes that such assessments may not be rational, they are based on the only models and examples that low–SES students and their families have available in their immediate environment.

Intersections of Race, Class, and Gender: Low-SES White Males and Education

Several scholars have qualitatively examined the educational experiences of low–SES White males (Archer et al., 2001; Freie, 2007; MacLeod, 2009; Quinn et al., 2006; Willis, 1977; Weis, 1990, 2004). Though typically based on the experiences of urban men from the United States and the United Kingdom, this research does share consistent themes with studies of rural low–SES White males (Whiting, 1999). The themes consistent across studies of low–SES White males and schooling include school as a site of lowered expectations, overtly policed behavior, curriculum tracking, and persistent disengagement. As Quinn et al. (2006) profess, "working-class whiteness is a particularly interesting and neglected issue for lifelong learning. Performing the supposedly superior position of White male, within an overwhelmingly White, but also disregarded and disrespected community, is a confusing business" (pp. 739–740). Specifically, Morris (2005) notes that while Whiteness is generally privileged in secondary and postsecondary education, White school personnel specifically tend to view low–SES Whites as aberrant and backwards. Based on the research on low–SES White men and schooling, their experience in education follows a rather predictable pattern of structural marginalization, leveled aspirations, and failure.

In what appears to be the only study specifically dedicated to low–SES males and their attitudes towards postsecondary education participation, Archer et al. (2001) use discussion group data from 64 males from working-class and ethnically diverse backgrounds to examine how definitions of masculinity lead to self exclusion from postsecondary education. Similar to the aim of this chapter, Archer et al. suggest that their work serves to examine what are the complex interconnections of race, class, and gender and how the negotiation and performance of those concurrent identities influence postsecondary participation, and as I propose, their success. Though Archer et al.'s study primarily addresses reasons for enrolling or not enrolling in higher education among low-SES males, it serves to inform this chapter by providing some qualitative insight into what might be similar reasons for low-SES males not persisting to graduation. Though the relationship may be indirect, as suggested by Tinto (2002), the fact remains that "patterns of access play an important role in shaping persistence" (n.p.).

Using data from the University of North London's Social Class and Widening Participation in Higher Education Project, Archer et al. (2001) conducted multiple focus groups organized around student decisions about their education and their participation or non-participation in higher education. Researchers found that the non-participation of low-SES White males in postsecondary education is a direct result of the males' perception of the incompatibility between schooling and working-class masculinity. Based on their extensive work with young low-SES White males, these researchers consistently found that this group conceptualized college attendance as a largely middle-class and anti-masculine endeavor. Within this framework, Archer et al.'s men profess that low-SES masculinity is most readily marked by physical prowess, endurance, and mechanical expertise, traits constructed in direct opposition to managerial masculinities that are deemed soft and effeminate (Leach, 1993; Pyke, 1996; Willis, 1977). Coupled with the traditional expectation of men as providers for the domestic household, work (specifically physical labor) and masculinity become fused (Leach, 1993). It is here that education, especially postsecondary education for the low-SES male, is inextricably linked with the masculinity of males from the managerial class. Archer et al.'s work clearly illustrates how the habitus created by the social class conditions of low-SES White males contributes to their sense of resignation concerning their educational potential as well as their desire to attain some semblance of masculine status via labor.

In addition, the males in Archer et al.'s (2001) study appear to lack any role models from similar class origins who were successful in higher education, and this lack of success among their social-class contemporaries appears to contribute to the leveling of aspirations for the low-SES men in the study. Furthermore, they found that low-SES White males perceived higher education as too difficult and with little to no guarantees for success. Moreover, these men noted that participation in higher education was a frightening proposition, given risk of loans and other related debt, and that early entry into manual labor provided immediate money. Last, while not all participants in the study had entirely ruled out enrolling in college, many simply felt that as a result of their social class circumstance, non-participation was a choice that had been made for them. This finding is also consistent with MacLeod (2009) and Moss' (2003) respective work with low-SES White males and low-SES White students in the United States.

Despite apprehensions about their success in postsecondary education and its ultimate utility in their lives, some low-SES males still attempt college study. However, the status inconsistency experienced by low-SES males and the sense of discontinuity that accompanies school struggle results in a deep skepticism about their potential within the contemporary U.S. achievement ideology (MacLeod, 2009). Despite the privilege often afforded them as a result of their race and gender, low-SES White males experience a paradoxical sense of powerlessness within the context of school and seek out other ways to assert their masculinity (Barker, 2005). As Connell (1989) suggests, the reaction of these men who fail is to claim other sources of power and definitions of masculinity (e.g., athletic ability, physical aggression, and sexual virility). Thus, not only are low-SES males, like all low-SES students, marginalized via factors such as low expectations and curriculum tracking, but they have traditionally constructed versions of masculinity that "may prevent them from perceiving participation [in school] as a 'manly' option" (Archer et al., 2001, p. 434).

Despite the fears and risks these low-SES men associate with participating in postsecondary education, as a result of changing economic conditions, Freie (2007) notes that this construction of masculinity appears to be giving way to a more favorable, though contradictory, view of postsecondary education as a growing necessity, even while they continue to code mental labor as feminine. For those who do attempt postsecondary education, their lingering assessment of education as anti-masculine and middle class, rooted as we know in their particular habitus, can lower their initial and subsequent commitments to education in general and the goal of graduation more specifically (Tinto, 1975).

Peer Influence

It appears that low-SES male's assessment of education as too difficult and in direct contradiction to valorized forms of masculinity is ever present in their male peer social networks. In their ethnographic study of Black teens at a racially diverse, yet divided, affluent California high school, Ogbu and Davis (2003) sought to understand the barriers to academic achievement and engagement faced by these students. One barrier that the authors detail is the degree to which peer influence undermines academic engagement. In line with Bourdieu's (1987) conceptualization of peer effects on academic success, Ogbu and Davis note that many of the Black teens abandoned or slacked in their academic efforts because they wanted to avoid teasing and accusations that they had abandoned their race.

In the same way that Ogbu and Davis' (2003) students reported immense pressure to not appear smart to their friends as to avoid being accused of "acting White," both Willis (1977) and MacLeod (2009) note that the low-SES White males in particular also resorted to such disengagement as to avoid a similar ostracism based on their social class. Leach (2003) states that this form of solidarity is used by low–SES males in particular as a means of coping with the limited prospects they have in the labor and education hierarchies. Specifically, among low–SES males this deference to male peers may be employed as a defense mechanism to garner male peer acceptance and support when they perceive that they have little hope of social mobility and when school has little to offer them in way of affirming their masculinity (Barker, 2005) or helping them become more socially mobile.

Summary

In summary, for many low–SES males entering the labor force stands as a masculine rite of passage, a masculinity marked by provision, caretaking, and production (Leach, 1993). It is through labor, despite their often low status as hourly wage earners, that low–SES males derive their unique sense of masculinity apart from the marginalization of the larger society and the organizational context of school. As a result of their marginalization and subordination, these men develop long standing and durable dispositions, known as habitus, that situates postsecondary study as effeminate and not worth the investments and risks for persons of their particular gender and SES. However, as the United States continues its shift to a knowledge- and technology-based economy, marked by rapid deindustrialization and labor union dissolution, education beyond high school will be required to maintain the most basic standard of living (Fine, Weis, Addelston, & Hall, 1997; Freie, 2007; Weis, 1990, 2004). Overall, research on low–SES males shares a basic belief that due to their class marginalization particularly, these men employ a hyper-masculinized and labor-focused sense of self to combat the emasculation they feel in not attaining the power and privilege, both inside and outside school, they feel should be afforded them as male in contemporary society.

Moreover, low–SES male's reluctance to see postsecondary education as a viable and realistic option for persons of their circumstance presents compelling obstacles to their college success if and when they do enroll. That is, for those low–SES males who do go to college, lingering doubt about chances of success can make persistence and college completion all the more difficult. However, without a postsecondary education in the changing labor market, masculinity as constructed and performed through manual labor may fail to be a viable and sustaining option for low–SES males in the immediate years ahead.

Recommendations

As part of their effort to increase the access and success of low-income students in postsecondary education in general, the College Board's Commission on Access, Admissions and Success in Higher Education has made several policy related recommendations to combat the persistent disparities plaguing students from low-income backgrounds. Here I borrow from their action agenda to make recommendations for administrators concerning low-SES males' persistence. Though much of this chapter focuses specifically on low-SES males, many of the recommendations below might also prove useful in assisting low-SES females and the diversity of low-SES males as well. Also, while many of the recommendations below are pre-college based, colleges and universities would do well to partner with local school systems and parents to combat the noted inequalities in low-SES student education in general and the cultural definitions and formations of masculinity in particular, if not for moral and ethical imperatives then for the increase in potential applicants and political good will. Moreover, because low-SES male habitus results from the earliest of experiences, pre-college interventions appear to make the most theoretical and practical sense.

Make Head-Start More Accessible for Low-Income Families

Because children from low-SES households begin their school experience with less vocabulary and reading sophistication, enrollment in universally available pre-school programs provides low-SES children with a better foundation by which to begin their formal education. The College Board (2008) recommends high-quality half-day programs for 3-year-olds and half- and full-day programs for 4-year-olds. While participation in such programs cannot guarantee a low-SES student's educational success, it does stand to close the gaps in their access to vital educational and cultural resources. Moreover, teachers and volunteers involved in these programs should be aware of how both programmatic and social structures unduly emphasize gender differences and the social messages that boys and girls receive quite early concerning gender roles and stereotypes. Pollack (1998) and Kivel (1999) are particularly instructive authors in the area of education and gender.

Improve and Increase Low-SES Student College Counseling

Because low-SES students tend to lack the same information and understanding of the college preparation and application process of their high-SES peers, the College Board (2008) recommends vast improvements in the quality and number of college counselors. College counseling, they say, should begin early in a student's academic career, and counseling should pay particular attention to low-SES students. This counseling can and should include help with selection of college prep courses, understanding financial aid, and standardized test preparation (College Board). I additionally recommend that such counseling, when conducted with low-SES males, be sensitive to the potential resignation that some low-SES males feel regarding their postsecondary prospects and should seek to counteract low-SES habitus with more positive messages regarding their educational opportunities and potential. Such programs can be paired with mentoring programs where socially and academically thriving low-SES college males act as mentors for elementary and high school low-SES males.

Curriculum Alignment

Because the rigor of high school curriculum is cited as the greatest predictor of student success once in postsecondary education, the College Board (2008) recommends that school systems work with higher education to align the K–12 curriculum with postsecondary entry requirements. As these authors note, many low-SES students typically begin their postsecondary careers underprepared. Curtis (2008) and King (2006) note that low-SES males particularly lack the strong curricular preparation required for postsecondary study. As the commission recommends, a rigorous curriculum should include:

- 4-year long units of English and literature;
- four units of college-preparatory mathematics;
- three units of laboratory science;
- two units of foreign language; and
- three units of history and social science.

Focus on Gender

Rather than create new programs that focus on low-SES males, I recommend providing gender based interventions within already existing early intervention programs such as Upward Bound, Talent Search, and GEAR-UP that counteract messages that equate schooling with femininity and femininity as negative. Such interventions might also benefit from time and space provided for single sex cohorts to discuss their educational goals, plans, and apprehensions, where masculine posturing and fears of vulnerability might be reduced without the presence of female peers. Initiatives like the Men's Leadership Program at the University of Virginia utilize mentor and mentee relationships among college males and middle-school males to do just this by using a critical gender framework in large group and one-on-one settings.

I also recommend that colleges and universities work with K–12 institutions to implement gendered based social norms campaigns, similar to the ones recommended in Chapter 12 of this text by Alan Berkowitz, containing positive messages about school and postsecondary education. Such a campaign could utilize multiple media to drive home the message that schooling does not make one less of a man or a traitor to one's social class.

Parent Support

As the research of Hossler et al. (1999) suggests, parent support (e.g., discussion, campus visits, savings) and encouragement for postsecondary study is the single greatest predictor of student enrollment, and has been theorized by Walpole (2003) and Wells (2008) to positively influence persistence. As such, colleges and universities, in collaboration with K–12, should focus on educating parents as well about the college preparation and application process. The good news is that based on Perna and Swail's (2002) analysis, many early intervention programs already require parental participation. However, as noted, low-SES students' parents are more likely to view a high school diploma and full-time employment following high school as the standards of success for their children (Walpole, 2003). In addition, many of these programs do not specifically work with parents on how they too can counteract culturally embedded messages their low-SES male student receives regarding postsecondary education opportunities. Thus, partnerships among schools and parents must also focus on each group emphasizing to low-SES males that higher education does not disqualify men from their particular social class background as masculine. Moreover, schools and parents can and must work cooperatively to interrupt messages of hegemonic masculinity altogether.

Acknowledging the Terrain

Whether employed in K–12 interventions or once low-SES males have enrolled and matriculated in postsecondary education, the presence of adults who understand and affirm the terrain of masculinity and class marginalization, while also appropriately challenging male privilege, is essential in young mens' development. While much of what I have discussed above refers specifically to encouraging low-SES males' college participation and success, the larger message is that the gender and class scripts that limit low-SES male potential must be interrogated and disrupted. However, this often requires the presence of adults, both men and women, who understand gender identity development, gender socialization, and how identities of class, race, and gender inform and influence the other. Thus, it is imperative that educators and parents familiarize themselves with the theoretical and practical resources available so that they might help the young men in their lives cope with and challenge the current gender structure.

Conclusion

Among other factors, research consistently shows that persistence to graduation in postsecondary education is greatly influenced by SES (Gerald & Haycock, 2006; Paulsen & St. John, 2002: Tinto, 2004; Walpole, 2003, 2007) and gender (King, 2000, 2006). Moreover, despite nearly three decades of research dedicated to its study (Astin, 1975; Tinto, 1975, 1993), solutions to the problem of student departure have been elusive, and as Walpole (2003) notes, have often neglected the conditions affecting low-SES student success. More specifically, this research has bothered little with the disparities in persistence-to-graduation across both class and gender, and consequently how the construction, negotiation, and performance of low–SES masculinities informs male perceptions of opportunities and limits in postsecondary education.

With little research having been dedicated to low–SES student success and the heterogeneity of low–SES students, it is evident that more research into the diversity of low–SES students and the factors influencing their persistence to graduation trends is warranted. What is more, the ongoing underrepresentation of low–SES males in college completing cohorts not only affects national and state economic goals, but also has significant impact on individual low–SES males, particularly earnings. For those low–SES males who do enroll in higher education despite external and self-imposed limitations, many arrive with lingering doubts about their rightful place in college and their abilities to succeed. I suggest in this chapter that Bourdieu's (1987) discussion of habitus may be a particularly novel theoretical supposition by which to examine these attitudes and behaviors.

To truly assist low–SES males in their efforts to complete college, we must first acknowledge that all men do not exact the same degree of power and privilege from patriarchy and sexism. As a result of their marginalized and subordinated class identity, these men will not benefit equally in the division of social, economic, and political capital. This does not excuse men who are victims of classism from their individual responsibilities in making every effort to persist to graduation if and once enrolled, but these distinctions are significant when we enter into research and policy formation regarding low–SES male's educational outcomes and how the formation of their specific masculinities inform their understandings of postsecondary education success. In addition, programs and services, such as those recommended by the College Board (2008), can and should be adapted to include more gender and class conscious information so that the unique interests of low–SES males can be addressed. To this end, administrators must resist the temptation to form policy and practice for low–SES males and low–SES females as if they were the same. Research (Archer et al., 2001; Freie, 2007) suggests that the needs of low–SES students can be different across and even within gender, and administrators should acknowledge this fact so that each population's distinctive needs can be met.

Notes

1. Success is used interchangeably with persistence-to-graduation and college completion.
2. It may be argued that this incentive has diminished steadily since the late 1970s with de-industrialization and union-dissolution (Fine, Weis, Addelston, & Hall, 1997; Freie, 2007; Weis, 1990) and now more rapidly as new jobs require greater levels of education (National Commission on Community Colleges, 2008). In addition the largest job growth for low-skilled laborers is in the service industry, a labor sector viewed by many men as anti-masculine and requiring a deferential customer service orientation that Nixon (2009) suggests many low–SES males have rejected.

References

Archer, L., Pratt, S. D., & Phillips, D. (2001). Working-class men's construction of masculinity and negotiations of (non) participation in higher education. *Gender and Education, 13*(4), 431–449.

Astin, A.W. (1975). *Preventing students from dropping out.* San Francisco, CA: Jossey-Bass.

Astin, A. W., & Oseguera, L. (2004). The declining "equity" of American higher education. *The Review of Higher Education, 27*(3), 321–341.

Bailey, T., Jenkins, D., & Leinbach, T. (2005). *What we know about community college low-income and minority student outcomes: Descriptive statistics from national surveys.* New York, NY: Community College Research Center.

Barker, G. T. (2005). *Dying to be men: Youth, masculinity, and social exclusion.* New York, NY: Routledge.

Bill and Melinda Gates Foundation (2009). *Postsecondary success.* Seattle, WA: Author.

Bourdieu, P. (1987). The forms of capital. In J. G. Richardson (Ed.), *Handbook of theory and research for the sociology of education* (pp. 241–258). New York, NY: Greenwood Press.

Bowen, W. G., Chingos, M. M., & McPherson, M. S. (2009). *Crossing the finish line: Completing college at America's public universities.* Princeton, NJ: Princeton University Press.

Carter, D. F. (2006). Key issues in the persistence of underrepresented minority students. *New Directions for Institutional Research, 130*, 33–46.

College Board. (2008, December). *Coming to our senses: Education and the American future.* New York, NY: The College Board.

Connell, R. W. (1989). Cool guys, swots, and wimps: The interplay of masculinity and education, *Oxford Review of Education, 15*, 291–303.

Connell, R. W. (2005). *Masculinities* (2nd ed.). Berkeley: University of California Press.

Cooper, M. A. (2006). Dreams deferred?-Exploring the relationship between early and later postsecondary educational aspirations among racial/ethnic groups (Doctoral Dissertation, University of Maryland). *Dissertation Abstracts International, 67/03*, 244.

Curtis, P. (2008, February 1). 85% of poorer white boys fall short in GCSEs. *Guardian.* Retrieved on March 13, 2009, from http://www.guardian.co.uk/politics/2008/feb/01/uk.gcses

Dimaria, F. (2006). Working-class students: Lost in a college's middle-class culture. *The Education Digest, 72*, 60–65.

Edley, N., & Wetherell, M. (1995). *Men in perspective: Practice, power, and identity.* London: Prentice Hall/Harvester Wheatseaf.

Engle, J., & Tinto, V. (2008). *Moving beyond access: College success for low-income, first generation students.* Washington, DC: The Pell Institute.

Engle, J., & Lynch, M. (2009). *Charting a necessary path: The baseline report of public higher education systems in the access to success initiative.* Washington, DC: The Education Trust.

Fine, M., Weis, L., Addelston, A., & Hall, J. M. (1997). In secure times: Constructing white working-class masculinities in the late 20th century. *Gender & Society, 11*(1), 52–68.

Freie, C. (2007). *Class construction: White working-class student identity in the new millennium.* Lanham, MD: Lexington Books.

Gerald, D., & Haycock, K. (2006). *Engines of inequality: Diminishing equity in the nation's premier public universities.* Washington, DC: The Education Trust.

Gladieux, L. E., & Swail, W. S. (1999). Financial aid is not enough: Improving the odds of college success." In J. King (Ed.), *Financing a college education: How it works, how it's changing.* Washington, DC: ACE/Oryx Press.

Goldrick-Rab, S. (2006). *Getting off track: Path-dependence and socioeconomic inequality in college completion.* Paper presented at the annual meeting of the Association for Institutional Research, Chicago, IL.

Haveman, R. H., & Smeeding, T. M. (2006). The role of higher education in social mobility. *The Future of Children, 16*(2), 125–150.

Horvat, E. (2001). Understanding equity and access in higher education: The potential contribution of Pierre Bourdieu. In J. C. Smart & W. Tierney (Eds.), *The higher education handbook of theory and research* (pp. 195–238). Hingham, MA: Kluwer Academic.

Hossler, D., Schmidt, J., & Vesper, N. (1999). *Going to college: How social, economic, and education factors influence the decisions students make*. Baltimore, MD: Johns Hopkins University Press.

Hsiao, K. P. (1992). *First-generation college students* (ERIC ED351079). Los Angeles, CA: Eric Clearinghouse.

Kimmel, M., & Messner, M. (Eds.). (2004). *Men's lives* (6th ed.). Boston, MA: Allyn and Bacon.

King, J. E. (2000). *Gender equity in higher education: Are male students at a disadvantage*. Washington, DC: American Council on Education.

King, J. E. (2006). *Gender equity in higher education: 2006*. Washington, DC: American Council on Education.

Kivel, P. (1999). *Boys will be men: Raising our sons for courage, caring, and community*. Gabriola Island, BC: New Society Publishers.

Leach, M. (1993). Hard yakkin'. Retrieved January 1, 2008, from http://www.xyonline.net/Yakkin.shtml

Lehmann, W. (2007). 'I just didn't feel like I fit in:' The role of habitus in university drop-out decisions. *Canadian Journal of Higher Education, 37*(2), 89–110.

Lotkowski, V. A., Robbins, S. B., & Noeth, R. J. (2004). The role of academic and non-academic factors in improving college retention. Retrieved January 5, 2010, from http://www.act.org/research/policymakers/pdf/college_retention.pdf

MacLeod, J. (2009). *Ain't no makin it* (3rd ed.). Boulder, CO: Westview Press.

McDonough, P. M. (1997). *Choosing colleges: How social class and schools structure opportunity*. Albany: State University of New York Press.

Mead, S. (2006). *The truth about boys and girls*. Washington, DC: Education Sector.

Messerschmidt, J. W. (1993). *Masculinities and crime: Critique and reconceptualization of theory*. Lanham, MD: Rowman & Littlefield.

Morris, E. W. (2005). From "middle class" to "trailer trash:" Teachers perceptions of white students in a predominantly minority school. *Sociology of Education, 78*, 99–121.

Mortenson, T. (2003). *Fact sheet: What's wrong with the guys?* Retrieved April 10, 2009, from http://www.postsecondary.org/archives/previous/GuysFacts.pdf

Moss, K. (2003). *The color of class: Poor whites and the paradox of privilege*. Philadelphia: University of Pennsylvania Press.

National Commission on Community Colleges. (2008). *Winning the skills race and strengthening America's middle class: An action agenda for competitiveness through community colleges*. New York, NY: The College Board.

Nixon, D. (2009). "I can't put a smiley face on': Working-class masculinity, emotional labour and service work in the "new economy." *Gender, Work and Organization, 16*(3), 300–322

Ogbu, J. U., & Davis, A. (2003). *Black American students in an affluent suburb: a study of academic disengagement*. Mahwah, NJ: Erlbaum.

Paulsen, M. B., & St. John, E. P. (2002). Social class and college costs: Examining the financial nexus between college choice and persistence. *The Journal of Higher Education, 73*(2), 189–236.

Perna, L. W. (2000). Differences in the decision to attend college among African-Americans, Hispanics, and Whites. *Journal of Higher Education, 71*, 117–141.

Perna, L. W., & Swail, W. S. (2002). Pre-college outreach and early intervention programs. In D. E. Heller (Ed.), *Condition of access: Higher education for lower income students* (pp. 97–112). Westport, CT: Praeger.

Pollack, W. (1998). *Real boys: Rescuing our sons from the myth of boyhood*. New York, NY: Owl Books.

Postsecondary Education Opportunity. (2008, February). *College participation rates for students from low-income families by state fy1993 to fy2006, 188*. Oskaloosa, IA: Postsecondary Education Opportunity.

Pyke, K. D. (1996). Class-based masculinities: The interdependence of gender, class, and personal power. *Gender & Society, 10*(5), 527–549.

Quinn, J., Thomas, L., Slack, K., Casey, L., Thexton, W., & Noble, J. (2006). Lifting the Hood: Lifelong learning and young white masculinities, *British Educational Research Journal, 32*(5), 735–750.

Reason, R. D. (2009). An examination of persistence research through the lens of a comprehensive conceptual framework. *Journal of College Student Development, 50*(6), 659–682.

Sax, L. J. (2008). *The gender gap in college: Maximizing the developmental potential of women and men.* San Francisco, CA: Jossey-Bass.

Tinto, V. (1975). Dropouts from higher education: A theoretical synthesis of recent research. *Review of Educational Research, 45,* 89–125.

Tinto, V. (1993). *Leaving college: Rethinking the cause and cures of student attrition* (2nd ed.). Chicago, IL: University of Chicago Press.

Tinto, V. (2002, October). *Enhancing persistence: Connecting the dots.* Paper presented at the Optimizing the Nation's Investment: Persistence and Success in Postsecondary Education Conference.

Tinto, V. (2004). *Student retention and graduation: Facing the truth, living with the consequences.* Washington, DC: The Pell Institute.

Tinto, V. (2007). Research and practice of student retention: What next? *Journal of College Student Retention: Research, Theory & Practice, 8,* 1–19.

Titus, M.A. (2006). Understanding college degree completion of students with low socioeconomic status: The influence of the institutional financial context. *Research in Higher Education, 47*(4), 371–398.

U.S. Department of Education (2002). *The economic imperative for improving education.* Washington, DC: U.S. Department of Education, National Center for Educational Statistics.

U.S. Department of Education (2003). *The condition of education 2003.* Washington, DC: U.S. Department of Education, National Center for Educational Statistics.

U.S. Department of Labor. (2000). The outlook for college graduates, 1998–2000. In *Getting ready pays off!* Washington, DC: U.S. Department of Labor, Bureau of Labor Statistics.

Walpole, M. (2003). Socioeconomic status and college: How SES affects college experiences and outcomes. *The Review of Higher Education, 27,* 45–73.

Walpole, M. (2007). *Economically and educationally challenged students in higher education: Access to Outcomes* (ASHE Higher Education Rep. No. 33–3). Hoboken, NJ: Wiley.

Weis, L. (1990). *Working class without work.* New York, NY: Routledge.

Weis, L. (2004*). Class reunion: The remaking of the American white working class.* New York, NY: Routledge.

Wellman, J. W., Desrochers, D. M., Lenihan, C. M., Kirshstein, R. J., Hurlburt, S., & Honneger, S. (2009). *Trends in college spending: Where does the money come from?* Washington, DC: The Delta Cost Project.

Wells, R. (2008). The effects of social and cultural capital on student persistence. *Community College Review, 36,* 25–46.

Whiting, M. E., (1999). The university and the rural white male. *Journal of Research in Rural Education, 15*(3), 157–164.

Willis, P. (1977). *Learning to labor: How working-class kids get working-class jobs.* New York, NY: Columbia University Press.

8

DISABILITY IDENTITY INTERSECTIONS WITH MASCULINITIES

Thomas J. Gerschick

ILLINOIS STATE UNIVERSITY

In 2000, women in the United States earned more bachelor's degrees than men for the first time. According to the U.S. Census Bureau in 2009, among people in the 25–29 age group, women held more advanced and professional degrees. As gender-divergence in educational degree accomplishment has expanded, so have calls for more focus on men in postsecondary education (see, for instance, Kaufman & Laker, 2007; Davis & Laker, 2004; Laker, 2003). This chapter explores the experiences of a particular group of college men: those with physical disabilities. Specifically, it will address the wide variety of challenges such men face, including those of negotiating acceptance, achievement, and a sense of parity with other male students. To conclude, I will offer suggestions that student life professionals can utilize to assist men with physical disabilities in successfully completing college, developing an empowered sense of manhood, establishing and cultivating meaningful male friendships, and managing multiple identities.

There are three parameters which bound this chapter. First, the focus will be on the United States because this is where research literature and data are most readily available. Second, due to very limited research on the intersection of physical disability and race, class, gender, and ethnicity, there is little that I can say beyond calling for such research to be undertaken. Finally, while the focus in this chapter is on men with physical disabilities, much of what is written below will hold true for many people with disabilities.

There are excellent reasons to attend to the challenges, experiences, conditions, and needs of men with physical disabilities pursuing postsecondary education. First, the population of college students with disabilities is large and continues to grow. In 2007–2008, estimates were that 10.7% of male college students had a disability (Chronicle of Higher Education, 2009). The number of students with disabilities pursuing postsecondary education increased almost three-fold between 1978 and 2003 due to legislation such as Individuals with Disabilities Education Act and the Americans with Disabilities Act which mandate equal access to education (Rothstein, 2003). Second ,"While federal law requires a full array of supports and services for students with disabilities through their high school years," notes the National Council on Disability (2004a), "there is little that has prepared them for the barriers and lack of adequate disability related supports and services they will face in university systems." Third, as a consequence, their postsecondary results pale in comparison with their non-disabled peers (National Council on Disability, 2003). Thus men with disabilities, including physical disabilities, lag their able-bodied counterparts on a range of quality of life measures. For instance in 2008, the employment rate of working-age people with disabilities in the United States was 39.5% or less than one-half of what it was for working-age people without disabilities: 79.9% (Erickson, Lee, & von Schrader, 2009). Similarly, in 2008 the poverty rate of working-age Americans with disabilities was two and a half times what it was for working-age people without disabilities: 25.3% vs. 9.6% (Erickson et al., 2009). The importance of meaningful and fairly remunerated employment cannot be stressed enough. Such employment is critical to the social integration, economic self-sufficiency, and quality of life of working-age people with disabilities (Erickson et al., 2009; National Council on Disability, 2004a). Postsecondary education is key to achieving these positive outcomes. Finally, there is also a moral and ethical dimension to this. All students, including men with physical disabilities, deserve the opportunity to successfully complete the academic and social aspects of a collegiate education.

Size and Selected Characteristics of the Population

Determining the number and percentage of men with physical disabilities on college campuses is challenging due to the varied nature of definitions of disability, data collection techniques and presentation practices. In addition to the decennial census and the American Community Survey (ACS), the U.S. Census Bureau utilizes seven other household surveys to estimate disability. These include the Current Population Survey (CPS) and the Panel Study of Income Dynamics (Brault, 2008a). These surveys do not utilize the same definitions or age categorizations when collecting and reporting data and/or have changed definitions over time within surveys, thereby making meaningful comparisons impossible (Erickson et al., 2009). Furthermore, when researchers collect data on disability on campuses, they tend not to disaggregate it for specific types of disabilities. Thus it is frequently impossible to separate physical disabilities from cognitive or learning disabilities. Co-occurring disabilities additionally complicate the statistics. Given the limitations on the reported data, the following statistics and observations provide context and a snapshot of the population of men with physical disabilities who are pursuing secondary education:

- In 2008, 12.6% of the non-institutionalized population of the United States reported in the ACS having one or more disabilities (Erickson et al., 2009).
- Disability rates vary by race and ethnicity. Native Americans of working ages 21–64 have the highest prevalence of disability at 18.8% followed by African Americans at 14.3%. Whites' predominance is 10.2% and the rate among Hispanics is 8.4%. Asian and Pacific Islanders have the lowest incidence at 4.6% (Erickson et al., 2009).
- Not surprisingly, disability prevalence varies by age. In 2005, 10.4% of the population aged 15–24 had a disability and 5% of this group had a severe disability. For the age group 25–44, the respective numbers were 11.4% and 7.5% (Brault, 2008b).
- Disability rates also vary by gender. In the aggregate, women have slightly higher rates of disability than do men: 12.9% versus 12.2% (Erickson et al., 2009). Men, however, tend to acquire their disabilities at younger ages than do women.
- Overall, ambulatory disability (FKA physical disability) was the most prevalent of the six types identified in the 2008 ACS at 6.9%. However the prevalence of this type of disability was only .9% in the 16- to 20-year-old age group and 5.4% in the 21–64 grouping (Erickson et al., 2009).
- Students with any type of disability are significantly more likely to drop out of high school thereby decreasing their likelihood of pursuing postsecondary education. For instance in 2004, the percentage of students with disabilities who dropped out of school was about 30%. This is about three times the rate of their able-bodied peers (National Council on Disability, 2004b).
- Postsecondary educational enrollment for people with physical disabilities is approximately one-half that of their able-bodied counterparts. The 2006 ACS estimated that 12.7% of the 18- to 34-year-olds of the civilian non-institutionalized population with a physical disability were enrolled in college or graduate school. In comparison, approximately 24.2% of the comparable temporarily able-bodied 18- to 34-year-olds were enrolled (U.S. Census Bureau, 2006). Thus, fewer men with disabilities pursue higher education than their able-bodied peers. One of the reasons for this may be that students with disabilities have reported lower educational aspirations than their able-bodied peers (U.S. Department of Education, 1999).
- According to the Chronicle of Higher Education's profile of Undergraduate Students, 2007–08, 10.7% of men on college campuses reported having a disability (2009). Of those men reporting a disability, 14.3% reported having an orthopedic disability.
- Men, regardless of their disability status, lag women in pursuing postsecondary education. According to the National Center for Educational Statistics (2008), in 2003–04, men comprised 42.1% of the population of undergradu-

ate students with disabilities. This is almost identical to the percentage of male undergraduate students (42.4%) who did not have disabilities.

- Among undergraduate students with disabilities in 2003–04, Whites comprised 65% of the population followed by African Americans at 13.2% and Hispanics at 12.3%. Asian and Pacific Islanders comprised 3.8% of the population and Native Americans/Alaskan natives were 1.2% (National Center for Educational Statistics, 2008).
- Students with disabilities are more likely than their able-bodied peers to begin their postsecondary education at a community college rather than a 4-year institution. For instance, according to the U.S. Department of Education, almost 60% of students with disabilities pursuing postsecondary education in 2002 attended two or less year programs (Savukinas, n.d.). Furthermore, a majority of students who enroll in the 2-year postsecondary educational sector with the intent of transferring to a 4-year institution do not (U.S. Department of Education, 1999).
- Students with disabilities are less likely to attend college full time, all year. The National Center for Educational Statistics (2008) reported that in 2003–2004 two-thirds of undergraduate students with disabilities attended part-time or part year. This figure rose to 71.1% for graduate students with disabilities.
- Undergraduate students with disabilities tend to be older than their non-disabled peers (the respective percentages for the non-disabled population are included in parentheses for easy comparison). According to the National Center for Educational Statistics (2008), in 2003–04, 45.8% (58.2%) of postsecondary students with disabilities were aged 15–23, 15.5% (17.5%) were aged 24–29 and 38.7% (24.3%) were over the age of 30. On average, undergraduate students with disabilities' pursuit of postsecondary education lags their non-disabled peers by nearly 3 years (GW Heath Resource Center, n.d.).
- A high proportion of undergraduate students with disabilities pursuing a postsecondary education reside off-campus. In 2003–2004, that figure was 61.5%. An additional 27.7% lived with parents or relatives; only 10.7% lived on campus (National Council for Educational Statistics, 2008).
- Past research found that postsecondary dropout rates are higher for students with disabilities in comparison to those without. Based on 1989–1994 data, the U.S. Department of Education (1999) indicated that 47% of students with disabilities had left college within 5 years without earning a degree whereas only 36% of able-bodied students had.
- Not surprisingly, college degree attainment for people with disabilities significantly trails that for people without disabilities. In 2008, the percentage of non-institutionalized, working-age people with disabilities who had earned a bachelor's degree or more in the United States was 12.3%. For people without disabilities, the rate was 30.6% (Erickson et al., 2009). This represents a difference of 2.5 times.

Taken together, these data indicate that having a disability poses substantial obstacles to earning a degree from a 4-year college or university (GW Heath Resource Center, n.d.; U.S. Department of Education, 1999). These outcomes do not arise in a vacuum but are rather the product of a wide range of educational, economic, political, and social dynamics that occur over the life course of people with disabilities. In order to be maximally effective in educating the whole student, student life personnel must be mindful of the circumstances men with physical disabilities face prior to arriving on campuses. The more that student life personnel can then anticipate the kinds of challenges that men with physical disabilities will face once on their campuses, the better able they will be to proactively address their needs thereby increasing the likelihood of these men's academic and social success.

The Transition from Secondary to Postsecondary Education

There are two primary dynamics which frame the transition from high school to postsecondary education for students with disabilities, including men with physical disabilities. They are uneven academic training and a lack of transitional preparation.

The degree of postsecondary academic preparation of students with disabilities will vary significantly depending on the high school district a student attended and the resources available to her/his family. Students with disabilities tend to face reduced expectations and as a consequence they lag their able-bodied counterparts in regard to their collegiate preparation. According to the U.S. Department of Education (1999, p. v.), "Those with disabilities were more likely to have taken remedial mathematics and English courses in high school, less likely to have taken advanced placement courses, had lower school GPAs, and had lower average SAT entrance exam scores." Among students ranked according to how qualified they were for matriculation to a 4-year institution, students with disabilities were much less likely than their able-bodied peers to be even minimally qualified (National Center for Educational Statistics, 2008; Ward, n.d.; U.S. Department of Education, 1999).

Given that high schools underprepare students with disabilities for future academic success, it should come as no surprise that they also do not prepare them for social or personal success. "Too many students with disabilities exit high school with limited self-determination and self-advocacy skills because school and parents assume responsibility for advocating for their educational needs rather than fostering the development of these skills in students" (Izzo & Lamb, 2002, in Ward, n.d., p. 1). This leaves students with disabilities unprepared for the changes in levels of institutional support they will receive in college vis-à-vis what they received in high school. Thus, such students are not sufficiently prepared or informed about how to obtain their rightful accommodations. Families are often similarly uninformed about transition issues and consequently are typically not able to provide help (Ward, n.d.).

There is a significant and rich body of literature which addresses the maturation process and outcomes that students experience in conjunction with post-secondary education. Space restrictions prevent me from including a discussion of these desired outcomes. Fortunately, they are addressed elsewhere in this volume. Very little research attention has been paid to the systematic exploration of gender identity development during this time period in students' lives, especially when disability is involved (Davis & Wagner, 2005; Davis & Laker, 2004; Davis, 2002). To be sure, we have many essays, narratives, memoirs and biographies that at least partially address the intersection of sex, gender, and disability. While these accounts are important and enlightening, they don't focus on the postsecondary years and their focus is too narrow to provide a full understanding of how gender impacts disability and how disability impacts gender during these formative years.

Social science research in this area is in its infancy. A comprehensive literature search in conjunction with this chapter revealed little empirical work that is based on systematic, aggregated, empirical data on college-aged men and gender. Thus researchers have little understanding of how college-age men develop their gender identities or how additional social factors such as race, class, and ethnicity mediate social interaction and identity. The purpose of this next section is to review what we know more generally about the junction of gender and disability.

The Intersection of Masculinity and Physical Disability[1]

To further contextualize the experience of men with physical disabilities in postsecondary education, three sets of social dynamics need to be attended. The first involves the stigma associated with having a physical disability, the second concerns gender as an interactional process and accomplishment, and the third is the hegemonic masculine standard to which men with physical disabilities are held (Gerschick, 1998).

As many commentators have noted, to have a disability is not only a physical or mental condition, it is also a social and stigmatized one (Goffman, 1963; Kriegel, 1991; Zola, 1982). This stigma is embodied in the popular stereotypes of people with disabilities; they are perceived to be weak, passive, and dependent (Shapiro, 1993). Our language exemplifies this stigmatization: people with disabilities are de-formed, dis-eased, dis-abled, dis-ordered, ab-normal, and in-valid (Zola, 1982 p. 206). Sociologist Erving Goffman (1963) noted that stigmatized people are both socially tainted and discounted.

This stigma is enacted in the daily interactions between people with disabilities and the temporarily-able-bodied. People with disabilities are evaluated in terms of normative expectations and are, because of their disability, frequently found wanting. As a consequence, they experience a range of reactions from those without disabilities from subtle indignities and slights to overt hostility and outright cruelty. More commonly people with disabilities are stereotyped, avoided, marginalized and discriminated against (Goffman, 1963; Fine & Asch, 1988). This treatment creates formidable physical, educational, economic, psychological, architectural and social obstacles to their participation in all aspects of social life. Having a disability frequently becomes a primary identity which overshadows almost all other aspects of one's identity. As a consequence, it influences all interactions with the temporarily-able-bodied, including gendered interactions. In light of these dynamics, disability must be understood as a reflection of social, economic and political power relations which impact stigmatized persons' life chances (Link & Phelan, 2001).

The degree to which stigmatization of men with physical disabilities occurs is dependent on the type of disability, its visibility, its severity, and the social context. For instance, a severe case of the Epstein-Barr virus can lead to disability; however, typically the condition is not readily apparent and, as a consequence, does not trigger stigmatization and devaluation. Conversely, having quadriplegia and using a wheelchair for mobility is highly visual, is perceived to be severe, and frequently elicits invalidation. Moreover, the degree to which a person with a disability is legitimized or delegitimized is context-specific and has both material and nonmaterial consequences (Gerschick, 2000).

In order to accomplish gender, each person in a social situation needs to be recognized by others as appropriately masculine or feminine. Those with whom we interact continuously assess our gender performance and decide whether we are "doing gender" appropriately in that situation. Our "audience" or interaction partners then hold us accountable and sanction us in a variety of ways in order to encourage compliance (West & Zimmerman, 1987). Our need for social approval and validation as gendered beings further encourages conformity. Much is at stake in this process as one's sense of self rests precariously upon the audience's decision to validate or reject one's gender performance. Successful enactment bestows status and acceptance, failure invites embarrassment and humiliation (West & Zimmerman, 1987).

In the contemporary United States, men's gender performance tends to be judged using the standard of hegemonic masculinity which represents the optimal attributes, activities, behaviors and values expected of men in a culture (Connell & Messerschmidt, 2005). Career-orientation, activeness, athleticism, sexual desirability and virility, independence, and self-reliance are exalted masculine attributes in the United States (Connell & Messerschmidt, 2005; Gerschick & Miller, 1994). Consequently, the physical body is central to the attainment of hegemonic masculinity. Men whose bodies allow them to evidence the identified characteristics are differentially rewarded in U.S. dominant culture over those who cannot. Despite the fact that attaining these attributes is often unrealistic and more based in fantasy than reality, men continue to internalize them as ideals and strive to demonstrate them as well as judge themselves and other men using them. Thus for men with physical disabilities, masculine gender privilege collides with the stigmatized status of having a disability, thereby causing status inconsistency, as having a disability erodes much, but not all, masculine privilege (Gerschick, 2000).

These social dynamics are exceedingly powerful; however, it would be a grave mistake to discount the human agency and resourcefulness of men with physical disabilities. Such men have significant amount of experience navigating both bodily and gender expectations. Low's (1996) research demonstrates that various interaction strategies with the able-bodied are differentially efficacious. For instance, adopting aggressive or assertive attitudes when interacting with them was perceived by people with disabilities as being less successful than speaking out and reasoning. Other strategies which have been successful for men with physical disabilities include creating alternative subcultures which validate their gender performance, rejecting the demands of hegemonic masculinity and formulating more self-satisfactory gender identities (Gerschick, 1998; Gerschick & Miller, 1994). Thus, having a physical disability does not equate to being helpless, passive or acquiescent. Furthermore, disability need not be central to a person with a disability's sense of self, their reference groups, or their public identity (Fine & Asch, 1988). As Link & Phelan (1991, p. 378) observe, "people artfully dodge or constructively challenge stigmatizing processes." In short, while men with physical disabilities have lower social power than their able-bodied counterparts, they are not powerless in creating self-satisfactory gender identities and relations.

Suggestions

The number of men with physical disabilities on college campuses is likely to increase, fueled in part by wounded military veterans returning from the conflicts in Iraq and Afghanistan who will pursue postsecondary education with their benefits. In the future, then, student life personnel should have excellent opportunities to work with men with physical disabilities to ensure that they develop both academic success and a healthy sense of masculinity. As readers consider the following suggestions, they should not lose track of the success that people with disabilities, including men with physical disabilities have had in earning postsecondary degrees and creating self-satisfactory gender identities. The challenges have been great and many have succeeded.

As student affairs professionals design programs to assist men with physical disabilities, they would be wise to keep the following information in mind. First, they will have more limited access to men with physical disabilities than other types of students. For example, men with physical disabilities are more likely to be transfer students rather than matriculating freshmen. Consequently, they will be on campus for fewer years than first-year students. This dynamic will be tempered somewhat by the fact that these men will typically take longer to complete their degrees. Additionally, according to the most recent statistics, less than 11% of them will live on campus. They are also more likely than able-bodied students to have dependents who will compete for their time and energy (National Center for Educational Statistics, 2008). Finally, managing their disability and their academic studies will leave these men with less time for co-curricular or extra-curricular activities. Student affairs practitioners are going to need to make the most of their time with them.

Second, student affairs professionals would be wise to contextualize their work with men with physical disabilities within their work with men more generally. As practitioners have noted, working with men on college campuses is challenging (Davis & Wagner, 2005; Davis & Laker, 2004; Davis, 2002). Men use their privilege within patriarchy to ignore issues of social justice. Furthermore, the dictates of independence and self-sufficiency embedded within hegemonic masculinity discourage men from acknowledging problems or seeking assistance. All of this makes it very difficult to motivate and engage male students.

Third, the current economic crisis in the United States has hit university budgets extremely hard. Typically universities have responded by disproportionately cutting student services budgets as opposed to those of academic departments. Consequently, student life personnel will likely be working with much tighter budgets as they seek to expand programs and/or outreach. One way this can be mitigated is by creating partnerships. Student affairs professionals are not alone in their desire to assist men with physical disabilities to succeed. Potential partners on campuses include Disability Services and Diversity Initiative offices, gender studies programs, ADA compliance coordinators, at-risk student offices, academic advisors and parents. Such partnerships are attractive because they have the potential to pool resources such as money, time, and skills.

Fourth, it is crucial that men with physical disabilities remain in good academic standing. Nothing that student life personnel do or plan for will do any good for a student who is dismissed from the university due to poor grades. Remaining in such standing will be a challenge due to academic responsibilities, possible poor educational preparation and the demands caused by one's disability. Academic support must be available to men with physical disabilities when they need it. Fortunately, many universities have offices or programs dedicated to student success that men with physical disabilities can access. However, they are likely to need significant coaxing to access these services (Ward, n.d.).

Fifth, how student life personnel engage with men with physical disabilities will depend, in part, on where and when they choose to intervene. For instance, personnel need to determine what role, if any, they will play in the challenging shift from high school to college/university. The transitional pathways are not well-paved and as a consequence fewer men with physical disabilities pursue secondary education than would otherwise. Second, of those men who do pursue college, many never move beyond the community college level. Thus, student affairs professionals might wish to provide men with physical disabilities with additional transitional assistance. Such support is crucial to increasing the number of men with physical disabilities on college and university campuses.

With the aforementioned information in mind, the following represent an array of potential interventions to improve the academic, social and gender success of men with physical disabilities. Many of these recommendations overlap or dovetail into one another; thus practitioners should think in terms of a multifaceted approach.

Train student life personnel in disability and gender issues. Men with physical disabilities clearly face a range of challenges in terms of creating male friendships and self-satisfactory gender identities. The more that student affairs professionals are aware of these challenges, the more efficacious they can be in their assistance.

To the extent possible, treat each man with a physical disability as an individual but remain aware of the social context. Each student's history, maturity, experience, values, and the type and severity of physical disability will shape particular requirements. While recognizing the need to provide individual services based on each man with physical disabilities' circumstances, it is also incumbent upon student life personnel not to lose sight of the social elements of the situation.

Create research agendas. Despite almost 30 years of judicial and federal action, practitioners continue to lack knowledge of effective interventions and academic outcomes regarding students with disabilities (Rothstein, n.d.). Notwithstanding many opportunities during these years, the National Council on Disability (2004B) notes that there is scant scientific and evidence-based research to help guide policy makers and practitioners regarding the most effective ways to transition and educate people with disabilities. "While prior research has suggested that students with disabilities encounter numerous barriers to postsecondary education, the particular factors that may inhibit or facilitate postsecondary success are less clear. Research and policy issues related to academic preparation, economic and social independence, financial aid, and services, accommodations, and supports for students with disabilities are especially important in this context" (GW Heath Resource Center, n.d.). Similar gaps exist regarding strategies to assist students in developing an empowered sense of masculinity, establishing and cultivating meaningful male friendships and comfortably managing the multiple facets of their identities (Laker & Davis, 2009, personal communication). Student life personnel can play a key role in catalyzing such research. In the absence of research on this range of topics, professionals should look at the extant research literature on the experience of other minorities in secondary education including racial and ethnic ones.

Involve men with physical disabilities in that research. Research studies need to be conducted not only about men with disabilities' experiences on campuses but *with* them regarding what strategies and practices work and under what circumstances. Given the paucity of quality research regarding the experiences of students with disabilities, practitioners and policy makers would be wise to tap the practical knowledge of students with disabilities and their families while simultaneously developing rigorous empirical research agendas (National Council on Disability, 2004b). Men with physical disabilities are the experts on their disabilities and their gender identities. They will have typically worked their way through many challenges and consequently will have a good sense of the most effective strategies given their strengths, limitations, and needs for accommodation. Seeking such knowledge can be a key strategy in student life personnel reaching out to such students but time and money are going to be major barriers.

Draw on existing knowledge. There are additional sources of knowledge that can be applied to working with men with physical disabilities. Over the last decade, universities have placed a tremendous amount of attention on the overall well-being and matriculation, retention and graduation of students representing a range of races and ethnicities. There is much to be learned from the literature which resulted from these efforts. Strategies from this literature can be adapted to work with men with physical disabilities.

Recruit significant numbers of men with physical disabilities to campus. Men with physical disabilities must not be tokens. One of the primary ways of normalizing disability, including physical disability, is to make it ubiquitous. In order for such recruitment to occur, campuses must be fully accessible, accommodative services must be in place, and a welcoming environment established. In order for this strategy to work, men with physical disabilities will need to be fully assimilated into the campus community.

Improve the campus climate. One of the most effective areas for student life personnel is work with the non-disabled population to alter perceptions of men with physical disabilities. This can be done in a myriad of ways, including creating joint volunteer opportunities so that able bodied people can interact with men with physical disabilities while pursuing external goals. Given the tendency of the able-bodied to ignore and avoid people with disabilities, the more interaction that can be facilitated, the better. Challenging the hegemony of able-bodiness on college campuses will be a long and arduous process given how deeply entrenched that hegemony is. However, if successful, it creates social space for men with physical disabilities to experiment with and express a range of gender identities. A more accepting campus climate also reduces social barriers to friendships between men with physical disabilities and their able-bodied peers.

Support disability awareness and pride. Nationally, October is designated as disability awareness month, though some states vary in their designation of it. The goal of any activity during such commemorations should be to educate the campus community about the wide range of abilities and contributions of persons with disabilities while simultaneously affirming people with disabilities' identities. Consequently, disability-acceptance should become a central component of the multicultural education that is part of the collegiate experience. Student affairs personnel can lead the way in enhancing their universities' commitment to disability awareness. In so doing, professionals should be aware that some men with physical disabilities will avoid participation as a strategy of disability avoidance and disavowal. They will be reluctant to identify with their devalued status (Low, 1996).

Undermine disability as a primary identity. There is clearly a tension here regarding encouraging identification with disability through disability pride while seeking to undermine it as a primary identity. However, this tension can be resolved if student life personnel help men with physical disabilities accept that their impairment is only one component of their identity. This can be accomplished by creating opportunities to highlight other aspects of one's identity such as artist, musician, student, or friend (Low, 1996).

Encourage alternative forms of masculinity. Multiple masculinities exist in every culture and compete with hegemonic masculinity for adherents. As Gerschick and Miller (1994) and Gerschick (1998) have demonstrated, men with physical disabilities are quite capable of adopting masculinities which stress cooperation rather than competitiveness, accommodation rather than strict-independence, and letting go rather than control. In order to accomplish alternative masculinities successfully, men with physical disabilities must alter their reference group, resist internalizing the stigma associated with having a disability and reject or redefine hegemonic standards (Gerschick, 1998). Student affairs professionals can provide opportunities for men with physical disabilities to practice gender self-definition. Providing students with opportunities for gender explorations and risk-taking will facilitate their sense of self worth and self-determination. On college campuses across the United States, non-hegemonic men without disabilities are involved in similar gender exploration and provide excellent opportunities for meaningful male friendships.

Create outreach and mentorship programs. Many men with physical disabilities have successfully negotiated the collegiate experience and have developed self-satisfactory gender identities. They represent powerful advocates, confidants, and role models for men with physical disabilities who find themselves in challenging circumstances. Mentors can share strategies, provide a sympathetic ear and help men with disabilities better integrate into the academic and alternative social communities. Men with physical disabilities, by virtue of being male, are going to be less likely to seek assistance when they encounter difficulties and/or challenges. Thus, a mentorship program could double as an outreach strategy.

Be prepared to allow men with physical disabilities to fail.   Whether it is in terms of academic success or the creation of self-satisfactory gender identities, student life personnel are going to have to avoid facilitating learned helplessness or being over-protective of men with physical disabilities. They must also avoid pitying or infantilizing these students. They are adults and as such are not only capable but also responsible for making their own decisions. While student affairs professionals are well-aware of the importance of encouraging self-advocacy, autonomy, and self-determination, it will be a challenge to determine where to draw the line regarding their efforts.

Conclusion

All students with disabilities, including men with physical disabilities, face significant academic and social challenges while pursuing postsecondary education. Many of the problems that create these challenges are not located within men with physical disabilities but rather are the products of the social environment. While these men have lower social power vis-à-vis their able-bodied peers, they are not powerless. Student affairs professions can form valuable partnerships to assist such men not only with academic success but also in the development of an empowered sense of masculinity and meaningful male friendships. The more that student life personnel are aware of the challenges such men face, the better able they are to assist in creating these desired outcomes.

Notes

1. This section draws heavily upon Gerschick and Miller (1994), Gerschick (1998), Gerschick (2000), and Gerschick (2005).

References

Brault, M. (2008a). *Disability status and the characteristics of people in group quarters*. Washington, DC: U.S. Census Bureau.

Brault, M. (2008b). *Americans with disabilities: 2005*. Washington, DC: U.S. Census Bureau.

Chronicle of Higher Education, Almanac of Higher Education. (2009). *Profile of undergraduate students 2007-08*. Retrieved January 27, 2010, from http://chronicle.com/article/Profile-of-Undergraduate-St/48078/

Connell, R. W., & Messerschmidt, J. W. (2005). Hegemonic masculinity: rethinking the concept. *Gender & Society, 19*(6), 829–859.

Davis, T. L. (2002). Voices of gender role conflict: The social construction of college men's identity. *Journal of College Student Development, 43*(4), 508–521.

Davis, T. L., & Laker, J. A. (2004). Connecting men to academic and student affairs programs and services. In G. Kellom (Ed.), *New directions for student services* (pp. 47–57). Wilmington, DE: Wiley.

Davis, T. L., & Wagner, R. (2005). Increasing men's development of social justice attitudes and actions. In R. D. Reason, E. M. Broido, T. L. Davis, & N. J. Evans (Eds.), *New directions for student services* (pp. 29–41). Wilmington, DE: Wiley.

Erickson, W. Lee, C., & von Schrader, S. (2009). *2008 Disability status report: The United States.* Ithaca, NY: Cornell University Rehabilitation Research and Training Center on Disability Demographics and Statistics.

Fine, M., & Asch, A. (Eds.). (1988). *Women with disabilities: essays in psychology, culture, and politics.* Philadelphia: Temple University Press.

Gerschick, T. J. (1998). Sisyphus in a wheelchair: Men with physical disabilities confront gender domination. In J. O'Brien & J. A. Howard, (Eds.), *Everyday inequalities: Critical inquiries* (pp. 189–211). Malden, MA: Blackwell.

Gerschick, T. J. (2000). Toward a theory of disability and gender, *Signs, 25*(4), 1263–1268.

Gerschick, T. J. (2005). Masculinity and degrees of bodily normativity in western culture. In M. Kimmel, J. Hearn, & R.W. Connell (Eds.), *Handbook of studies on men and masculinities* (pp. 367–378). Thousand Oaks, CA: Sage.

Gerschick, T. J., & Miller, A. S. (1994). Gender identities at the crossroads of masculinity and physical disability. *Masculinities 2*(1), 34–55.

Goffman, E. (1963). *Stigma: notes on the management of spoiled identity.* New York: Simon and Schuster.

GW Heath Resource Center (n.d.). *Postsecondary students with disabilities: recent data from the 2000 national postsecondary student aid survey.* Informally published manuscript. GW Heath Resource Center, George Washington University, Washington, DC. Retrieved from http://www.heath.gwu.edu/files/active/2000_student_ai

Kaufman, M., & Laker, J. A. (2007, February). Masculinity in the quad. *Academic Matters,* 16–17.

Kriegel, L. (1991). *Falling into life.* San Francisco: North Point Press.

Laker, J. A. (2003). *Bad dogs: rethinking our engagement of male students.* American College Personnel Association Minneapolis Conference 2003, http://www.myacpa.org/sc/scm/files/newsletters/SCM%20Brief%202003%20-%20Bad%20Dog.pdf

Link, B. G., & Phelan, J. C. (2001). Conceptualizing stigma. In K. S. Cook & J. Hagan (Eds.), *Annual review of sociology* (pp. 363–385). Palo Alto, CA: Annual Reviews.

Low, J. (1996). Negotiating identities, negotiating environments: an interpretation of the experiences of students with disabilities. *Disability & Society, 11*(2), 235–248.

National Center for Educational Statistics. (2008). *Number and percentage of students enrolled in postsecondary institutions by level, disability status and selected student characteristics: 2003–04* (Table 231). Washington, DC: National Center for Educational Statistics. Retrieved from http://nces.ed.gov/programs/digest/d08/tables/dt08_231

National Council on Disability. (2003). *People with disabilities and postsecondary education.* Washington, DC: National Council on Disability. Retrieved from http://www.ncd.gov/newsroom/publications/2003/education.htm

National Council on Disability. (2004a). *Higher education act fact sheet.* Washington, D.C. National Council on Disability. Retrieved from http://www.ncd.gov/newsroom/publications/2004/hea_factsheet.htm

National Council on Disability. (2004b). *Improving educational outcomes for students with disabilities.* Washington, DC: National Council on Disability. Retrieved from http://www.ncd.gov/newsroom/publications/2004/educationoutcomes.htm

Rothstein, L. (2003). *Students with disabilities and higher education: A disconnect in expectations and realities.* Informally published manuscript, Heath Resource Center, George Washington University, Washington, DC. Retrieved from http://www.eric.ed.gov/PDFS/ED482310.pdf

Savukinas, R. (n.d.). *Community colleges and students with disabilities.* Informally published manuscript, Heath Resource Center, George Washington University, Washington, D. C. Retrieved from http://www.heath.gwu.edu/index.php?option=com_content&task=view& id=118&Itemid=51

Shapiro, J. P. (1993). *No pity: people with disabilities forging a new civil rights movement.* New York: Random House.

U.S. Census Bureau. (2009). *Census bureau reports nearly 6 in 10 advanced degree holders age 25–29 are women.* Washington, DC: U.S. Census Bureau.

U.S. Census Bureau, American Community Survey. (2006). *Physical disability by school enrollment and educational attainment for the civilian noninstitutionalized populations 18 to 34 years* (Table B18012). Washington, DC: U.S. Census Bureau. Retrieved from http://factfinder.census. gov/servlet/DTTable?_bm=y&-geo_id=01000US&-ds_name=ACS_2006_EST_G00_&-_ lang=en&-_caller=geoselect&-state=dt&-format=&-mt_name=ACS_2006_EST_G2000_ B18012

U.S. Department of Education, National Center for Education Statistics. (1999). *Students with disabilities in postsecondary education: a profile of preparation, participation and outcomes.* (NCES 1999-187). Washington, DC: U.S Department of Education. Retrieved from http://nces.ed.gov/ pubsearch/pubsinfo.asp?pubid=1999187

Ward, M.J. (n.d.). *Self-advocacy for college students in plain, simple language.* Informally published manuscript, Heath Resource Center, George Washington University, Washington, DC. Retrieved from http://www.heath.gwu.edu/index.php?option=com_content&task=view& id=118&Itemid=51

West, C., & Zimmerman, D. H. (1987). Doing gender. *Gender & Society, 1*(2), 125–151.

Zola, I. K. (1982). *Missing pieces: A chronicle of living with a disability.* Philadelphia: Temple University Press.

SECTION C

Effective Interventions with College Men

Section Editors, Jason Laker and Tracy Davis

9

MASCULINITIES REVIEWED AND REINTERPRETED

Using a Critical Approach to Working with Men in Groups

Tracy Davis, James LaPrad, and Sean Dixon

WESTERN ILLINOIS UNIVERSITY

As any practitioner knows, there are gaps between theory and practice. What works under theoretically ideal circumstances, does not always hold up under the weight of developmental complexities, political realities, and contextual nuances. While any professional practice requires negotiating theory-to-practice translation issues, there are specific stumbling blocks associated with contemporary efforts to effectively re-envision masculinities. Often the most fundamental obstacle is the traditional debate between biological and social influences on gender formation. We, however, find this debate an unnecessary distraction. Genetics may help explain some male and female behavior and evolutionary biology certainly has an intrinsic influence, but we also know that culture and history deeply affect the construction of gender. Here we agree with Tiger (2005) that the conflict between nature and nurture paradigms "is unfortunate and scientifically unnecessary … and the distinctions commonly made in practice if not in theory between the (curiously described) natural and social sciences are scientifically impractical and probably even malignant" (p. xxxv). Reinterpreting masculinities must begin with mindful recognition of the contributions of both nature and nurture in a manner that doesn't circumscribe our thinking to the narrow either/or dogma typically associated with this debate.

Related to the nature-nature debate and a second hurdle in reinterpreting masculinities, are assumptions about the importance of gender differences. Here, the *"Men are from Mars and Women are from Venus"* faithful are contrasted with those who believe there are no differences. Research is clear that essentially men and women are psychologically basically the same (Sax, 2008; Hyde, 2005). While there are salient biological differences, according to a comprehensive meta-analysis by Hyde (2005) most of the disparities found between men and women tend to be quite small. Moreover, like ethnicity, spirituality, sexual orientation, and other identity related factors, gender differences *within* group tend to be much larger than the differences between sexes. In our view, then, higher education professionals must be reflexively mindful regarding practices that assume significant differences both in terms of programmatic and individual intervention. Any observation of difference can easily be exaggerated to support static political perspectives that may, in fact, *construct* reality rather than provide a scientific description of it.

A third hurdle is the legitimate fear that a reinterpretation of masculinities is really the proverbial wolf in sheep's clothing. Some men's religious groups, men's rights groups, and other variations on the men's movement have formed in reaction to the advances of women and needed efforts to promote equal rights. As Demetrakis (2001) warns, we need to "avoid falling into the trap of believing that patriarchy has disappeared simply because heterosexual men have worn earrings" (p. 19). One of the insidious beauties of hegemony is that through negotiation and appropriation, what appears to be counter-hegemonic and forward-moving, can really be steps toward patriarchal reproduction (Brookfield, 2005; Demetrakis, 2001). Taking an explicit critical perspective, we encourage rigorous skepticism and debate about our claims in this chapter. We also feel it is important to communicate our values. Each of us has been transformed in some way by feminist theory and pedagogy and takes an explicitly pro-feminist position. Many forms of feminism promote freedom for both men and women. We believe that working to inhibit violence against women, for example, will liberate men as well.

An additional threat to successfully reimagining masculinities is our failure to recognize the critical contextual and intersectional nature of identity development. We too often forget that "masculinity comes in many forms and packages and these multiple masculinities are informed, limited, and modified by race, ethnicity, class background, sexual orientation, and personal predilections" (Tarrant & Katz, 2008, p. 10). There is, in fact, nothing particularly universal or eternal about conventions related to masculinities. That is not to say that there isn't an attempt to value only one form of masculinity. As is persuasively argued throughout this text, hegemonic masculinity is a social process in which one form of institutionalized masculinity is "culturally exalted" above all others (Connell, 2005). A model that more fully portrays development resulting from the wide array of masculinities is the Jones and McEwen (2000) Multiple Dimensions of Identity (MDI) model. In this model, sexual orientation, ethnicity, culture, class, religion, and gender are dimensions central to one's identity. The salience of a particular dimension to one's core identity depends on changing contexts that include current experiences, family background, sociocultural conditions, and career decisions and life planning. The MDI is a mental model we use to be mindful about making assumptions about individual men. This model encourages us to consider how intersections of sexual orientation, ethnicity, culture, religion, and gender might impact a specific individual. Rather than assuming, for example, that sexual orientation is a central aspect of one's identity or even making assumptions about a student's sexuality, practitioners are encouraged to consider the range of possibilities. Another example is the all-too-human tendency to assume that men are masculine gendered. Spence and Helmreich (1978) have persuasively demonstrated that men can be feminine gendered. We tend to ascribe relational and nurturing qualities such as emotional expression and gentle demeanor to femininity and to women. If one believes that such qualities are, in fact, human rather than feminine per se, then how might this possibly impact our interactions with, for example, a 6'4" man who is both emotionally expressive and is active in traditionally masculine pursuits such as rugby or football?

Finally, context and history dramatically impact one's performance of gender. As Berila describes in Chapter 6, there is no essential man or woman, and what we mean by masculinity and femininity is created by performing a series of acts. In fact, according to the prolific feminist scholar, Judith Butler (1990), performativity describes how individuals create gender and sexual identities through everyday behaviors. Moreover, as performatives, actions do not represent identity; instead, actions create identity. Like an actor on a stage, we are influenced by the audience, our scripts, and larger cultural mores such that we seldom act independent of the salient influences of context. Consider the above example of the gender performance in the body of the 6'4" male athlete compared to a 5'2" female. Reflect on what it means to express oneself in front of an audience of all men or all women. How is gender performed by men in the athletic arena compared to a hospital where a close friend is critically injured? Or examine the career counseling women generally received 30 years ago compared to today. As captured by the MDI, the salience of particular identities shift according to both history and other activities that are occurring in the broader social milieu.

Reinterpreting masculinities, then, requires a critical theoretical approach that is cognizant of history, sensitive to sex role expectations, aware of identity intersections, and ready to interrogate underlying assumptions. Rather than essentializing identity, critical theory recognizes time and place changes, causing identities to be "multiple, contradictory, fragmented, incoherent, disciplinary, disunified, unstable, and fluid (Gamson, 2000, p. 356). Such an approach, by combining theoretical models with critical processes, offers the nexus between theory and practice that can guide our work with college men to promote their learning and development. Theory can help practitioners become more understanding of and empathetic toward men to effectively implement the critical strategies that can advance social change. In addition, we believe that not only do men who adhere to unhealthy rigid masculine norms have the capacity to change, but that organizations and institutions can promote counter-hegemonic gender values and norms that promote a full range of human expression. Anderson (2008), for example, recently described a popular college fraternity that constructed an institutionalized form of 'inclusive masculinity' that successfully rivaled the hegemonic form of social dominance. The rest of this chapter will focus on describing how professionals can use a critical approach with groups of men to promote positive, inclusive masculinities.

Working Effectively with Men in Groups

Male bonding may be the most common phrase to describe relationships among men. In fact, the phrase "male bonding" has humorous undertones that, under scrutiny, illustrate the sometimes comedic contortions men go through to build intimacy with another man in light of traditional masculine norms. There is a scene in the movie *Gran Torino*, for example, that illustrates this point. Walt (Clint Eastwood) takes his new neighbor Thao (Bee Vang), a Hmong immigrant, to the barbershop to talk with Martin (John Carroll Lynch), an Italian American barber, to teach him how to "talk like a man." The scene illustrates the put downs, racial epithets, and swearing that in some contorted way have come to symbolize male friendship. These bonds are most often developed in groups and are almost always activity based. Consider college men's participation in athletics, fraternities, working out, watching sports, and partying together in groups. This activity sharing, as opposed to direct emotional sharing, follows the contours of hegemonic masculinity and anyone interested in understanding men's behavior in groups would be absolutely confused absent such an awareness.

Although history, as well as recent events, are riddled with men in groups who perform horrible atrocities (e.g., Sept. 11, Madrid bombings, gang activity, mercenary troops, athletic and fraternity hazing), we believe that groups also offer one of the most significant opportunities to challenge patriarchal norms and promote positive masculinities. Male bonding, the social relationships that are the basis for men in groups, can become congruent with inclusive, pro-social, and healthy masculinities if we begin to raise consciousness about the absurdly restrictive rules of hegemonic masculinity. What follows are examples of men's consciousness groups, Greek organizations, service-learning activities, and outdoor learning experiences that can provide space for men to be vulnerable and honest, as well as begin to reinterpret masculinities for themselves.

Men's Psycho-Educational or Consciousness Groups

Conventional wisdom indicates that men collectively and overwhelmingly hold power in our society. Statistics continue to show men still maintain the majority of high-level positions, earn higher wages, and enjoy privileges sometimes out of reach for women. To some it must seem absurd that men would seek out support groups that have been more commonly associated with oppressed groups struggling to make institutional gains. Indeed, the suggestion of men's groups or men's studies rankles many in the academy who fear such a focus would only perpetuate the hegemony that they have struggled against for so many years.

While it is true that men enjoy patriarchal power, it is generally wealthy White men who hold the lion's share. While all men have been painted with the broad brush of membership to this power elite (and all men do enjoy some privilege associated with being a man), men of color, men of middle and lower economic class, and gay men do not enjoy the same level of benefits that are assumed to be characteristic of this gender advantage. Kaufman (1999), for example, suggests that men's experience of power is confusing to most men. This confusion, if left unarticulated and unrecognized, can both inhibit our ability to hear men's pain and serve as an obstruction to men's development of a healthy gender identity. The paradox of masculinity is that "in objective social analysis, men as a group have power over women as a group: but in their subjective experience of the world, men as individuals do not feel powerful. In fact, they often feel powerless (Capraro, 2004, p. 192). Too often we hear men's expression of feeling powerless as a denial of privilege. This is not necessarily a denial of privilege, which exists whether or not it is felt or recognized. Essentially men's contradictory experience of power suggests that men's social power is both the source of individual privilege and also the basis of an individual's experience of pain and alienation. For example, a gay man or a Latino man or a man with a disability experience some patriarchal privilege, but also experiences the powerlessness associated with the part of his identity that is targeted by oppression. According to Kaufman (1999), "The social power of a poor man is different than a rich one, a working class black man from a working class white man, a gay man from a bisexual man from a straight man, a Jewish man in Ethiopia from a Jewish man in Israel, a teenage boy from an adult" (p. 68). What is needed are professionals who work with groups of men who have the capacity to first hear the personal pain men experience, and then raise consciousness about institutional privilege. Even the most apparently privileged man has been targeted by hegemonic masculinity and can become conscious of the gender role straightjacket that has limited him. Professionals need to first understand men's pain and difficulties before trying to promote change. That is, we encourage seeking understanding before seeking to be understood.

The 1960s and 1970s gave rise to movements of personal growth and introspection. Men became more aware of their changing role in society, their vulnerability, the change in their power status as well as a growing sense of isolation (Castellini, 2005). Men also began questioning what constitutes being a man thanks to emerging demands of the women's movement which challenged the narrow and confining roles afforded to women. The hegemonic model of masculinity portrays men as physically dominant, aggressive, independent, pragmatic, narcissistic, and sexually prolific. Yet studies find that men rank such characteristics as self-exploration and personal growth, family, helping others, and religion as being more in line with their ideal sense of what it means to be a man (Keen, 1991). There is an obvious disconnect with the perception of what constitutes masculinity as dictated by social institutions and what men value individually. Culturally, men are raised to be self-sufficient. To seek support or affirmation from others, especially other men, is often judged to be a sign of weakness. This characterization has kept many men from connecting with other men and in turn has stunted their personal growth similar to the institutional limits on women that spurred the women's movement. Space for men to reflect on the impact of gender role expectations on their own identity development is, therefore, virtually absent.

The men's group movement has been an attempt to provide the space for men to reflect on socially prescribed roles and help men reach a healthier, self-authored identity. As such, the focus is not only to celebrate the masculine, but to embrace the feminine as well. These groups serve to bridge the artificial dualism which implies that to be a man means shunning femininity. Men can, in these groups, begin to share universal emotions related to doubts, fears, and existential anxiety. Through connecting with other men about these shared experiences men can transcend the shackles of isolation and radical individualism inherent in hegemonic masculinity.

Historically, in many cultures it was customary for boys to be removed from their homes by older men of the community and taken to the woods, hunting grounds, sweat lodges, or other sacred spaces to participate in a rite of passage into manhood. Contrary to many of the depictions of rites of passage ceremonies in contemporary literature, the intent was not simply to test survival or physical skills. Boys were often mentored with compassion about the values of integrity, authenticity, responsibility to family and community, respect for others, respect for life, and respect for self. The duality of feminine and masculine stereotypes were not taught as distinct characteristics of men and women, but rather as aspects within each individual (Keen, 1991).

These rites, more often than not, took place in physical settings where the connection to important values could be viscerally experienced. Immersed in the rustic wild, boys learned the value of depending upon each other as well as the realization that they too were being depended upon by others. Examples of the feminine and masculine working in concert are evident in nature (e.g., protection and nurturing, competition and cooperation). The natural world was described in feminine and masculine terms such as father sky and mother earth. Neither was deemed more important than the other. On the contrary, they were depicted as depending upon one another to maintain harmony.

Many of the men's groups today orchestrate intensive weekend experiences in remote wooded locations for these reasons. The intention is to remove men from the trappings of daily distractions and connect instead with the natural world to better focus on inner selves. These groups strive to address the externally defined standards of masculinity and create a more self-defined, fully-human masculine identity that fosters integrity regarding their relationship to community and family.

For college-aged men, identity and becoming a man are central developmental concerns. College men are on the precipice of entering into the responsibilities of adulthood, fatherhood, life partnerships, community leadership, and serve as role models for other boys and men. What resources are available to these young men to ensure they have the support they desire and ensure they are not alone as they establish their identities and roles in society? Absent the experience of mentorship, guidance, or a simple rite of passage, these young men get swept up into what Kimmel and Davis describe in Chapter 1 as the culture of "Guyland" where apprentices are being socialized not by experienced mentors but by other novices. It should be no surprise, then, that behaviors like binge drinking, drug abuse, sexual assault, and unsafe sex practices get passed down. While educational programs and significant resources are directed to address these issues, we too often succumb to the "boys will be boys" mentality that fails to fundamentally address the lack of public discourse about and effective mentoring of young boys and men.

Men's groups are needed that create dialogue about how one becomes a man, how one can choose to construct relationships with those around him, the responsibilities to his community, and the healthy process of challenging hegemony to construct a more self-authored identity. Without a solid sense of self and positive male role modeling (including the necessity for embracing and incorporating the feminine), men risk falling victim to the trappings of the objectification of and predatory actions toward women, the justification and encouragement of disingenuous behavior for personal gain, the desperate seeking of others' acceptance, and the abuse of competition and dominance in an attempt to gain a degree of self-worth. These are the attitudes, skills, values, and judgments that men's groups are designed to address. The limitation of these men's groups is that they often come too late in life. It is a common lament among men involved in these groups that they didn't have the experience earlier in life such as during adolescence or college.

A significant challenge for proponents of men's groups is addressing the vast amount of misinformation and ridicule used to describe these groups. Images of overly sensitive men parading awkwardly through the woods in Native American costuming and crumbling into a puddle of tears with only minimal prodding is fodder for TV comedy. It portrays group members to be a bunch of emasculated men that represent the exact opposite of the image we socially associate with masculinity. As such, even mention of interest in these groups is often met with a chuckle or rolling eyes. Although some successful examples exist, much of what is portrayed in media is satire (e.g., drumming, animal names, men hugging and crying, etc.). The ridicule expressed in such portrayals function to discipline men into avoiding exploration of critical questions in favor of adhering to hegemonic norms and standards. And, it does so effectively because men who begin to question their socialization are at one of the most tentative and fragile beginnings of the process. Therefore, ridicule or other challenges can be quite effective in keeping people from changing. As such, these portrayals also stand in stark contrast to the primary aim of men's groups: to empower men with an emphasis on accountability and integrity. Given the very real limitations just described, one may have more success in working with men's groups that already exist for other purposes: fraternities, athletic teams, and all-male residence hall floors.

Fraternities, Athletic Teams, and Other Existing Groups of Men

Men's athletic teams and Greek organizations are typically found at most colleges and universities. They can provide opportunities for improving one's self esteem, building relationships, learning important social skills, leadership and other benefits. They can also be the source of shame, ostracism, peer pressure, misogyny, physical abuse, and glorification of conquest over compassion or cooperation. These groups can either exacerbate or help to overcome men's fear of peer rejection, negative bystander behavior, and secrecy and blind loyalty that often leads to unethical decision-making. We believe it is critical to take advantage of these groups of men to promote the kind of critical mindfulness that leads to healthy masculinities. Each of us has personally witnessed both the tremendous benefits of brotherhood that resulted from a meaningful masculine culture of fraternity, athletic team and/or other group of men, as well as the negative impact of patriarchal privilege unchecked by men competing to perform socially constructed roles. Organizations, like people, left unchallenged to consider critical developmental tasks will certainly yield the latter. The advantage these groups have is that they typically have educational programming requirements and their members do not have to individually decide to attend an educational program designed to discuss that which goes against their gender role socialization: talking about masculinities and gender roles.

The first task is to get buy-in from the coach or leadership of the fraternity or other men's group. It is not only important in terms of sending a message to the other men in the group that the intervention is to be taken seriously, but also because the leadership and coaching staff can provide an insider's cultural perspective that will help shape the intervention. There are cultural nuances (language, norms, etc.) as well as unique issues associated with fraternities and sports teams about which program designers and presenters need to be familiar. In addition, any intervention needs to be fundamentally informed by the social construction of masculinities. Men have been taught specific gender roles and keeping this invisible leads to a reification of hegemonic masculinity which essentially keeps things "as they are." One of the most effective strategies for beginning a discussion about hegemonic masculinity is to use commercials, television shows, and popular movies to illustrate how messages about gender are sold. Davis (2004), for example, offers a series of examples related to using media to inform interventions related to promoting understanding of gender. In addition, Media Education Foundation offers excellent videos featuring Jackson Katz (*Tough Guise,* 1999), Jeane Kilbourne (*Killing Us Softly 4,* 2010), Byron Hurt (*Hip Hop: Beyond Beats and Rhymes,* 2006), and Sut Jhally (*Dreamworld 3,* 2007). Using media can help create an environment where men are willing to talk about issues like sexuality, gender identity, racial issues, women's rights, personal fears, etc.

Professionals designing the educational interventions need to be guided by three fundamental questions: Are they consistent with what we know about developmental theory and the social construction processes that shape men's development? Do they recognize important differences among men and masculinities? Do they balance challenge with support? Our answers to these questions will determine, to a large extent, our success in effectively promoting men's growth and development.

As mentioned earlier in this chapter, Anderson (2008) provides an example of an all-male culture where healthy, counter-hegemonic standards of masculinities are evident. He did an ethnographic study, interviewing more than 30 men and performing intensive participant observation over two years, and found what he calls a culture of "inclusive masculinity" described as "a form of masculinity ... based on social equality for gay men, respect for women, and racial parity and one in which fraternity men bond over emotional intimacy" (p. 604). The key factor helping to construct a culture of inclusive masculinity appears to be a fundamental institutional commitment to change. National-level leadership for this organization passed a national bylaw forbidding discrimination based on sexuality and actively promoted a national directive that encourages something they call being a "new age man," part of which includes discussions of homosexuality. This helped reduce homophobic discourse and members were generally affirming of openly gay members. Moreover, a culture was created where "social stigma is doled out to those who act in accord with hegemonic masculinity, not to those who distance themselves from it" (p. 617). Other cultural artifacts include values of emotional expression where members feel free to share anxieties, troubles, secrets, and fears; the routine development of nonsexual friendships with women; and, the absence of structural or social ethnic discrimination.

The intention of men's groups is to provide new models of manhood as alternatives to that which is projected through media or perpetuated through generations. Male bonding, as described by Tiger (2005) characterizes a fundamental process that is biologically extended through many other primate species, cross-culturally validated as a powerful phenomenon, and represented in human groups as varied as the St. Louis Cardinals, the Masons, Lakota Tribes, and the Vatican Council. This important factor of human social organization has had a major impact on men's development and offers an opportunity to provide new rituals, new rites of passage, and new more fully-human forms of masculinities that promote equal rights and liberation.

Outdoors and Service Learning Spaces for Healthy Men's Development

In addition to men's psycho-educational groups, athletic teams, and fraternities, we can look at both the outdoors and service learning programs as potential educational environments for men's development. In both cases, the context and approach creates unique opportunities for modeling and dialogue that are generally consistent with some of the practical and action-oriented ways boys and men tend to learn (Pollack, 1999). In outdoor learning retreats, programs and classes, participants are physically and psychologically removed from their familiar surroundings (which are generally saturated with messages related to hegemonic masculinity) into a potentially different environment where implicit and explicit cues might invite experiential, holistic and relational ways of being with oneself and others. Here, dialogue can evolve regarding personal experiences of masculinity, so that meanings, values, and behaviors can be explored, tested, and realigned in a more self-authored, rather than externally driven, manner, thus disrupting traditional patters of thought. Discussions may lead into deeper exploration of manhood, privilege, hegemony, personal paths, political alliances and structures that allow participants to develop a healthier identity and to critique the processes they have experienced related to becoming more fully developed men and human beings.

Outdoor programs may take on many shapes and forms, yet all are designed to take advantage of the resources available in nature. Interventions may range from walking through the woods, to backpacking on a hiking excursion, or even setting up a campsite for an overnight campout or retreat. Regardless of the initiative's mechanics, the purpose or goal of the initiative itself is most important. Some initiatives may be part of larger activities, as in backpacking, while other initiatives may be goal orientated as in a team building or high ropes course. The common thread in all outdoor activities is that there is a set of initiatives that are clearly defined and they are acted upon or viscerally experienced, as opposed to being only conceptualized. Kolb (1984) provides the foundation for work in this field by defining pinnacle points in the learning process as the *what* (experience), *so what* (reflection), and *now what* (transformation/action). Educators continue to draw on Kolb's work as they reconstruct learning in their own work (La Prad, Mink, & O'Steen, 2008).

While conceptually simple, this methodological framework is important for understanding the transformational potential of these learning environments.

In outdoors learning environments, experience is phase I of the experiential model (the *what*). It is this experience that becomes discussed and reflected on later in phase II (the *so what*) that can then be facilitated to promote meaning making and metaphor construction, plans for further action, and the transformation of self that potentially occurs in phase III (the *now what*). Phases II and phase III provide an excellent opportunity to focus on men's development. Facilitators will need to be versed in the models and processes discussed throughout this text in order to focus in on particular issues associated with the initiative itself or extended naturally from the initiative. A good example of this is a discussion regarding spread loading the group gear after an overnight expedition hike. Discussions may include the difference between equality and equity, machismo and feminism, egotism or self-sacrifice and how these terms influence behaviors and practice and shape conceptions of manhood and masculinity. As Warren (2005) explains, "The mind, body, spirit connection of experiential education makes it an appropriate vehicle for addressing social justice issues … students do not drop their social identities when they go on a trip" (p. 96).

Similar to outdoor programs, service-learning trips or experiences can provide activity-based reflection that is more consistent with masculine gender role socialization. This service involves partners in service who are the recipients of the service. Pedagogically, service itself is the experience in phase I of the experiential model (the *what*) and the dialogue and reflection on the service are phase II (the *so what*) regarding the service are opportunities to promote discussion and opportunities for meaning making and metaphor construction that lead into phase III of the model. It is critical for partners in service to have opportunities to reflect on and share their perspectives on the meaning of the service during dialogue sessions with the service participants. Such dialogue may naturally evoke political and identity questions regarding privilege, position in the larger social order (i.e., positionality), responsibility and gender roles. Facilitators versed in men's developmental theories can make observations and focus discussion on matters related to men's identity development. Robert Coles (1993) validates this potential in *The Call to Service* which includes an analysis of service in one's development into manhood and personhood.

The German educator Kurt Hahn recognized the therapeutic and educational value of nature and the outdoors. At the Salem School in the 1920s in Germany, "Each day, the students took a silent walk to commune with nature and revitalize their powers of reflection" (James, 1990, p. 7). Many cultures have long recognized the beneficial and potentially transformative power of nature as in Native American's vision quest or the Australian Aborigines' walkabout or the European's hike in the Alps. At the Gordonstoun School in the 1930s in Scotland, Hahn's students "engaged in service activities, experiencing the value of compassion through direct action on behalf of the community or specific people in need" (James, 1990, p. 15). He recognized the need for learners to discover their place in society along with developing self worth and compassion. As such, these activities may have potential to serve as an effective antidote to the aimless wondering characteristic of "Guyland" discussed in Chapter 1. An example of an effective pragmatic outdoors service activity is Hahn's coastal watch search and rescue program in England during World War II. This effort was created to provide opportunities for youths too young to serve in the armed forces or wartime industries to contribute needed services to their country and community.

Hahn recognized the value in developing the compassionate character of young people. John Dewey (1938) further developed these ideas by providing the central philosophical tenants for practical, outdoor, and service-learning. Dewey's University of Chicago sociology colleague George Herbert Mead (1934, 1964) foundationally described the psychological effects that the call to service has on the development of self and empathy both philosophically and politically; as service potentially can transform individuals and society. Rhoads (2000) explains, "Mead's social self seems particularly helpful in understanding the service context. In fact, the kinds of reflections offered to students by fellow volunteers and by community members are likely to be positive sources of self-development" (p. 40). It is in Mead's essay on the philosophical aspects of benevolence, where he shares a story of running into a beggar after leaving a restaurant following dinner. Mead explains that psychologically a person may have the desire to reach into his or her pocket to provide the person some loose change. However, "Even the immediate identification of the self with the other does not in itself take us beyond the impulsive attitude of relieving suffering" (Mead, 1964, pp. 397–398). Mead argues that our benevolent feelings must go beyond handing the person some change as he outlines the educational and political aspects of engaging with, rather than dismissively giving to others. Foundationally, service experiences can be designed to evoke such emotional engagement and focused specifically on healthy men's development.

Conclusion

The first step toward reinterpreting masculinities so that we move beyond static, monolithic constructions, is to employ a critical perspective that (a) avoids exaggerating differences and the pitfalls of either nature or nurture essentialism, (b) is mindful of both the blinders of privilege and men's contradictory experiences of power, (c) illuminates multiple dimensions of identity and values their intersections, and (d) recognizes contextual and historical dynamics that influence gender performance.

We must also believe in men's capacity to change as well as reflect on the ways we may be complicit in hindering such transformation. It is important to remember that individual men are generally not the problem; rather, the crisis lies more centrally in gender hegemony located within our larger institutions, policies and practices. Knowing this allows us to focus compassion and empathy toward individual men, while simultaneously holding everyone accountable for their behavior and meeting community standards. Feminism has paved a way for men to also become liberated from sex role stereotypes that are externally driven as opposed to individually defined. Change is difficult, both in terms of initially questioning long-held beliefs and practices, and in sustaining new ways of living. As such, our students (in this case, our male students) or even ourselves and our colleagues can seem resistant to change. But anyone who doesn't have a story about transformations that were precipitated by being presented with new ideas, like for example "inclusive masculinity," has not been in the business of promoting learning and development.

As Kimmel and Davis claim in Chapter 1, the need for a band of brothers is stronger than ever. Boys and men need a place where they can be vulnerable, honest, and open with each other and learn how to become men. Psycho-educational or consciousness groups, fraternities, athletic teams, and outdoor and service-learning environments hold significant promise for providing such a place. If designed according to the principles in this text, men can come together to critically examine the relative advantages in relation to the high costs (to self and others) associated with adherence to hegemonic masculinity. This presents an opportunity to courageously reinterpret masculinities toward a more healthy, adaptive, self-authored identity.

References

Anderson, E. (2008). Inclusive masculinity in a fraternal setting. *Men and Masculinities*, *10*(5), 604–620.

Berman, B., Kahn, J., Moore, T., Richman A. (Producers), & Eastwood, C. (Director). (2008). *Gran Torino* [Motion picture]. United States: Warner Brothers Pictures.

Brookfield, S. (2005). *The power of critical theory for adult learning and teaching*. Berkshire, UK: Open University Press.

Butler, J. (1990). *Gender trouble: Feminism and the subversion of identity*. New York: Routledge.

Capraro, R. L. (2004). Why college men drink: Alcohol, adventure, and the paradox of masculinity. In M. S. Kimmel & M. A. Messner (Eds.), *Men's lives* (6th ed.). Needham Heights, MA: Allyn and Bacon.

Castellini, J. D., Nelson III, W. M., Barrett, J. J., Nagy, M. S., & Quatman, G. L. (2005). Male spirituality and the men's movement: A factorial examination of motivations. *Journal of Psychology and Theology*, *33*(1), 41–55.

Coles, R. (1993). *The call to service: A witness to idealism*. Boston: Houghton Mifflin.

Connell, R. W. (2005). *Masculinities* (2nd ed). Berkeley: University of California Press.

Davis, T. (2004). Using media to inform teaching related to sex and gender. In D. Forney & T. Cawthon (Eds.), *Using entertainment media in student affairs teaching and practice* (New Directions in Student Services, No. 108, pp. 49–59). San Francisco: Jossey-Bass.

Dewey, J. (1938). *Experience and education*. New York: Simon & Schuster.

Demetrakis, Z. D. (2001). Connell's concept of hegemonic masculinity: A critique. *Theory and Society*, *30*(3), 337–361.

Gamson, J. (2000). Sexualities, queer theory, and qualitative research. In N. K. Denzin & Y. S. Lincoln (Eds.), *Handbook of qualitative research* (2nd ed., pp. 347–365). Thousand Oaks, CA: Sage.

Hyde, J. S. (2005). The gender similarities hypothesis. *American Psychologist, 60*(6), 581–592.

James, T. (1990). Kurt Hahn and the aims of education. *Journal of Experiential Education, 13*(1), 6–13.

Jones, S. R., & McEwen, M. K. (2000). A conceptual model of multiple dimensions of identity. *Journal of College Student Development, 41*(4), 405–414.

Jhally, S. (Producer), & Katz, J. (Director). (1999). *Tough guise: Violence, media, and the crisis in masculinity* [Documentary]. United States: Media Education Foundation.

Jhally, S. (Producer), & Hurt, B. (Director). (2006). *Hip hop: Beyond beats and rhymes* [Documentary]. United States: Media Education Foundation.

Jhally, S. (Producer), & Jhally, S. (Director). (2007). *Dreamworlds 3 (unabridged) desire, sex & power in music video* [Documentary]. United States: Media Education Foundation.

Jhally, S. (Producer), & Kilbourne, J. (Director). (2010). *Killing us softly 4 advertising's image of women* [Documentary]. United States: Media Education Foundation.

Kaufman, M. (1999). Men, feminism, and men's contradictory experiences of power. In J. A. Kuypers (Ed.), *Men and power.* Halifax, Nova Scotia: Fernwood Books.

Keen, S. (1991). *Fire in the belly: On being a man.* New York: Bantam.

Kolb, D. A., (1984). *Experiential learning: Experience as the source of learning and development.* Englewood Cliffs, NJ: Prentice Hall.

La Prad, J., Mink, A., & O'Steen, B. (2008). Explore, create, harvest, own: An experiential approach to professional development. In L. Adams & S. Galloway (Eds.), *The confluence proceedings,* Wellington, New Zealand: Outdoors New Zealand.

Mead, G. H. (1934). *Mind, self, and society: From the standpoint of a social behaviorist.* Chicago: University of Chicago Press.

Mead, G. H. (1964). *Selected writings* (Andrew J. Reck, Ed). Chicago: University of Chicago Press.

Pollack, W. (1999). *Real boys: Rescuing our sons from the myths of boyhood.* New York: Henry Holt and Company.

Rhoads, R. (2000). Democratic citizenship and service learning: Advancing the caring self. *New Directions for Teaching and Learning, 82,* 37–44.

Sax, L. (2008). *The gender gap in college: Maximizing the developmental potential of women and men.* San Francisco: Jossey-Bass.

Spence, J. T., & Helmreich, R. (1978). *Masculinity & femininity: Their psychological dimensions, correlates, antecedents.* Austin: University of Texas Press.

Tarrant, S., & Katz, J. (2008). *Men speak out: Views on gender, sex, and power.* New York: Routledge.

Tiger, L. (2005). *Men in groups* (3rd ed.). Piscataway, NJ: Transaction Publishers.

Warren, K. (2005). A path worth taking: The development of social justice in outdoor experiential education. *Equity & Excellence in Education, 38*(1), 89–99.

10

USING HOW COLLEGE MEN FEEL ABOUT BEING MEN AND "DOING THE RIGHT THING" TO PROMOTE MEN'S DEVELOPMENT

Alan D. Berkowitz

INDEPENDENT CONSULTANT

There is a pervasive theme in the literature on college men: men are uncomfortable with the way that they have been taught to be men. This creates conflict between how one wants to be and how one thinks one is supposed to be a man. Another theme is that men want to be accepted and appreciated by other men, to be seen as "normal" and as "one of the guys." Men's motivation to be accepted by other men results in many men not caring about women and tolerating other men's abusive behavior towards men and women. In general, men—in all the different identities that men have—want and try to be accepted as manly by other men. These issues about how to be a man reflect a larger culture in which the masculine and feminine are out of balance, with dangerous consequences for each of us as individuals, and for the planet as a whole.

This understanding of men reveals a paradox that is the central theme of this chapter. Most men don't want to be the kind of men they have been taught to be, but do not always know that other men share this discomfort. As a result, men may squeeze themselves into an uncomfortable "man box" in order to be accepted by other men, even when other men don't like the box either. The term used to describe the phenomenon of incorrectly thinking that one is in the minority when one is in fact in the majority is "pluralistic ignorance." This phenomenon influences how people behave, for example, in places of worship, in social groups, with respect to political views, consumption of alcohol, sexual activity, prejudicial behavior and masculinity (Miller & McFarland, 1991). Simply put, the majority of men secretly disagree with how we have been taught to be men, but act as if we don't. Why? Because we wrongly assume that most other men believe in what we have been taught to be as men, and also because we fear their disapproval were we to reveal the truth. The result is "role-conflict," a state of inner conflict and stress resulting in impaired mental and physical health.

Men often conform to an ideal of masculinity that we don't like because the consequences of non-conforming can be serious. A minority of men act as "enforcers" to punish and ostracize men who are seen as deviant. This is ironic, because the men who are labeled as "deviant" are probably the majority with the enforcers and exponents of "real" masculinity in the minority. Fear of being ostracized leads men to hide their discomfort in order to fit in with and be accepted by other men. The enforcers think that they speak for all men when in fact they do not. This pattern of behavior may occur among men in general, as well as within sub-groups of men who share a particular identity. As described earlier in this book (see, for example, Berila's insights in Chapter 6) men from non-dominant groups can feel oppressed by what they perceive as dominant norms of masculinity and struggle against it.

The power and influence of the enforcers comes from the misunderstanding—technically called "false consensus"—that they are the majority when in fact they are the minority. As long as these men and the silent majority of other men accept that the enforcers represent the kind of man that most men want to be, then they in turn will have the power to censor, ostracize, bully, and isolate men who are perceived as not fitting in. This norm of masculinity endures because "for a norm to be perpetuated it is not necessary for the majority to believe it, but only for the majority to believe that the majority believes it" (Berkowitz, 2003, p. 261).

How Men Feel about Being Men

A recent ethnographic study paints a distressing picture of the perceived norm for collegiate male culture (Kimmel, 2008). The term "Guyland" is used to describe a culture of men who perceive that they never measure up to their peers, to the masculine ideal, or to their own sense of self (see Chapter 1). Guyland is composed of men who feel inauthentic. It emphasizes the "guy code"—a sense of entitlement, of maintaining silence about one's own feelings and other's actions, and on men's protecting each other from being accountable for misbehavior. Guyland guys get drunk, abuse women, take risks, dismiss authority, talk and behave in sexist and homophobic ways, and expect other men to protect them from any consequences. Kimmel notes: "men subscribe to these ideals not because they want to impress women … (but) because they want to be positively evaluated by other men" (2008, p. 47). Enforcement of the rules is accomplished by innuendos and challenges to men's masculinity. Kimmel makes it clear however, that the majority of men are probably uncomfortable with this situation and only conform to it because they fear being ostracized by other men. In other words, "Guyland" is perpetuated by men's need for approval from other men, secret shame about not living up to the masculine ideal, and the false perception that most men believe in it.

Let's take a deeper look at what the research says regarding how men feel about being men—i.e., how men feel about the man-box. Table 10.1 shows what college men have said regarding how they feel about the masculinity they learned as children.

In addition, men are clearly uncomfortable with behavior of other men that is supposed to foster a sense of male bonding and proof of one's masculinity. In answer to the question, what are some things that men do when there are no women present that bothers you (Berkowitz, 1994), college men gave the following responses:

"When they talk about the sexual habits of girls that they know nothing about"

"Demands by friends to know how far sexually you've gone in a relationship"

"Bragging about sexual acts and giving details"

"Talking about women in crude sexual terms"

"Swearing"

These two sets of quotations, taken from men's workshops I have conducted, indicate that college men would like to be different from how they have been taught to be men and that they are uncomfortable with hyper-masculine behavior. These anecdotal findings are supported by a number of empirical studies.

TABLE 10.1 How Men Feel about Being Men

"I would like to experience women more as human beings and not as sexual partners. My past has been marred by a male chauvinistic upbringing in school and at home"

"I would like to be able to be more outgoing and emotional with my friends, rather than being cool, too cool for words."

"Being more comfortable with showing emotions—people are surprised when men cry."

"I would like to express my emotions more freely."

"I'd like to be able to be more human in the sense that I'd like to be more open to receiving help"

"I want to be able to be closer to male friends in the area of talking about problems. Many guys can't open up when it comes to certain topics."

"I definitely wish I could cook. My best effort in the kitchen is making toast."

"I'd like to be more human in the sense that I'd like to be more open about receiving help."

"I want to be closer to male friends in the area of talking about problems."

"Why can women dance together but not men?"

Based on responses in workshops to the question: "what would you like to change about how you were taught to be a man"

Gottfried (2002) surveyed college men to determine if they endorsed traditional masculine norms and to what extent they perceived other men as endorsing them. Participants overestimated the degree of other men's belief in stereotypical male characteristics, with most men not endorsing them but thinking that most men did. In addition, lower self-esteem was reported by men who perceived a disparity between their own and other males' beliefs about being a man. This study confirms the theme of this chapter that men are uncomfortable with how we are taught to be men, but try and act like "men" because we incorrectly think that other men expect us to.

Gottfried's (2002) study also determined that men were not influenced by how they thought women defined masculinity. Fabiano, Perkins, Berkowitz, Linkenbach, and Stark (2003) documented a similar phenomenon: men's willingness to intervene to prevent sexual assault was predicted by what men thought other men would do, but not by what men thought women would do. In other words, what is important to men about being a man is what they think other men think, not what they think women think.

To demonstrate this phenomenon, we can use a perhaps humorous example pertaining to how one decides what to wear to a party.

Box 10.1

A Thought Experiment for Men about Perceptions of Others

Imagine that you have been invited to a party by a group of people you are hoping to get to know better. You have the impression that this group likes to dress in black, and that it's "sophisticated." Actually you don't like black and it doesn't feel like "you." But you put your feelings aside and dress black. It turns out that almost everyone at the party does the same thing. Not caring for black, they dress in black.

Now imagine yourself at the party with these people who you want to be accepted by, who are mostly dressed in black. People say things like "You look so good!" "Black really becomes you," etc. And what do people say or think about the few who are not in black? How would you respond if someone told a joke about someone one of them? Most importantly, how does it feel to dress in a way that is not "you" while thinking that for everyone else it is the "real" them? How does it feel to think that you are perhaps the only person dressed in black who does like black?

In truth, almost everyone dressed in black is uncomfortable but thinks that everyone else is. Dressing one way and feeling another creates a sense of in-authenticity and conflict between how one looks from the outside and how one feels on the inside. This is not the case for the few people who actually like black, who feel comfortable and a sense of belonging.

They assume that they represent the majority when in fact they are a small minority.

Now imagine that this example is about something more fundamental, such as gender or another significant identity. Instead of "putting on black" you are "putting your face on" or "acting tough" or something else that allows you to fit in with what you think other men think about being male.

Now let's go back to the party. What if everyone found out that most people didn't care for black? How would they dress the next time? Would this change how those who like black feel and would they act differently? Would others behave differently to them?

While some may be non-conformists and do what feels right regardless of what others think, most of us take others into consideration to some degree. To the extent that we consider others it is important to know the truth about them. The truth about men is that most men are uncomfortable with normative masculinity but conform to this "false norm" because they think that this will produce acceptance from other men.

Now that the secret is out, how will you "dress" for the next party? Be yourself. And find out how your friends really feel about themselves. It will help you to be a happier person and the world to be a better place as a result.

Recent qualitative research on men's experiences supports this hypothesis and provides examples from the everyday experiences of college men. Edwards and Jones (2009) called it "Putting My Man Face On." They conducted extensive interviews with 10 traditionally aged college men from diverse backgrounds and found that "in order to try to meet these (society's) expectations and be seen as men, the participants in the study put on a performance that was like wearing a mask." (p. 214). Men moved through stages of "feeling a need to put on a mask," "wearing a mask," "experiencing and recognizing the consequences of wearing a mask," and finally, "beginning to transcend external expectations." Men continued to put on their "man face" despite the negative consequences that it had in all aspects of their lives.

In another qualitative study of men's experiences a similar conclusion was reached (Davis, 2002). "When these men were with a group of other men, even friends, there was some level of performance associated with their communication" (p. 515). Even though participants were clear "that they did not see themselves as typical of most men" and "communicated a general sense of unease with masculinity" they felt a need to hide this unease. Davis concluded that men had a strong inner need to be honest, empathic, communicative, and in other ways, break the "guy code," and that student affairs practitioners should create intentional environments where this is possible.

These qualitative studies confirm what has been frequently documented in the quantitative research on men's role conflict and gender-role strain—that men feel conflicted about how they are supposed to be men, which generates shame and which causes physical and emotion suffering. Underlying this problem is a "discrepancy between the real self and the gender role" (O'Neil, 1990, p. 24).

The Consequences of Mens' Mis-Perceiving Each Other

In this discussion we are following a thread to see where it leads us. If we accept the premise that men want to act differently as men but are held back by fear of what other men might think and shame about feeling deviant, what are the consequences? In what specific ways do men act differently than they would wish to act because of what they think other men think? And how might men act differently if they knew the truth about other men?

The assumption that misperceptions influence behavior is a central assumption of the "social norms approach"—a research-based theory that examines the impact of perceptions in different areas of life (Berkowitz, 2003, 2005a; Perkins, 2003). Social norms research has established that much human social behavior is based on misperceptions (or pluralistic ignorance), that these misperceptions are more extreme and influential among individuals who engage in problem behaviors, and that misperceptions predict how people act. Pluralistic ignorance is strongest when fear of social disapproval motivates behavior (Miller & McFarland, 1991). Thus, men's fear of disapproval from other men intensifies the influence of pluralistic ignorance on men's behavior.

Social norms research has established that high-school and college students consume more alcohol, cigarettes and marijuana when they think that their peers use more of these substances than they really do, and feel more pressure to have sex because they overestimate peer's sexually activity. The belief that others engage in more of a behavior than is really the case is most strongly held by those who engage in more of the behavior themselves—i.e., the false consensus group. In the case of masculinity, it is the hyper-masculine men who are the most committed to believing that most men believe the way they do.

The social norms approach has been used to reduce alcohol and other drug use, increase use of seat-belts and other healthy-behaviors, foster healthy relationships and encourage individual's to act from a place of conscience to intervene against negative behaviors. It is also a cutting edge strategy for engaging men in the prevention of violence against women (Berkowitz, 2007, Kilmartin & Berkowitz, 2005). In almost all areas of human life the negative is seen as more prevalent than it really is and the positive is underestimated. Not surprisingly, this is also true for gender, with both college men and women misperceiving the attitudes and behavior of their own gender as well as the other.

What do we know about men's experience from the perspective of the social norms approach? Table 10.2 provides examples of men's incorrect perceptions of each other that have been documented in empirical research.

These findings indicate that most men want to "do the right thing" and make healthy choices but may suppress this desire in order to fit in with what they think is true for other men. Men drink more alcohol (than they would otherwise), have more sex, blame sexual assault victims, talk and act in sexist and homophobic ways, and watch with silence when men degrade women verbally and physically because they think that these other men support these behaviors more than they really do, and also because they want to be accepted by these men.

Thus, although some men do terrible things and get bad attention for it, most men are "good guys" who don't agree with these behaviors but who are complicit by not acting to stop them. While men's bad behavior is broadcasted, much of men's good behavior is hidden or suppressed.

Let's look more closely at some of the studies that examine how men's misperceptions of each other influence men's behavior.

Three studies reported that college men (and women) overestimate prevalence of sexual activity among peers and their average number of sexual partners while underestimating the prevalence of safe-sex practices (Lynch, Mowrey, Nesbitt, & O'Neil, 2004; Martens et al., 2006; Scholly, Katz, Gascoigne, & Holk, 2005). Among high school students, Hillebrand-Gunn,

TABLE 10.2 College Men's Misperceptions of Each Other

College men *over*estimate other men's:
use of alcohol and other drugs
amount of sexual activity
desire to "hook-up"
belief in rape myths
interest in gambling
willingness to use force to have sex
frequency of unwanted sexual activity
acceptance of homophobia
College men *under*estimate other men's:
discomfort with language or behavior that objectifies or degrades women
willingness to intervene to prevent a sexual assault
desire to make sure that they have consent when sexually active
desire for a socially just world and to act against injustice

Heppner, Mauch, and Park (2010) found that most boys overestimated their peers support of rape myths and rape supportive behavior.

Lambert, Kahn, and Apple (2003) examined the culture of "hooking-up" and found that "participants believed that other college students were more comfortable with the amount of hooking up than they were" (p. 131). While this was true for both men and women, the pattern was more pronounced for men, who overestimated other men's comfort with hooking-up culture more than women overestimated other women's comfort with it.

Other researchers report similar findings for college men in relation to attitudes about sexual assault, willingness to engage in behaviors which will ensure consent, willingness to intervene to prevent a sexual assault, and/or peers discomfort with inappropriate language and actions towards women (Brown & Messman-Moore, 2009; Burn, 2010; Fabiano et al., 2003; Loh, Gidycz, Lobo, & Luthra, 2005; Kilmartin et al., 2008; Stein, 2007).

In one of these studies, Loh et al. (2005) reported that:

> Compared to themselves, participants believed that the average college man demonstrated more rape-myth acceptance, was less likely to intervene in situations where a woman was being mistreated, and was more comfortable in situations where women are being mistreated.

(p. 1334)

In this study perceived rape-myth acceptance of peers predicted sexual assault perpetration for members of fraternities at a three month follow-up.

In two studies of rape proclivity and misperception of peer support for rape myths, men reported greater willingness to rape when they were given information suggesting that other men believed in rape myths, with this being strongest for men with greater rape-proclivity (Bohner, Siebler, & Schmelcher, 2006; Eyssel, Bohner, & Seibler, 2006). Similarly, among domestic violence perpetrators, "men who are engaging in intimate partner violence tend to overestimate how often these behaviors are engaged in by other men" (Neighbors et al., 2010). These overestimations were associated with violence against their partners during the previous 90 days.

Regarding alcohol use, college men believe that other college men drink more alcohol than they really do, with problem drinkers overestimating the most. Perceptions of how much other men drink is the strongest influence on how much an individual man drinks himself, and is a stronger influence on drinking behavior than men's perception of how much women drink (Korcuska & Thombs, 2003; Lewis & Neighbors, 2004). Most men also incorrectly feel that they are more concerned about other men's drinking than are their male peers (Suls & Green, 2003). Among fraternity men, the strongest predictor of alcohol use is a fraternity man's perception of how much his brothers drink (Bartholow, Sher, & Krull, 2003). Furthermore, perceptions of fraternity brother's alcohol use predicts personal drinking, with these perceptions being "largely responsible for the prevalence of heavy drinking among fraternity and sorority members" (Sher, Bartholow, & Nanda, 2001, p. 50). Overestimations of other men's drinking is also correlated with personal drinking for men's "pre-partying" drinking and for amount consumed during drinking games (Pederson & LaBrie, 2008). The way in which these misperceptions interact with other influences on men's drinking is discussed in an insightful article by Capraro (2000).

Similar findings are revealed when researchers examine social justice attitudes, in this case heterosexual men's (and women's) homophobia. Thus, heterosexual individuals were found to overestimate the homophobia of their peers in two studies (Bowen & Bourgeois, 2001; Dubuque, Ciano-Boyce, & Shelley-Sireci, 2002), and a social justice educator reported that sharing accurate norms about heterosexual's homophobia—that it is less than what is perceived—empowers individuals to take more action against it (Smolinsky, 2002). Regarding men's sexism, Kilmartin et al. (2008) found that men overestimated other men's sexism and underestimated other men's discomfort with sexist behaviors. These findings are consistent with other research establishing that individuals are more likely to express prejudices when they believe that other's share them (Crandall, Eshleman, & O'Brien, 2002). Thus, in the case of prejudiced men, the false belief that other men are in agreement allows them to be vocal in expressing their biases, with the pluralistic ignorance of the uncomfortable majority causing them to be silent.

Cumulatively, these studies suggest that misperceptions of other men's attitudes and behaviors with respect to alcohol, sexual assault, other health-risk behaviors, and social justice attitudes may inhibit men who are bystanders from intervening to stop them, and that they also function to facilitate violent and other abusive behavior in men who are pre-disposed to these problems. This supports the hypothesis that "Guyland" is perpetuated by myths—the myth that the enforcers are the true men, and the myth that the bystanders agree with them.

Misperceptions and Willingness to Intervene

Recent research on bystander behavior supports the conclusion that misperceptions function to inhibit individuals from intervening against problem language and behavior. In one pilot study, Berkowitz (2006) assessed college students' experiences of second-hand effects of drinking and documented that students underestimated of the extent to which their peers were bothered by these behaviors, and also their peers' interest in having someone intervene to stop them.

A number of studies examining the role of college men as allies in ending sexual assault, have found that men overestimate other men's adherence to rape-supportive attitudes and underestimate other men's willingness to intervene to prevent sexual assault (Brown & Messman-Moore, 2009; Fabiano et al., 2003; Stein, 2007). In these studies, the strongest or only significant predictor of men's willingness to prevent a sexual assault was a man's perception of other men's willingness to intervene to prevent a sexual assault.

In these studies, men report having pro-social attitudes and intentions but are inhibited from expressing them because of the incorrect perception that other men are less pro-social. This misperception also functions to allow anti-social men to justify and encourage their misbehavior.

Social norms efforts to reduce men's violence against women. Recent efforts to apply the social norms approach to men's violence against women have determined that misperceptions can be corrected with this correction resulting in more positive attitudes and/or behavior, including reductions in sexual assault and increases in men's intervening to prevent it. These results have implications for addressing other forms of men's problem behavior.

In a three-part workshop for high school boys and girls Hillebrand-Gunn and her colleagues (2010) incorporated a normative feedback component for boys. At follow-up experimental group, participants reported reduced misperceptions of peers' attitudes conducive to rape coupled with a reduction in personal attitudes conducive to rape, without these changes occurring in a matched control group. Similarly, Kilmartin et al. (2008) conducted a small-group social norms intervention to correct college men's attitudes about rape and sexist attitudes and reported a significant decrease in perceptions of peer's sexism in the intervention group at three-week follow-up. Finally, in a study by Gidycz et al. (2011) testing a rape prevention workshop for college men developed by the author which included group social norms exercises and bystander intervention techniques, the men in the experimental group committed fewer sexual assaults after three months than men in the control group, along with other beneficial effects.

A small-group norms intervention developed by the White Ribbon Campaign (Berkowitz, 2005b) incorporates normative feedback into small group workshops that address gender stereotypes and promote gender equity for middle and high-school students. After filling out a survey assessing personal attitudes about gender equity along with their perception of the gender attitudes and behaviors of other students in the class, feedback is provided indicating that a majority misperceive their class-mates adherence to gender stereotypical norms. Preliminary results show boys have extreme misperceptions of their peer's attitudes about gender equity.

Bruce (2002) implemented a social norms media campaign to change men's intimate behavior towards women. The campaign was followed by a significant increase in the percentage of men who indicated that they "stop the first time a date says no to sexual activity" and a significant decrease in the percentage of men who said that "when I want to touch someone sexually, I try and see how they react." In a similar high school campaign focusing on healthy dating relationships, boys at 2-year follow-up reported more accurate perceptions of other boy's discomfort with boys "trash-talking girls" and this change was correlated with an increase in the number of boys who did something when they heard trash-talk (Moran & Berkowitz, 2007).

Collectively these studies, although preliminary, indicate that correcting men's misperceptions of each other holds promise as a violence prevention strategy engaging men and boys in the prevention of violence against women, and more broadly as a strategy that gives men permission to act on pro-social impulses that are being stifled by a desire to fit in with a false norm of masculinity.

Let's Tell Men the Truth about Each Other

The research reviewed here indicates that men would be more likely to express positive attitudes and behaviors if they knew the truth about other men. Men's role conflict, passivity in the face of other men's problematic behavior, and reticence to express a social conscience might all be reduced if men knew how other men really feel. Thus, student affairs practitioners should develop a research agenda that would document men's misperceptions of each other, and implement programs to correct them.

While this strategy would not by itself create healthy men, or solve the problems of men's bad behavior and men's internal conflict about being men, misperception correction could act as a powerful catalyst nudging men in the right direction, creating a more permissive environment for men to be their healthy selves, and in turn creating a space for men to do the difficult emotional and transformational work necessary to be more mature, socially engaged human beings.

William Perry (1970), in his well-known study of college students' intellectual development, used the terms "temporizing" and "retreat" to describe students who felt overwhelmed by a developmental challenge and who were either treading water in the face of it (temporizing), or actively moving in an opposite direction to avoid it (retreat). Perhaps among college men the silent majority who are bystanders are "temporizers" while the enforcers and perpetrators are in "retreat". In either case, men's misperceptions of each other reinforce and congeal these developmental regressions and may prevent men from moving forward.

Numerous researchers have written about the emotional and developmental challenges that men face as a result of our socialization to be male in unhealthy ways, of the guilt and shame that it engenders, and how this blocks men's healthy development (for example, Davis & Wagner, 2005; and Johnson, 1997). In addition, Edwards and Jones (2009) examined how the culture of "putting my man face on" resulted in men's moving through a series of developmental stages in relation to it: "feeling the need to wear a mask," "experiencing and recognizing the consequences of wearing a mask," and "beginning to transcend external expectations." Research and theory reviewed here leads to the conclusion that men might move more easily through these stages if they knew the truth of how other men feel about themselves as men. Correcting men's misperceptions of each other could unfreeze men so that development could move forward and other group and environmental interventions could be more effective.

If a social norms approach to masculinity offers benefits and could be part of a comprehensive approach to addressing men's issues on campus, how should student affairs practitioners make use of it?

Recommendations for Student Affairs Practitioners

The following recommendations inspired by the social norms approach are offered to student affairs professionals to help us understand college men, to design effective programs to foster their development, and to address unhealthy behavior.

> **Recommendation #1. Develop a social norms research agenda for college men.** What are the strengths and pro-social attitudes and behaviors of college men? For example, how many have intervened against a sexist remark or to prevent abusive behavior? To what extent are men interested in attending lectures or taking courses that are outside of the "gender box?" Briodo and Reason (2005), Edwards and Jones (2009), Davis and Wagner (2005) and others have identified critical ingredients of campus environments that serve to engage men (and women) in social justice ally behavior and in healthy development. What are men's perceptions about these elements, to what extent are men willing to participate in them, and are these intentions misperceived with respect to other men? Are men with privileged identities uncomfortable with the behavior of other men in their group(s)? Finally, are the patterns of misperceptions suggested in this chapter prevalent in different communities of men, for example, gay and bi-sexual men, African American, Latino and/or Asian men, etc.? There are endless possibilities for examining the positives of men's attitudes and behaviors and the misperceptions of other men that cause men to closet them. Emphasizing the positive and revealing men's misperceptions have also been recommended by Fabiano et al. (2003) and Stein (2007).
>
> **Recommendation #2. Integrate normative feedback and normative feedback exercises into existing student affairs programs at all levels of prevention.** Consistent with the principles of the social norms approach, normative feedback can be provided

to individuals who engage in problem behavior, as Neighbors et al. (2010) have recommended for domestic violence perpetrators; to groups of men and boys, as Smolinsky (2002) recommends for homophobia education and as the White Ribbon Campaign proposes to foster gender equity (Berkowitz, 2005b), and in campus-wide media campaigns, as have been successfully utilized by Bruce (2002) and Moran and Berkowitz (2007). This can be done both for men in general, and for specific identity groups among men.

Recommendation #3. Consider a social norms approach to masculinity as a student affairs philosophy. The social norms approach, with its emphasis on the role of misperceptions, can be synthesized and integrated with other theories and approaches to men's development, and should not be considered only as a specific strategy or technique. The phenomenon of pluralistic ignorance and false consensus are consistent with theories of men's development, as well as student development in general, and help to explain many of the phenomenon described by them. Misperception correction could also serve as a catalyst to make existing student affairs practices more effective.

Recommendation #4. Offer skills training to men who want to be change agents. As men realize that they and other men want to "do the right thing," they become more ready to act on their pro-social impulses. This requires attending skills-training in order to overcome the emotional and interpersonal challenges to intervening and to learn how to do so effectively (Berkowitz, 2009).

I would like to conclude by sharing the results of an interesting study that examined how college men perceive other men's and women's attitudes towards alcohol (Suls & Green, 2003). When surveyed about campus drinking norms and their willingness to express concern about another's drinking, men perceived themselves to be different from other men but similar to women. This can be interpreted symbolically. Privately men feel in some ways to be more similar to women but hide this "feminine" side from other men because it is incorrectly felt to be deviant. Providing men the opportunity to become authentic and whole requires giving men permission to acknowledge and express this hidden "feminine" and to realize that other men are similar. Men's health requires replacing of denial of the feminine with acknowledgment of the male-female polarity that exists within each of us along with healthy expression of both.

Student affairs practitioners have traditionally tried to solve problems caused by men by focusing on the negative. In this chapter I have argued that an important element in changing men lies in a different direction—by focusing on the positive (on men's desires to act and be men in a positive way) and on releasing men from a false and destructive sense of peer pressure and gender dichotomies by revealing the truth about men to each other.

References

Bartholow, B. D., Sher, K., & Krull, J. L. (2003). Changes in heavy drinking over the third decade of life as a function of fraternity and sorority involvement: A prospective, multilevel analysis. *Health Psychology, 22*, 616–626.

Berkowitz, A. D. (1994). The role of coaches in rape prevention programs for athletes. In A. Parrott, N. Cummings, & T. Marchell (Eds.), *Rape 101: Sexual assault prevention for college athletes* (pp. 61–65). Holmes Beach, FL: Learning Publications.

Berkowitz, A. D. (2003). Applications of social norms theory to other health and social justice issues. In H. W. Perkins (Ed.), *The social norms approach to preventing school and college age substance abuse: A handbook for educators, counselors, clinicians* (pp. 257–279). San Francisco: Jossey-Bass.

Berkowitz, A. D. (2005a). An overview of the social norms approach. In L. Lederman, L. Stewart, F. Goodhart, & L. Laitman (Eds.), *Changing the culture of college drinking: A socially situated prevention campaign* (pp. 187–208). Cresskill, NJ: Hampton Press.

Berkowitz, A. D. (2005b). Social norms snowball survey. In *Education and action kit*. Toronto, Ontario: White Ribbon Campaign.

Berkowitz, A. D. (2006, October). *Understanding the role of bystander behavior.* Presented at the U.S. Department of Education's 20th Annual National Meeting on Alcohol and Other Drug Abuse Prevention and Violence Prevention in Higher Education. Arlington, VA.

Berkowitz, A. D. (2007). An interview with Alan Berkowitz. In C. Kilmartin &, J. Allison (Eds.), *Men's violence against women: Theory, research and activism* (pp. 190–197). Mahwah, NJ: Erlbaum.

Berkowitz, A. D. (2009). *Response Ability: A complete guide to bystander intervention.* Chicago: Beck and Company.

Bohner, G., Siebler, F., & Schmelcher, J. (2006). Social norms and the likelihood of raping: Perceived rape myth acceptance of others affects men's rape proclivity. *Personality and Social Psychology Bulletin, 32*, 286–297.

Bowen, A. M., & Bourgeois, M. J. (2001). Attitudes towards lesbian, gay, and bisexual college students: The contribution of pluralistic ignorance, dynamic social impact, and contact theories. *Journal of American College Health, 50*(2), 91–96.

Broido, E.. & Reason, B. (2005). The development of social justice attitudes and actions: An overview of current understandings. In R. D. Reason, E. M. Broido, T. L. Davis, & N. J. Evans, (Eds.), *Developing social justice allies* (pp. 17–28). San Francisco: Jossey-Bass.

Brown, A. L., & Messman-Moore, T. L. (2009). Personal and perceived peer attitudes supporting sexual aggression as predictors of male college students' willingness to intervene against sexual aggression. *Journal of Interpersonal Violence, 25*(3), 503–517.

Bruce, S. (2002). The "a man" campaign: Marketing social norms to men to prevent sexual assault. *The report on social norms: Working paper #5.* Little Falls, NJ: PaperClip Communications.

Burn, S. M. (2010). *The influence of peer norms on men's sexual consent behavior.* Manuscript submitted for publication.

Capraro, R. L. (2000). Why college men drink: Alcohol, adventure and the paradox of masculinity. *Journal of American College Health, 48*(6), 307–315.

Crandall, C. S., Eshleman, A., & O'Brien, L. (2002). Social norms and the expression of prejudice: The struggle for internalization. *Journal of Personality and Social Psychology, 82*(3), 359–378.

Davis, T. (2002). Voices of gender role conflict: The social construction of college men's identity. *Journal of College Student Development, 43*(4), 508–521.

Davis, T., & Wagner, R. (2005). Increasing men's development of social justice attitudes and actions. In R. D. Reason, E. M. Broido, T. L. Davis, & N. J. Evans (Eds.), *Developing social justice allies* (pp. 29–41). San Francisco: Jossey Bass.

Dubuque, E., Ciano-Boyce, C., & Shelley-Sireci, L. (2002). Measuring misperceptions of homophobia on campus. *The Report on Social Norms: Working Paper #4.* Little Falls, NJ: PaperClip Communications. Available from http://www.socialnorm.org

Edwards, K. E., & Jones, S. R. (2009). Putting my face on: A grounded theory of college men's gender identity development. *Journal of College Student Development, 50*(2), 210–228.

Eyssel, F., Bohner, G., & Seibler, F. (2006). Perceived rape myth acceptance of others predicts rape proclivity: Social norms or judgmental anchoring? *Swiss Journal of Psychology, 65*(2), 93–99.

Fabiano, P., Perkins, H. W., Berkowitz, A., Linkenbach, J., & Stark, C. (2003). Engaging men as social justice allies in ending violence against women: Evidence for a social norms approach. *Journal of American College Health, 52*(3), 105–111.

Gidycz, C. A., Orchowski, C. M., Probst, D., Edwards, K., Murphy, M., Tansill, E., & Berkowitz, A. (2011). Preventing sexual assault among college students: An outcome evaluation. *Violence Against Women*, Summer, 2001.

Gottfried, M. G. S. (2002, August). *Perceptions of others' masculinity beliefs: Conforming to a false norm?* Presented at the 110th Conference of the American Psychological Association, Chicago, Illinois.

Hillebrand-Gunn, T., Heppner, M. J., Mauch, P. A., & Park, H. J. (2010). Men as allies: The efficacy of a high school rape prevention intervention. *Journal of Counseling and Development, 88*, 43–51.

Johnson, A. G. (1997). *The gender knot: Unravelng our patriarchal legacy.* Philadelphia: Temple University Press._

Kilmartin, C. T., & Berkowitz, A. D. (2005). *Sexual assault in context: Teaching college men about gender.* Mahwah, NJ: Erlbaum.

Kilmartin, C. T., Smith, T., Green, A., Heinzen, H., Kuchler, M., & Kolar, D. (2008). A real-time social norms intervention to reduce college mens' sexism. *Sex Roles, 59*, 264–273.

Kimmel, M. (2008). *Guyland: The perilous world where boys become men.* New York: Harper Collins.

Korcuska, J. S., & Thombs, D. L. (2003). Gender role conflicts and sex-specific drinking norms: Relationships to alcohol use in undergraduate women and men. *Journal of College Student Development, 44*(2), 204–215.

Lambert, T. A., Kahn, A. S., & Apple, K. J. (2003). Pluralistic ignorance and hooking up. *The Journal of Sex Research, 40*(2), 129–133.

Lewis, M. A., & Neighbors, C. (2004). Gender-specific misperceptions of college student drinking norms. *Psychology of Addictive Behaviors, 18*, 340–349.

Loh, C., Gidycz, C. A., Lobo, T. R., & Luthra, R. (2005). A prospective analysis of sexual assault perpetration: Risk factor related to perpetrator characteristics. *Journal of Interpersonal Violence. 20*(10), 1385–1348.

Lynch, J., Mowrey, R., Nesbitt, G., & O'Neil, D. (2004). Risky business: Misperceived norms of sexual behavior among college students. *NASPA Journal, 42*(1), 21–35.

Martens, M., Page, J., Mowry, E., Damann, K., Taylor, K., & Cimini, D. (2006). Differences between actual and perceived student norms: An examination of alcohol use, drug use, and sexual behavior. *Journal of American College Health, 54*(5), 295–300.

Miller, D. T., & McFarland, C. (1991). When social comparison goes awry: The case of pluralistic ignorance. In J. Suls & T. Wills (Eds.), *Social comparison: Contemporary theory and research* (pp. 287–313). Hillsdale, NJ: Erlbaum.

Moran, M., & Berkowitz, A. (2007, July). *Using social norms to prevent teen dating violence at gateway high school.* Presented at the Tenth Annual National Social Norms Conference. Boston, MA.

Neighbors, C., Walker, D., Mbilinyi, L., O'Rourke, A., Edleson, J. L., Zegree, J., & Roffman, R. A. (2010). Normative misperceptions of abuse among perpetrators of intimate partner violence. *Violence Against Women, 16*, 370–386.

O'Neil, J. (1990). Assessing men's gender role conflict. In D. Moore & F. Leafren (Eds.), *Problem solving strategies and interventions for men in conflict.* (pp. 23–38). Alexandria, VA. American Association for Counseling and Development.

Pederson, E. R., & LaBrie, J. W. (2008). Normative misperceptions of drinking among college students: A look at the specific contexts of prepartying and drinking games. *Journal of Studies on Alcohol and Drugs, 69*, 406–411.

Perkins, H. W. (2003). (Ed.), *The social norms approach to preventing school and college age substance abuse: A handbook for educators, counselors, clinicians*. San Francisco: Jossey-Bass.

Perry, W. G., Jr. (1970). *Forms of intellectual and ethical development in the college years: A scheme*. New York: Holt, Rinehart, & Winston.

Sher, K., Bartholow, B. D., & Nanda, S. (2001). Short- and long-term effects of fraternity and sorority membership on heavy drinking: A social norms perspective. *Psychology of Addictive Behaviors, 15*, 42–51.

Scholly, K., Katz, A., Gascoigne, J., & Holk, P. (2005). Using social norms theory to explain perceptions and sexual health behaviors of undergraduate college students: An exploratory study. *Journal of American College Health, 53*(4), 159–166.

Smolinsky, T. (2002). What do we really think? A group exercise to increase heterosexual ally behavior. *The Report on Social Norms: Working Paper #4,* Little Falls, NJ: PaperClip Communications. Available from http://www.socialnorm.org

Stein, J. (2007). Peer educators and close friends as predictors of male college willingness to prevent rape. *Journal of College Student Development, 48*(1), 1–15.

Suls, J., & Green, P. (2003). Pluralistic ignorance and college student perceptions of gender-specific alcohol norms. *Health Psychology, 22*, 479–486.

11

BEST PRACTICES FOR IMPROVING COLLEGE MEN'S HEALTH

Designing Effective Programs and Services for College Men

Will Courtenay

MEN'S HEALTH CONSULTING

The greatest gender gap in mortality occurs among 15- to 24-year-olds (DHHS, 2000). Three out of every four deaths annually in this age group are male (DHHS, 2007). The death rate is highest for African American men, followed by Hispanic and European American men. Although disease, injury, and death rates are unavailable for college students specifically, a general profile of college men's health can be inferred from the risks of this approximate age group. Among adolescents, males are more likely than females to be hospitalized for injuries. Fatal injuries account for more than 80% of all deaths among 15- to 24-year-old men, and 3 out of 4 injury deaths in this age group are male. Young men of this age are also at far greater risk than women for sexually transmitted diseases or infections (STDs/STIs). Despite these risks, the gender-specific health care needs of college men have only recently begun to be examined (Courtenay, 1998, 1999; Courtenay & Keeling, 2000a, 2000b).

Explaining College Men's Poor Health

The gender gap in longevity is explained largely by men's health behaviors and beliefs—including men's beliefs about manhood.

Beliefs and Behaviors

Biological factors are relatively poor predictors of gender differences in disease and death, which are explained largely by men's health beliefs and behaviors (Courtenay, 2003, 2011). For example, men are less likely than women to believe that personal behaviors contribute to good health or to accept personal responsibility for their health (Courtenay, 2001a, 2003, 2011). Similarly, men respond to stress in less healthy ways than women do. They are less likely than women to employ healthy, vigilant coping strategies and more likely to use avoidant coping strategies such as denial, distraction, and increased alcohol consumption (Stanton & Courtenay, 2003).

Men are also more likely than women to engage in more than 30 behaviors that are associated with an increased risk of disease, injury, and death (Courtenay, 2000a, 2011). Among college students specifically, men engage in fewer health-promoting behaviors than women—including wearing safety belts; eating well; conducting self-examinations for cancer; and behaviors related to driving, sleep, and exercise (Courtenay, 1998, 2000a, 2011). College men also engage in more risky behaviors than college women do, among them behaviors related to sex, drug use, carrying weapons, and physically fighting; and they take greater risks while playing sports and driving.

Compared to college women, college men are more likely to drink alcohol, to drink more of it, and to drink more often—as well as drive under the influence of alcohol. Consequently, college men experience more negative health consequences of drinking, notably physical injury, infection from STDs/STIs and HIV, drowning, and motor vehicle death. College men are also more likely to use tobacco and have more dangerous smoking habits such as smoking more cigarettes per day (Courtenay, 1998, 2000a, 2011). Consumption of smokeless tobacco has increased among young men between 250% and 300% since the 1970s and is typically initiated during college. These gender differences in health beliefs and behaviors remain among college students across various ethnic groups (Courtenay, McCreary, & Merighi, 2002).

Masculinity

Although simply being male is linked with poor health behavior and increased health risks, so is gender, or men's beliefs about "being a man." Men who adopt traditional attitudes about manhood have greater health risks than men with less traditional attitudes (Courtenay, 2011). Among college students, traditional attitudes have been linked with a higher level of anxiety, greater cardiovascular reactions to stress, maladaptive coping, depression, and poor health behaviors related to smoking, alcohol and drug use, safety, diet, sleep, and sexual practices. Furthermore, these men are more likely than nontraditional men not to seek help from others and underuse professional services on campus. African American men are more likely than men of other ethnic groups to endorse traditional attitudes about masculinity (Courtenay, 2000b, 2001b, 2002).

How College Men Learn Unhealthy Beliefs and Behaviors

There is high agreement in U.S. society about what are considered to be typically feminine and typically masculine characteristics (see Courtenay, 2000c, 2011).

It is not surprising then that people treat girls and boys differently from the very first day of life. In fact, regardless of gender, people interact with an infant on the basis of what they believe to be the infant's gender. Similarly, clear distinctions are drawn in the media between men's and women's behaviors— including men's and women's health behaviors. These lessons can last a lifetime.

Peers, Parents, and Other Adults

From birth, parents treat girls and boys differently (Courtenay, 2000c, 2011). Despite the fact that boys are at relatively greater risk, parents are less concerned about the safety of their sons than they are about the safety of their daughters. Boys are handled more roughly, are engaged in more intense and competitive play, are physically punished more, and are exposed to more violence. Boys are also more likely than girls to be discouraged from seeking help, and to be punished when they do seek help. This differential treatment has both short- and long-term effects on the health of men and boys (Courtenay, 2000b, 2000c).

It is not only parents but peers and other adults who teach boys unhealthy beliefs and behaviors (Courtenay, 2000b, 2000c, 2003, 2011). North Americans strongly endorse the cultural (and health-related) beliefs or stereotypes that men are independent, self-reliant, strong, robust, and tough. When people are told that an infant is male regardless of its actual gender, they are more likely to believe that it is "firmer" and "less fragile" than when they are told that the same infant is female. Men and boys experience comparatively greater social pressure than women and girls to endorse traditional beliefs about gender.

Media

On television and in films, men are shown smoking 3 to 7 times more often than women. Two-thirds of all characters who drink in prime-time television programs are men. In general, women and girls are portrayed in the media as having the greatest health risks and being the most likely to die, while men and boys are portrayed as engaging in unhealthy or high-risk behaviors—and as being healthy and invulnerable to the risks that their high-risk behaviors pose.

Alcohol and tobacco advertisements are strategically placed in magazines and television programs with predominantly male audiences. For example, *Sports Illustrated,* the magazine most often read by college men, has more tobacco and alcohol advertisements than any other. Advertisers also often portray men in high-risk activities to sell their products. Beer commercials, for example, have been found to link men's drinking with taking risks and facing danger without fear. Tobacco companies link the use of smokeless tobacco with virility and athletic performance in marketing to men. These media representations of gender and health have been found to contribute to negative health effects for men and boys (Courtenay, 2000c, 2011).

Conflicting Messages About Manhood and Health

College men receive contradictory (and consequently confusing) messages about health (Courtenay, 1998). Even though health education campaigns attempt to teach young men that it is wrong to be violent, on television men and boys are more likely than women and girls to initiate and engage in physically violent behavior, which typically is rewarded and without negative consequences (see Courtenay, 2000c, 2011). Not surprisingly, nearly 1 in 7 college men in California gets into a physical fight in one year (Patrick, Covin, Fulop, Calfas, & Lovato, 1997). Health messages encouraging abstinence and tobacco cessation similarly contradict consistent messages young men receive from the media, and society in general, indicating that both drinking and tobacco use are simply part of being a man (Courtenay, 2000c). Given this, it is not surprising that college men use more alcohol and tobacco than college women.

Evidence-Based Strategies for College Health Professionals: The Six-Point HEALTH Plan

Research indicates that students often need gender-specific interventions, such as safer-sex education specifically tailored for women and men (Courtenay, 1998). I have developed a clinical practice guideline for health professionals who work with men (Courtenay, 2001a, 2011; Stanton & Courtenay, 2003), which is summarized here. Its recommendations are based on an extensive review of research. This Six-Point HEALTH Plan identifies behavioral and psychosocial factors that affect the onset, progression, and management of men's health problems; reviews evidence demonstrating the effectiveness of various interventions; and outlines specific best practices for addressing these factors when working with college men. Whether a health professional is treating college men in a health service, developing gender-specific programming for men, conducting outreach, or designing health education materials, the same basic principles of the Six-Point Plan hold true.

Any contact a health professional has with a college man represents an important opportunity. In general, men (including college men) are less likely than women to seek health care (Courtenay, 1998, 2000b, 2011). Therefore any encounter a health professional has with a college man may be the *only* opportunity for assessment and intervention that *any* health professional will have with that man for a long time. Furthermore, even one contact with a male patient can have significantly positive effects on both behavioral and clinical outcomes (Courtenay, 2001a).

The practice guideline addresses communication between clinicians and their patients, which is associated with treatment compliance and patient health status (see Courtenay, 2001a, 2011). College health professionals whose responsibility it is to counsel men in any capacity are in a unique position to assist these men. Research indicates that people are more likely to be helped to prevent future disease by health professionals who ask, educate, and counsel them about personal health behaviors than by those who perform physical examinations or tests (Courtenay, 2001a, 2011).

Each of the six subsections here briefly summarizes one of six types of intervention discussed in the clinical practice guideline. Together, the titles of the six points form an acronym that spells HEALTH: Humanize, Educate, Assume the worst, Locate supports, Tailor a plan, and Harness strengths.

Humanize

Humanizing is a technique that validates or normalizes patients' health problems and concerns. Conveying to patients that their feelings and experiences are understandable or legitimate—and that other people would probably feel the same way—is considered essential to effective communication with patients (Courtenay, 2001a, 2011). Because disease, disability, and health-promoting responses to illness are antithetical to masculinity, men can experience embarrassment and shame when they do have health problems that they must address (Courtenay, 2001a, 2011). Clinicians can compensate for this and help men learn that asking for help, acknowledging pain, expressing fear, crying, or needing bed rest are normal, human experiences; they are not unmanly. Moderate self-disclosure on a clinician's part, particularly if the clinician is a man, may make a male patient feel safer and is associated with positive outcomes. You might say, "I know what you mean; I have hard time admitting when I'm sick too."

Humanize Help Seeking. Men have less intention to seek help from a variety of sources when they need it (Courtenay, 2001a, 2011). Seeking help can undermine a man's sense of independence and be experienced as demeaning, which may lead to feelings of inadequacy and shame. Reconceptualize a student's help seeking as positive behavior, and offer reinforcement by saying, "Coming to see me when you did was the best thing you could have done." Reframing a man's seeking help as an act of strength, courage, and self-determination may decrease any embarrassment or self-doubt that he may experience in reaching out for help.

Humanize Illness and Convalescence. Because illness threatens masculine ideals of competence, vitality, and strength, men may experience illness as a personal flaw or a failure to successfully demonstrate manhood (Courtenay, 2000c, 2011). Simply saying, "You know, everybody gets sick sometimes" can bring relief to a man and help to establish rapport. When they are ill, men are less likely than women to restrict activities or stay in bed for both acute and chronic conditions (Courtenay, 2001a, 2011). Some men consider staying in bed to recover to be unnecessary "pampering." A college man may think of himself as "lazy" if he misses school or sports practice after an injury or operation.

Humanize the need for convalescence by saying to a student, "Staying in bed and taking care of yourself when you're sick doesn't mean you're a not a team player."

Humanize Pain and Fear. Admitting or displaying fear and pain is largely unacceptable for men in our society. Not surprisingly, compared to women men report less pain for the same pathology, less severe pain, greater tolerance of pain, and a higher pain threshold. Although hormones may play some role in mediating the experience of pain, it is clear that psychosocial factors do too. Men report less pain to female clinicians than to male clinicians (Courtenay, 2003). The reluctance to acknowledge or report physical or emotional distress can have far-reaching implications for college men's health; it can influence help-seeking decisions, delay intervention, and undermine diagnosis and treatment planning.

In humanizing pain, health professionals should label conditions known to be painful as such: "Kidney stones can be very painful. I don't want you to hesitate for a moment if you think you might need to come back to get urgent care." Express surprise when a student denies that his kidney stones are painful. To more accurately assess a college man's level of pain, and to compensate for his potential minimization of pain, say, "There are no medals for enduring pain, so I want you to let me know if you experience even the *slightest* bit of discomfort."

Humanize Sexual Concerns. At least 1 out of 4 American men is unable to get or maintain an erection for sex, and almost all men—including college men— experience occasional and transient erectile problems. Erectile dysfunction is also a common side effect of a variety of medications (Courtenay, 2001a). These facts are inconsistent with the stereotype that men are perpetually interested in and ready for sex. Consequently, sexual dysfunction can threaten a student's self-image as a man, and it can be threatening to acknowledge it. Three out of four men with sexual concerns report being too embarrassed to discuss those concerns with their physician. To humanize college men's sexual concerns, problems, and fears say, "Most men have concerns about sex; it's normal. And I'd be surprised if you didn't." Help men identify unrealistic perceptions of manhood that contribute to sexual anxiety, and learn how human perceptions of sexuality can reduce stress and sexual dysfunction. You can say, "You're not a machine. Your body can't be expected to turn on and off at will."

Humanize Men's Body Image. Superhuman perceptions of manhood distort college men's perceptions of their bodies. Over the last several decades, cultural standards of the ideal male body have grown increasingly large and bulky. Not surprisingly, men and boys have become increasingly dissatisfied with their bodies. Research indicates that 28%–68% of normal-weight young men either try to or want to gain weight, and that the desire to be bigger and more muscular is linked with traditional masculinity (Courtenay, 2003; McCreary, Saucier, & Courtenay, 2005). This desire in young men is also associated with psychological distress, impaired social functioning, and substance abuse, including abuse of anabolic steroids. College health professionals can teach this to college men and help them make human their superhuman perceptions of the male body.

Educate

Health education interventions are an essential aspect of disease and injury prevention and can reduce risks, improve compliance, facilitate change, and promote health (Courtenay, 2001a). Furthermore, research consistently indicates that men, including college men, are less knowledgeable than women about health in general, and about specific diseases (Courtenay, 1998, 2003, 2011). College men, for example, know significantly less than college women about self-examinations for cancer and risk factors for HIV.

Despite these findings, health professionals often fail to provide health education to men. For example, men are provided with fewer and briefer explanations—as well as less information overall—from clinicians during medical examinations (Roter & Hall, 1997). Only 29% of physicians routinely provide age-appropriate instruction on performing testicular self-examination (TSE), compared to 86% providing age-appropriate instruction to women on performing breast self-examination. Additionally, although men engage in more unhealthy behaviors, they are less likely than women to be counseled by clinicians about changing those behaviors. For example, college men are less likely than college women to be questioned in medical visits about tobacco use.

Specific educational interventions vary depending on a college man's current health, his presenting concern, and his future risks. A good way to start educating men is by communicating that "Most of the things that have the biggest impact on your health are completely within your control." When educating college men, it is essential to include even quite basic knowledge (such as whom to call for an appointment) because many men have had relatively little experience with health care. Educators should keep the information simple, offer written materials, and make statements and written materials both clear and direct. They should also provide alternative responses to unhealthy behaviors. It is also important to encourage questions, because men ask clinicians fewer questions than women do (Courtenay, 2001a, 2011). You can say, "I've explained a lot to you. I'd be surprised if you didn't have some questions."

College men also need to be taught the importance of early detection of disease. Screening tests and self-examinations are essential for preventing disease and identifying a variety of diseases at an early stage, which is when successful treatment is more likely (Courtenay, 2001a). However, men in general and African American men in particular are less likely than women to practice self-examination or to attend health screenings (Courtenay, 2001b, 2003, 2011). Self-examinations particularly relevant to college men include those for skin and testicular cancer, and STDs/STIs.

Assume the Worst

One of the most common and enduring cultural stereotypes about men is that they are healthier and more resistant to disease or injury than women, despite a wealth of evidence to the contrary (Courtenay, 2000c, 2011). Men who conform to these cultural stereotypes increase their health risks. They may try to appear strong and healthy, believe that they are invulnerable to risk, minimize pain and deny feelings that others may perceive as signs of weakness, and report their health inaccurately.

Among college students, men perceive less risk than women for a variety of health threats, among them risks associated with the use of cigarettes, alcohol, and other drugs; sun exposure; physically dangerous sports; and driving. For example, college men perceive less risk associated with not using a safety belt, drinking and driving, and not making a full stop at a stop sign. These beliefs are inconsistent with the finding that (in California, for example) men are at fault in nearly 8 of 10 automobile accidents and 2 of 3 injury crashes (Courtenay, 2000a); and among 15- to 24-year-olds 20 times more men than women die in automobile accidents, which are the leading cause of death in this age group (DHHS, 2000). Furthermore, college men's perceived invulnerability prevents them from changing unhealthy behaviors (Courtenay 1998, 2011).

The desire to conceal vulnerability can influence college men's decision not to seek care and can affect assessment and diagnosis when they do get care. Compared to college women, men are less likely to confide in friends, express vulnerability, disclose their problems, or seek help or support from others when they need it (Courtenay 1998a, 2000b, 2000c, 2011). Among college students with depression, for example, men are more likely than women to rely on themselves, withdraw socially, or try to talk themselves out of it (Courtenay, 2000c, 2011). These behavioral responses to depression contribute to explaining why young men represent 6 of 7 deaths from suicide, which is the third leading cause of death in this age group (DHHS, 2000).

Taken together, these findings about men suggest that clinicians should assume the worst. An additional reason for assuming the worst is that health professionals can also be blinded by gender stereotypes and fooled by men's displays of invulnerability. Mental health clinicians, for example, are less likely to diagnose depression correctly in men than in women, which contributes to men's high suicide rate (Courtenay, 2003). Making matters worse, because of delays in their help seeking men's physical and mental conditions are often serious when they finally do seek help.

To diagnose a man's condition correctly and to plan his treatment, it is essential to elicit accurate information about his symptoms and emotional states. Asking a man, "How do you feel?" is not recommended. This question can be difficult for men to respond to, and it often elicits nothing more than a shrug of the shoulders or an unreflective "Fine." Instead, a health professional should inquire indirectly: "Tell me, how do you experience that?" Or, "What is that like for you?" These questions are uncommon and may be less likely to prompt an automatic response. In response to perceptions of vulnerability that are inconsistent with a man's actual risks, a clinician can say, "I know it's important to you to think of yourself as strong and healthy. But that attitude can lead you to take unnecessary risks with your health."

Locate Supports

Men are taught to value independence, autonomy, and self-sufficiency in themselves (Courtenay, 2000b, 2011). It is not surprising then that men (including college men) have fewer friendships and smaller social networks than women do, and that they tend not to use the support they do have. There is strong evidence that a lack of social support constitutes a risk factor for mortality, especially for men. Men with the lowest level of social support are much more likely to die than men with the highest level. In contrast, men with a higher level of social support maintain more positive health practices (Courtenay, 2000a, 2011).

It is essential for college health professionals to help men identify the sources of support that are available to them: significant others, friends, family, coworkers, classmates, and so forth. You can ask, "Who are the people you're most comfortable asking to give you a hand?" It is important then to encourage men to reach out to these people, because often they will not do so of their own accord. Health professionals can also help college men identify support or educational groups and social activities—such as church and organized sports—that can be valuable sources of social support. In talking with college men about social support, use concepts that are familiar to many men, such as teamwork and strategic planning. Suggest that the student set regular times to meet with friends. The routine ball game, movie, or dinner out gives a college man regular contact and support without his having to ask for it or betray his need for it.

Tailor Plan

Tailoring a plan means devising a health maintenance plan (like a maintenance schedule for a car). A man is more likely to have a maintenance plan for his car than for himself. Developing and implementing such a plan is associated with improved treatment follow-through and behavioral change (Courtenay, 2001a, 2011). The type of plan, the extent of the plan, and its specific components depend on each man's individual needs, as well as on the clinician's role and functions. Ideally, a man's comprehensive health maintenance plan includes periodic physicals, screenings, self-examinations, preventive behaviors, self-care techniques, and vitamin and medicine schedules.

Tailoring the plan means individualizing it to the student's needs, age, intellectual capacity, attitudes, cultural background, and circumstances; this is considered essential both in establishing a plan and in fostering adherence. For the plan to be successful, it must be realistic, it must be broken down into attainable steps, and the patient must have the skills necessary to carry it out. College health professionals should also invite the student's own input and suggestions, as well as help him identify potential obstacles. He may know, for example, that if he drinks he is not likely to use a condom. It is also beneficial to develop a verbal or written contract, with dates for achieving specific goals. All of these factors are associated with improved outcomes (Courtenay, 2001a, 2011).

Harness Strengths

Harnessing a patient's strengths fosters motivation and compliance. It also conveys respect for his efforts and achievements, which is an important aspect of effective patient-clinician communication (Courtenay, 2001a, 2011). Although endorsement of traditional masculinity in general is associated with increased health risks among men, there are certain masculine-identified characteristics that are highly adaptive for men (and women). Among them are having the ability to act independently, be assertive, and be decisive (Courtenay, 2001a, 2003). Reliance on some specific masculine characteristics such as these has been found to help enable men to cope with cancer and chronic illness. Some specific strengths that should be harnessed are intellectualized and goal-oriented coping, a need for control, and a teamwork approach.

Begin by commenting on a student's strength before exploring his physical symptoms or emotional states. An example is to say, "It's great that you took control of things the way you did and got yourself in here so quickly." Because being intellectual, logical, and rational are highly valued coping mechanisms among men (Courtenay, 2001a, 2011), health professionals should emphasize the intellectual aspects of health education. Similarly, men engage in more action-oriented, problem-solving, and goal-setting coping than women do (Courtenay, 2001a). Goal setting is also an effective way to modify behavior and improve health (Courtenay, 2001a, 2011), so college health professionals can frame health goals as targets to shoot for. Similarly, they can capitalize on a student's talent for keeping baseball scores when he is tracking cholesterol, blood pressure, or behavioral change.

To maintain healthy behaviors and modify unhealthy ones, it is essential that people have a sense of self-efficacy or control, and to believe that they can respond effectively to reduce a health threat. College men who have a personal sense of control over cancer, for example, are more likely to practice monthly TSE (Courtenay, 2001b). Illness, however, can threaten a man's sense of being in control. Additionally, men are more likely than women to believe they have little or no control over their future health (Courtenay, 1998b, 2003, 2011). College health professionals can foster a student's sense of self-efficacy by focusing on the positive aspects of control, and suggesting that he take "personal responsibility" for his well-being and "take charge" of his health.

Emphasize teamwork too. For most men, health care is something that is done *to* them; it is not something in which they see themselves as active participants. Clinicians need to invite a man's active involvement and emphasize teamwork, which can be ideal for a man; men are often most comfortable engaging in relationships through action and by doing things, such as projects, together. This kind of patient-clinician collaboration is associated with positive health outcomes (Courtenay, 2001a). Asking "Where do you want to start?" enlists a man's involvement and reinforces his active participation.

Evidence-Based Strategies for Educational Campaigns, Marketing, and Outreach

The Six-Point Plan can also be applied to educational campaigns and marketing to college men. For example, these interventions can humanize by addressing the contradiction between human health care needs and masculinity, and assume the worst by addressing college men's perceived invulnerability to risk. Additional evidence-based strategies should guide the development of gender-specific educational campaigns, marketing, and outreach to men, which I discuss briefly next.

One example is research related to TSE educational brochures provided at many colleges. These brochures typically diagram how to conduct a testicular self-examination. On the basis of prior success educating women with materials diagramming breast self-examinations, we might expect TSE brochures to be similarly effective. According to emerging research, TSE instruction in general is indeed effective. College men also prefer written materials, such as brochures, over video instruction; they also prefer brief, specific checklists on how to perform TSE rather than more detailed instructions. Most important, according to one study college men prefer written materials with *no* diagrams of the male anatomy. These materials were also the most effective in promoting TSE (Morman, 2002).

As the preceding example illustrates, health education, marketing, and outreach efforts must take gender-based research into account if they are to be successful; what is effective with women is not necessarily effective with men. Stages-of-change research is another example of this.

The stages-of-change, or transtheoretical, model identifies five stages of change that people move through in modifying their behavior. The stages are precontemplation, contemplation, preparation, action, and maintenance (Prochaska, Norcross, & DiClemente, 1994). Precontemplators typically deny their problems or unhealthy behaviors. Contemplators recognize their problems and begin to seriously think about solving them. Extensive research generally indicates that women are more likely than men to be contemplating changing unhealthy behavior or already maintaining healthy habits (Courtenay, 2003).

The transtheoretical model has also identified interventions that are effective in helping people adopt healthier behavior at each stage. What women contemplators need most is assistance in identifying the causes and consequences of their behaviors, help in considering the pros and cons of changing, and support in maintaining their healthy lifestyles. What men precontemplators need most is increased awareness of their problems and education to help them begin to consider change. These strategies can be applied to interventions with individuals, and to educational, marketing, and outreach interventions. In fact, interventions that neglect to apply stage-specific strategies, or neglect to take people's readiness to change into account, are likely to fail.

According to this model, public health campaigns are often unsuccessful because they are typically designed for the small minority of people who are ready to change unhealthy behavior. However, people who are not ready to change (people who are more likely to be men) actively resist these campaigns. Precontemplators in particular are the hardest people to reach, because they typically deny that they have a problem. Health campaigns for men not ready to change—the men at greatest risk—are more likely to be effective when they are designed for precontemplators. For example, one newspaper ad for a smoking cessation self-help program was directed to "smokers who do not wish to change." This unusually worded advertisement drew 400 precontemplators, which the researchers considered a great success (Prochaska et al., 1994). Interventions like this that effectively help men to simply *begin* contemplating the possibility of changing unhealthy behavior (which is the primary objective with precontemplators) actually double the probability that these men will ultimately change.

Another research-based approach that can be applied to gender-specific interventions with men is social norms marketing. According to social norms theory, unhealthy (and healthy) behavior is fostered by perceptions (often incorrect) of how one's peers behave (Berkowitz, 2003). For example, a college man might overestimate his peers' involvement in risky behavior, which would foster his own involvement in unhealthy behavior. Alternatively, he might underestimate his peers' adoption of healthy habits, which would discourage him from adopting healthy behavior. Social norms theory focuses on peers because they have been found to have the greatest influence in shaping individual behavior.

One common intervention based on this theory is a social norms marketing campaign, which promotes accurate, healthy norms. Research indicates that when college students' "perceived norm" is challenged with evidence of the "actual norm," the unhealthy behavior—such as heavy drinking—often decreases. Social norms marketing campaigns hold promise for addressing a variety of health concerns relevant to men. They can be used, for example, to change incorrect perceptions about men's indifference to health matters.

More than 500 men at a small midwestern liberal arts college were recently surveyed. Results of this survey indicated that these men misperceived that most other male students (55%) were either not at all concerned or only a little concerned about their health as men. Actually, only 35% of students were unconcerned; most (65%) reported being either somewhat or very concerned about their health as men (unpublished data). On the basis of these data, a social norms marketing campaign could be designed to promote the true norm that men on this campus *are* interested in their health as men. Although it has yet to be developed, we can hypothesize, from prior research, that interest in and concern about men's health would increase among men on this campus if such a campaign were implemented.

Unfortunately, social marketing campaigns do not always work (Keeling, 2000). For example, students sometimes *underestimate,* rather than overestimate, their peers' unhealthy behavior. Social marketing is particularly ineffective with specific groups within a larger campus—groups such as fraternity men, for whom norms are riskier than they are for other groups on campus. It has been argued recently that new, alternative intervention methods are needed for these high-risk men (Carter & Kahnweiler, 2000). One new, innovative, evidence-based approach is based on "sensation seeking" research.

Sensation seekers are disinhibited people who seek thrills and adventure, lust for new experiences, and are easily bored (Zuckerman, 1994). The instrument measuring this trait determines whether a person is a high or low sensation seeker. Thirty years of research consistently indicates that men are more likely than women to be high sensation seekers. It also shows that high sensation seekers are more likely than low sensation seekers to engage in a variety of risky behaviors such as heavy alcohol use, drug use, cigarette smoking, dangerous driving, high-risk sexual activity, high-risk sports, and criminal activity. For example, adolescent high sensation seekers are twice as likely as low sensation seekers to report using beer and liquor, and 2 to 7 times more likely to report drug use.

Recently, researchers at the University of Kentucky began studying intervention strategies based on these findings (Harrington and others, 2003). They hypothesized that because people who engage in unhealthy, high-risk behavior are more likely to be high sensation seekers who seek novel and stimulating experiences, health campaigns targeting this population would also need to be novel and stimulating. Findings from a growing body of research indicate that high sensation seekers do, in fact, prefer media and health campaigns that are novel, creative, or unusual. Additionally, campaigns are most effective when they are intense, exciting, and stimulating; are graphic and explicit; are complex and unconventional; are fast-paced; are suspenseful and dramatic; use close-ups; and have strong audio and visual effects. Although not all of these features need be included in a single message, the most effective messages have multiple features from this list. Research shows that high sensation seekers pay greater attention to antidrug public service announcements (PSAs) that incorporate these features than to PSAs that do not; they are also more likely to recall PSA content, phone a drug hotline, report a more negative attitude toward drug use, and report less intention to use. (Interestingly, high sensation seekers also prefer messages that do not preach, which is consistent with the transtheoretical model; preaching to, or nagging, a precontemplator about changing will actually make him more *resistant* to change.)

These findings are relevant to college health professionals (particularly those concerned about men's health) because sensation seekers are primarily men and because they include those students who engage in the riskiest behaviors. These are the men who, historically, have been the most difficult to reach and for whom traditional health campaigns are ineffective. Sensation-seeking intervention strategies can be applied to college radio PSAs and to flyers and posters. They can also be adopted when marketing to and conducting health fairs for men, which should be designed differently than health fairs for women. Another application of this evidence is to provide safe, high sensation-seeking alternatives to risky activities. For example, at an all-male, liberal arts college in the Midwest, a climbing wall was set up and made available on the most popular midweek drinking night. Although the effectiveness of this specific intervention has yet to be tested empirically, research suggests that this high sensation-seeking alternative would effectively reduce drinking on this campus. The overwhelmingly enthusiastic response from students certainly suggests that it has been effective.

Conclusion

This chapter has presented an overview of psychosocial and behavioral factors that influence men's health and identified evidence-based strategies for addressing these factors. If college health professionals adopt these best practices, research indicates that college men will live longer, healthier lives. The final section lists some additional interventions for promoting health and well-being among college men. Although these strategies may prove helpful, future research is needed to determine whether they are actually effective, and if so, with which men; and whether they are more effective with college men than with college women.

Health Promotion Strategies for College Men

- Offer convenient and free or low-cost services, such as screenings and immunizations.
- Provide a confidential telephone health line.

- Bring services and education to men (classes, sports events, fraternities, and fitness centers).
- Furnish incentives (such as free promotional items, food, tickets to sports events, academic credit for attendance, or requiring attendance).
- Offer free men's health kits or fanny packs with educational materials such as self-examination instructions and health service information, along with promotional items, such as healthy protein bars and toiletries.
- Develop a health mentoring project with upperclassmen educating lowerclassmen.
- Address the needs of special populations of men (for example, gay and bisexual men, men of color).
- Identify students who have experienced health problems (testicular cancer, auto accidents) as spokesmen and peer health educators.
- Use high-profile spokesmen to promote men's health through media campaigns or for special events (community leaders, athletes, actors or media personalities).
- Offer competitive contests with prizes for involvement in health promotion activities.
- Attach men's health education information to prescriptions.
- Develop health events with a theme (for instance, related to pop culture, rock music, or sports).
- Make available health promotion and education to men in urgent care.
- Use concepts that appeal to men (like "health coaching" and "teamwork") in marketing and education materials.
- Make use of men's bathrooms and locker rooms for distribution of health education materials and for health campaigns.
- Provide e-mail-based education and Internet survey tools or games.
- Offer a "sports and fitness expo" with health and wellness components, as well as sports events, competitions, sporting equipment, and exhibitions.
- Design activities around National Men's Health Week (the week including and ending on Father's Day), featuring lectures, forums, debates, media campaigns, displays, workshops, and presentations.
- Hire male staff and clinicians and make them available to men
- Create opportunities for men to talk about health issues in small discussion groups (for example, after peer educators speak to larger groups).
- Require entering freshmen to attend a workshop that addresses the health effects of masculinity and includes healthy strategies for adjusting to college life.

References

Berkowitz, A. D. (2003). Applications of social norms theory to other health and social justice issues. In H. W. Perkins (Ed.), *The social norms approach to preventing school and college-age substance abuse.* San Francisco: Jossey-Bass.

Carter, C. A., & Kahnweiler, W. M. (2000). The efficacy of the social norms approach to substance abuse prevention applied to fraternity men. *Journal of American College Health, 49*(2), 66–70.

Courtenay, W. H. (1998). College men's health: An overview and a call to action. *Journal of American College Health, 46*(6), 279–290.

Courtenay, W. H. (1999). Youth violence? Let's call it what it is. *Journal of American College Health, 48*(3), 141–142.

Courtenay, W. H. (2000a). Behavioral factors associated with disease, injury, and death among men: Evidence and implications for prevention. *Journal of Men's Studies, 9*(1), 81–142.

Courtenay, W. H. (2000b) Constructions of masculinity and their influence on men's well-being: A theory of gender and health. *Social Science and Medicine, 50*(10), 1385–1401.

Courtenay, W. H. (2000c). Engendering health: A social constructionist examination of men's health beliefs and behaviors. *Psychology of Men and Masculinity, 1,* 4–15.

Courtenay, W. H. (2001a). Counseling men in medical settings. In G. R. Brooks & G. E. Good (Eds.), *The new handbook of psychotherapy and counseling with men: A comprehensive guide to settings, problems, and treatment approaches* (Vol. 1, pp. 59–91). San Francisco: Jossey-Bass.

Courtenay, W. H. (2001b). Men's health: Ethnicity matters. *Social Work Today, 1*(8), 20–22.

Courtenay, W. H. (2002). A global perspective on the field of men's health. *International Journal of Men's Health, 1*(1), 1–13.

Courtenay, W. H. (2003). Key determinants of the health and well-being of men and boys. *International Journal of Men's Health, 2*(1), 1–30.

Courtenay, W. H. (2011). *Dying to be men: Psychosocial, environmental and biobehavioral directions in promoting the health of men and boys.* New York: Routledge.

Courtenay, W. H., & Keeling, R. P. (2000a). Men, gender, and health: Toward an interdisciplinary approach. *Journal of American College Health, 48*(6), 1–4.

Courtenay, W. H. (Guest Ed.), & Keeling, R. P. (Ed.). (2000b). Men's health: A theme issue [Special issue]. *Journal of American College Health, 48*(6).

Courtenay, W. H., McCreary, D. R., & Merighi, J. R. (2002). Gender and ethnic differences in health beliefs and behaviors. *Journal of Health Psychology, 7*(3), 219–231.

Department of Health and Human Services (DHHS). (2000). *Deaths: Final data for 1998.* (DHHS publication no. PHS 2000–1120.) *National Vital Statistics Reports.* Hyattsville, MD: National Center for Health Statistics.

Department of Health and Human Services (DHHS). (2000). *Deaths: Leading causes for 2004* (DHHS Publication No. [PHS] 2008-1120). Hyattsville, MD: National Center for Health Statistics.

Harrington, N. G., Lane, D. R., Donohew, L., Zimmerman, R. S., Norling, G. R., An, J. H., et al. (2003). Persuasive strategies for effective anti-drug messages. *Communication Monographs, 70*(1), 16–38.

Keeling, R. P. (2000). Social norms research in college health. *Journal of American College Health, 49*(2), 53–56.

McCreary, D. R., Saucier, D. M., & Courtenay, W. H. (2005). The drive for muscularity and masculinity: Testing the associations among gender role traits, behaviors, attitudes, and conflict. *Psychology of Men and Masculinity, 6*(2), 83–94.

Morman, M. T. (2002). Promoting the testicular self-exam as a preventative health care strategy: Do diagrams make a difference? *International Journal of Men's Health, 1*(1), 73–88.

Patrick, M. S., Covin, J. R., Fulop, M., Calfas, K., & Lovato, C. (1997). Health risk behaviors among California college students. *Journal of American College Health, 45*(6), 265–272.

Prochaska, J., Norcross, J., & DiClemente, C. (1994). *Changing for good: The revolutionary program that explains the six stages of change and teaches you how to free yourself from bad habits.* New York: Morrow.

Roter, D. L., & Hall, J. A. (1997). *Doctors talking with patients/patients talking with doctors: Improving communication in medical visits.* Westport, CT: Auburn House.

Stanton, A. L., & Courtenay, W. H. (2003). Gender, stress and health. In R. H. Rozensky, N. G. Johnson, C. D. Goodheart, & R. Hammond (Eds.), *Psychology builds a health world: Research and practice opportunities* (pp. 105–135). Washington, DC: American Psychological Association.

Zuckerman, M. (1994). *Behavioral expressions and biosocial bases of sensation seeking.* New York: Cambridge University Press.

12

SUCCESSFUL JUDICIAL INTERVENTIONS WITH COLLEGE MEN

Randall B. Ludeman

BEMIDJI STATE UNIVERSITY

American higher education continues to experience more frequent and complicated concerns related to college student behavior. Most of us have read about issues such as school shootings, sexual violence and harassment, abuse of alcohol and other drugs, rioting, and hate crimes. To complicate matters, more students are entering college with serious and persistent mental health issues (Farrell, 2008; Featherman, 2004). Few studies, however, have been conducted to explore strategies to address these problems in higher education.

Student development practitioners commonly deal with these issues and are increasingly attending to the behavior and development of college men (Davies et al., 2000; Harris III & Struve, 2009). College men are sanctioned more commonly than women for violent and disruptive behaviors (Dannells, 1997; Harper, Harris III, & Mmeje, 2004). Despite this unfortunate reality, we have only recently focused research on how men's experience and performance of gender is related to disruptive behavior. Even fewer studies have focused on developmental interventions for college students who violate campus conduct codes and participate in campus judicial processes.

The following chapter presents a critical challenge to higher education professionals dealing specifically with college men and behavioral issues. The chapter summarizes research in the areas of male gender role socialization, student development theory relating specifically to men, violent male behaviors, and judicial programs and services in higher education. The chapter concludes with recommendations regarding effective strategies for working with college men in student judicial affairs.

Male Gender Role Socialization

> In the United States a real boy climbs trees, disdains girls, dirties his knees, plays with soldiers, and takes blue for his favorite color. When they go to school, real boys prefer manual training, gym, and arithmetic. In college the boys smoke pipes, drink beer, and major in engineering or physics. The real boy matures into a "man's man" who plays poker, goes hunting, drinks brandy, and dies in war.
>
> (Brown, 1965, p. 161)

The male gender role is established early for boys. Society places a unique set of expectations on boys to deal autonomously with life, hide pain, and avoid behavior that shames themselves or family (Pollack, 1999). Pollack (1998, 1999) described boys as experiencing "gender straightjackets," which affect them by forcing the repression of emotions and needs for love and affection.

"Confused by society's mixed messages about what's expected of them as boys, and later as men, many feel a sadness and disconnection they cannot even name" (Pollack, 1998, p. xxi). As a result, it often is difficult for us to notice when boys are experiencing difficulty. Yet research continues to provide evidence that boys are experiencing crises in many ways: "Boys are failing at school, succeeding at suicide, engaging in homicide, and disconnecting from their own inner lives: losing their genuine voices and selves" (Pollack, 1999, p. 7). The crisis, thus, is not in the numbers of men coming to college, but the support and developmental success once they arrive.

Boys are influenced by parents, other adults, and peers to behave differently than girls. Boys are more likely to be encouraged to play aggressively (Hyde & Linn, 1986), and to be punished physically for inappropriate behavior (Hartley, 1974). Parents and peers are more likely to discourage behavior that diverges from prescribed gender norms (Fagot, 1985). Expressing emotion, such as crying, is discouraged by adult men, often fathers, who remind boys that only girls cry (Rabinowitz & Cochran, 1994). Television and other media portray male heroes as possessing strength, determination, and dominance (Greenberg, 1982). The messages begin early for boys that they should adhere to the traditional masculine code.

The socialization process has been purported to hinder the emotional development of boys and men. For many males, "one striking and far-reaching consequence of the male socialization ordeal is an inability to differentiate and identify their emotions" (Levant, 1997, p. 9). Levant (1997) has labeled this condition "normative male alexithymia" (p. 9), which is the inability for men to put feelings into words or even to be aware of them. According to Levant (1997), normative male alexithymia, in conjunction with the socialization of boys to suppress tender, vulnerable, and caring feelings, leaves only aggression and sexuality as accepted channels for the release of emotional energy.

As boys grow up and enter adulthood, society challenges them to develop further their identity, traditionally associated with the important tasks of choosing an occupation and establishing intimate relationships (Levinson, Darrow, Klein, Levinson, & McKee, 1978). For young men choosing to attend a college or university, entering the adult world often can be delayed. These men can explore and experiment with relationships, academic study, and work without assuming much of the responsibility of being an adult (Rabinowitz & Cochran, 1994). However, these college men are faced with the development of competence, learning to manage emotions, developing autonomy, establishing an identity, freeing interpersonal relationships, developing a purpose, and developing integrity (Chickering, 1969; Chickering & Reisser, 1993). These developmental tasks may conflict with their socialized experience and expectations of masculinity.

In facing these developmental tasks, college men find the expression of emotion and other traditionally defined feminine qualities more desirable and beneficial (Levinson et al., 1978). Expression of feminine qualities has been shown to create conflict for men, therefore college-aged men are likely to experience difficulty in expressing concern for others, disclosing vulnerabilities, and describing their feelings to others (Cournoyer & Mahalik, 1995). The fear of femininity in fact is central to the theory of male gender role conflict (MGRC) described by O'Neil (1981a, 1981b, 1982, 1990). O'Neil (1990) described gender role conflict as occurring when "rigid, sexist, or restricted gender roles learned during socialization result in the personal restriction, devaluation, or violation of others or self" (p. 25). As a result of conflict around appropriate masculine behaviors, men may engage in patterns of gender role conflict due to a fear of becoming or appearing feminine (Cournoyer & Mahalik, 1995). MGRC has been found to create liabilities for college men including self-destructive behaviors (Meth, 1990), increased stress (Stewart & Lykes, 1985), disregard for health (Courtenay, 1998; Nathanson, 1977), substance abuse and addiction (Blazina & Watkins, 1996; Capraro, 2000), and increased depression and anxiety (Sharpe & Heppner, 1991). Additional details regarding MGRC are illustrated in Chapter 2 of this book.

It is abundantly clear that research on MGRC and restricted emotionality of men holds promise for understanding why men behave they way they do and for designing effective interventions aimed at impacting college men and promoting development in the context of judicial programming. If the male socialization process shapes or restricts the emotional skills and development of boys and men, then it appears incumbent upon higher education educators to understand these processes in order to effectively promote learning and development. Understanding the impacts of hegemonic masculinity on male college students is critical to the effective delivery of student services in general, and judicial interventions in particular.

Student Development Theory Related to Men's Conduct

The emotional and psychological development of young adults has received much attention in psychology and education (e.g., Chickering, 1969; Chickering & Reisser, 1993; Gilligan, 1982; Perry, 1970). Prior to the 1970s, the majority of research on psychological, intellectual, and ethical development was conducted on men. Early theory on college student development also was based on studies using primarily male participants. Although these studies involved the use of males as participants, the research was not focused on understanding men within the contours of the social construction of male identity development (Davis, 2002). While men's development was taken as the default for all humanity, specific gender differences were not considered.

Applying a gendered perspective can illuminate critical nuances that can increase the effectiveness of educational interventions. Chickering (1969), for example, outlined a vector model of college student. Two vectors of this model are particularly relevant to men's socialization with respect to judicial affairs: managing emotions and developing autonomy. Young men entering the collegiate environment often become aware of their feelings, yet struggle with flexible control and expression of these feelings (Chickering, 1969; Chickering & Reisser, 1993). The difficulty college men experience with the management of emotions often is reflected in residence hall vandalism, conflicts with roommates, exploitive sexual encounters, and substance abuse. Men entering the college environment also experience emotional and instrumental autonomy often for the first time in their lives. Parental control and support is not as immediately available, and development of self-directedness and independence, as well as the recognition of interdependence with others, becomes a necessity. These two developmental tasks seem to relate significantly with the socialization of men, since men are typically expected to deal autonomously with life, hide pain, and avoid behavior that shames themselves or family (Pollack, 1999).

In the 1970s and 80s, research conducted by Gilligan (1982) introduced differences in developmental processes for women. While controversial at the time, this vital research opened the doors to an understanding of the different developmental processes experienced by women and men. Although much of the research on human development had been centered on men's lives, Gilligan's recognition of gender related differences also ignited the emergence of men's studies as a scholarly field. Much of the focus on how men are gendered is relatively recent. New research focusing on the effects of socialization, parenting, and masculinity on boys and men continues to develop (Pollack, 1999).

Since college men have been identified as more frequently violating student conduct codes and perpetrating violent behavior, it stands to reason that student development practitioners and scholars must better understand men's development in order to develop effective strategies for intervention.

Understanding men's emotional and gender identity development should provide insight as we continue the exploration into college men and behavior.

Etiology of Men's "Dark Side" Behavior

> It is easier, and riskier, than ever to write about the dark side of male behavior. After centuries of celebrating male patriarchal manhood, a new gender consciousness has arisen. Feminist scholarship has written women back into history, highlighting the former marginality of women and challenging the misogyny that is deeply imbedded in Western culture.
>
> (Brooks & Silverstein, 1995, p. 280)

Many authors have written about the disproportionate overrepresentation of men amongst both perpetrators and victims of violence (e.g., Brooks & Silverstein, 1995; Diamond, 1994; Hong, 2000; Pollack, 1998; Seidler, 1996). Research has suggested men most often are the perpetrators of homicide (U.S. Department of Health and Human Services, 1991), physical assaults (Valois, Vincent, McKeown, Garrison, & Kirby, 1993), sexual assaults (Koss, Gidycz, & Wisniewski, 1987), domestic abuse (Federal Bureau of Investigation, 1992), and bias-related crimes (Levin, 1993). Boys and men also are more likely than girls and women to bear weapons (Courtenay, 1998; Hong, 2000), which significantly increases their risk for violence. Finally, men have been cited as a significant proportion of the victims of violence (Hong, 2000).

A growing number of researchers and authors have argued that male violence has been prescribed by the traditional masculine norms of hegemonic masculinity (e.g., Brooks & Silverstein, 1995; Courtenay, 1998; Hong, 2000; Pollack, 1998). Creating what Brooks and Silverstein (1995) called the "dark side of masculinity" (p. 281), traditional masculine roles and norms have been purported to encourage behavior such as violence, sexual abuse and sexual harassment, substance abuse and other self-destructive behaviors, relationship inadequacies, absent fathering, and social-emotional withdrawal. These "dark side" behaviors commonly have been regarded as the problem of only a few deviant men; however, it has been argued more recently that these behaviors actually may "exist to a lesser degree in the *normative* masculine role socialization of all men" (Brooks & Silverstein, 1995, p. 281).

Many hypotheses have been purported regarding the etiology of males' inappropriate behavior. Brooks and Silverstein (1995) outlined five such explanations, including: The "aberrant male" hypothesis, the biological hypothesis, the social-developmental hypothesis, the social construction hypothesis, and the gender role strain/conflict hypothesis.

The aberrant male hypothesis has focused on the belief that inappropriate male behavior is a function of personality deficits of undersocialized men (Brooks & Silverstein, 1995). Many scholars have rejected this theory due to its placing blame on individual men rather than identifying problems inherent in the male socialization process.

Biological etiologies often have focused on testosterone as generating a tendency in males of all species to exhibit dark side behaviors (Brooks & Silverstein, 1995). Although research has claimed evidence of patterns of aggression, dominance, and sexual promiscuity in studies of primates, Haraway (1989) argued that these primate studies have traditionally reflected significant White, male, capitalist bias. Accounting for these biases suggests, "the biological hypothesis that differing levels of testosterone in males generate high levels of aggression and sexual promiscuity has not been supported by more recent interpretations of nonhuman primate behavior" (Brooks & Silverstein, 1995, p. 297).

A third etiology of males' dark side behaviors suggested by Brooks and Silverstein (1995) is the social-developmental hypothesis, which has focused on gender role identity (e.g., Chodorow, 1978; Pollack, 1990). This theory has purported that since boys are raised primarily by their mothers (opposite-sex parents) with little emotional connection to their fathers (same-sex parents), a conflicted gender role identity is generated that results in dark side behavior. The social-developmental theory has been criticized due to its focus on gender as biologically rather than culturally constructed, and the lack of empirical evidence supporting its position (Brooks & Silverstein, 1995).

The social construction hypothesis has focused on feminist explanations of male dark side behavior as a natural consequence of male power within patriarchal society. Male dark side behaviors have been described as "strategies for maintaining male entitlement and privilege" (Brooks & Silverstein, 1995, p. 307). For example, men's sexual violence has been explained as a result of both men's normative socialization and their desire to maintain control over women. Sattel (1976) argued that men's emotional inexpressiveness was more a sociopolitical strategy to maintain control of social situations than a result of troubled male socialization. "From this theoretical perspective, dark side behaviors are the result of unequal power relations between men and women within patriarchal culture" (Brooks & Silverstein, 1995, p. 307).

A fifth etiology regarding men's dark side behavior is the gender role strain/ conflict paradigm (O'Neil, Helms, Gable, David, & Wrightsman, 1986). This theory has suggested that gender differences as a result of cultural pressures on individuals to conform to gender role norms generates conflict/strain that results in men exhibiting dark side behaviors (Brooks & Silverstein, 1995). According to Brooks and Silverstein, "the men's studies of gender role strain paradigm is the best description to date of the dark side of masculinity" (p. 306).

Although all of the above theories may help explain men's dark side behaviors, the concept of gender role conflict seems to hold the most promise for working with men and misbehavior. Specifically, college men going through identity development are faced with tremendous pressure to conform to gender role expectations. For many men, the resulting conflict can lead to antisocial or otherwise destructive behaviors as competing value systems are explored, reconciliation is sought between internal feelings and external messages, and challenges to construct a self-authored identity go unsupported due to misunderstanding of men's gender role conflict.

Men's Misconduct in the College Context

There is little published research dealing specifically with college students' behavior, and most of what does exist is based on studies done before 1980 (Dannells, 1997). The research regarding disruptive college student behavior typically has focused on the effectiveness of judicial programs and services. However, several studies have focused on the characteristics of college student offenders. Van Kuren and Creamer (1989) reported that students whose parents have college degrees were less likely to violate student codes of conduct than were students whose parents did not have college degrees. They also found that "students who had positive feelings about the institution, in general, were less likely to be offenders" (p. 264).

Alcohol abuse has also been linked to behavior problems on college campuses (Dannells, 1997). Hanson and Engs (1995) reported that campus administrators indicated alcohol increasingly was involved in violations of campus policy and in violent behavior. Wechsler, Deutsch, and Dowdall (1995) found that at campuses where binge drinking is common, 87% of the non-binge drinkers who lived on campus reported they were affected adversely by the binge drinking of others.

Dannells and Stuber (1992) reported that psychopathology appears to be on the rise among college students, leading to more pathological origins of student misconduct. This explanation of student misbehavior is supported by the apparent increase in frequency of behaviors such as sexual harassment, acquaintance rape, dating and domestic violence, alcohol abuse, and stalking (Gallagher, Harmon, & Lingenfelter, 1994).

Moreover, behavior resulting in judicial hearings is disproportionately male. According Hong (2000), there is "a clear link between socialization into stereotypical norms of hegemonic masculinity and an increased risk for experiencing violence" (p. 269). However, many college campuses have failed to recognize this link between men, socialization, and violence, and have relied only on traditional approaches to violence prevention. In the college setting, the judicial system is the venue for handling disruptive behavior, including incidents of violence. It would seem beneficial, therefore, for student affairs practitioners, and male college students, to understand better how gender roles and socialization impact male students in the collegiate environment in order to proactively intervene at early stages of misconduct to prevent increasingly serve patterns of behavior.

While it is clear that more research is needed regarding the origins of student misconduct and appropriate intervention strategies, it seems clear that we must begin using what we know about men's development and college contextual factors in the design and implementation or judicial processes. We know the college context presents men with significant opportunities for identity development, and our interventions must challenge men to explore the potential consequences of hegemonic masculinity as they construct this identity. Men who participate in the judicial process may already be vulnerable to these consequences, and are afforded a developmental opportunity for guided reflection and learning. Our interventions in the judicial arena can be enhanced when we integrate our understanding of men's development with purposefully designed opportunities to explore positive masculine identity development.

Judicial Programs in Higher Education

> The development of student disciplinary systems in American colleges and universities in many ways reflects the development of these institutions in general. From the beginning of higher education in America, the social (or antisocial) behavior of students was considered as important as academic progress, and responses to this behavior reflected the atmosphere and philosophical disposition of the institutions.
>
> (Smith, 1994, p. 78)

Significant changes in the enforcement of behavioral expectations on college campuses have occurred over the past 300 years (Smith, 1994). From the early practices of "flogging" and "cuffing," to the more current practices of due process and fair and objective hearings, student judicial systems have undergone transformations related to the adjudication of student misconduct (Smith, 1994). As stated by Dannells (1997):

> Perhaps no other single subject so dramatically reflects our attitudes about students and how we define our duty and our relationship with them. From the earliest dissatisfaction with pious and moralistic paternalism in the colonial colleges, to recent controversies over hate speech and First Amendment rights, student behavior and institutional response have vexed faculty and administrators with a set of issues both fundamental and timely.
>
> (p. iii)

While legislative initiatives have sought more accountability from colleges and universities related to safety, judicial affairs has become a focus of much attention.

The term "judicial affairs" was coined as a result of the litigious 1960s when *in loco parentis* died and higher education administrators more commonly found themselves in the courtroom. The complicated nature of judicial affairs in higher education has led to research in the area, but this research has focused primarily on the nature of disciplinary systems or the protection of students' rights in the adjudication of misconduct (Dannells, 1991). A limited number of studies have dealt with the developmental component of judicial processes. Several of these articles are summarized below.

Boots (1987) discussed the importance of judicial practitioners understanding human and college student development theory as it relates to their practice. Boots stated, "Understanding developmental theory and applying it to student conduct interventions provide student development professionals with positive, proactive opportunities to influence students' growth and to benefit the campus environment" (p. 63). Boots argued that part of the judicial professional's role was assisting students to learn and grow from their judicial experience.

Focusing on specific developmental issues confronting college students, Mullane (1999) examined the relationship between perceptions of the fairness and educational value of campus judicial systems and moral development. The results of the study suggested that college students involved in judicial systems exhibited lower levels of moral development than other students (Mullane, 1999). Practitioners could, therefore, provide opportunities for moral development as a way of lessening the likelihood of student misconduct.

Consistent with the idea that judicial programs can be ideal landscapes for promoting learning, Bostic and Gonzalez (1999), in a survey of over 500 judicial affairs officers, reported that respondents recommended the use of developmental discipline, less legalistic models, and more training and development for judicial officers. The study clearly indicated "that the judicial officers surveyed believe that sanctions and discipline should focus on development" and that "recommendations also focused on the educational value of a disciplinary process that furthers educational learning by providing opportunities for behavior change and moral growth and development" (p. 178).

One of the more common trends in judicial services has been the use of disciplinary counseling (Dannells, 1991, 1997; Stone & Lucas, 1994). This approach to dealing with student misconduct has involved the counseling staff in developmental intervention. There has been little research regarding the effectiveness of disciplinary counseling in higher education. However, research in public schools and the criminal justice system have reported less than positive results. In a survey of counseling center directors on college campuses, Stone and Lucas (1994) reported a 37% overall increase in disciplinary referrals to counseling services on the campuses surveyed. Also, the authors recommended that disciplinary referrals were best served through educational rather than therapeutic intervention. Consolva and Dannells

(2000) found that 63% of institutions they surveyed had employed the use of disciplinary counseling. They argued that judicial affairs practitioners need to educate college counselors regarding the developmental and educational benefits of this intervention.

Further illustrating the potential of disciplinary counseling, Amada (1986) suggested that "The disruptive student, whether emotionally disturbed or not, often angers, baffles, alarms, and immobilizes those instructors and administrators who must cope directly and immediately with the disruptive behavior" (p. 222). Thus, referring disruptive students to mental health professionals for either therapy or educational intervention may help to mediate the volatile disciplinary situation in order to yield educational benefits. In addition, Howell (2005) described the opportunity for learning and development that exists in the judicial venue through focus on the consequences of the behaviors and the encouragement of the practice of empathy. Healy and Liddell (1998), furthermore, present a model for "developmental conversation" that could occur between the judicial officer and the student to facilitate cognitive and moral development.

A significant hurdle for those interested in using disciplinary hearings to promote growth and development is the overly legalistic nature of most judicial processes. Gehring (2001) discussed the incompatibility of the legalistic nature of judicial process in higher education and the student development outcomes they intend to provide. "The disciplinary process on campuses has been too procedural and mirrors an adversarial proceeding that precludes student development" (p. 466). Gehring suggested that higher education has allowed "creeping legalism" (Dannells, 1997, p. 69) to bring the due process rights and procedures way beyond what is required by the courts, and that campuses must review their disciplinary procedures to bring back the focus on education and student development.

When working with college men, we must challenge ourselves to design interventions that incorporate developmental learning opportunities, not just punitive sanctions, into the process. As we design interventions in judicial affairs, we must both explore the impact of our traditional approaches as well as incorporate our understanding of college student development in developing new approaches. What follows is a challenge to traditional judicial approaches as well a recommendations for more intentional developmental approaches for college men.

Traditional Judicial Interventions with College Men

As student development practitioners become more aware of the effects of hegemonic masculinity, we may be better able to assess current judicial affairs practices and make necessary changes in the provision of these practices. Judicial processes, while serving the function of accountability for behavior, can also provide opportunities for emotional growth and development. Judicial officers must develop an awareness of the emotional and gender identity development processes of college men. Judicial officers must also understand their own emotional needs and development in order to effectively role model and facilitate discussions with college men related to emotions and development. For college men to understand possible reasons for their inappropriate choices and behaviors, the judicial process venue must be open to men's exploration of their emotionality and its connection to their behavioral choices. This would mean incorporating emotional work with students into the judicial process.

Although judicial programs often reference learning and developing empathy as essential to the judicial outcomes, evidence of how the judicial process provides these elements is rarely presented. For example, referrals to counseling are common outcomes of judicial proceedings, but the actual counseling often occurs independently from the judicial process. In addition, judicial programs often incorporate the use of educational sanctions. These sanctions generally consist of referrals to learning experiences that also occur away from the judicial process. This suggests student development and learning are supplements to the judicial process rather than a central concern.

Traditional judicial programs also tend to reinforce static gender roles rather than providing opportunities to explore them. Consistent with Smith's (1987) notion of the existence of gender-specific work roles in society, judicial processes appear to separate functions related to the work of providing judicial services. Smith (1987) suggested that "feminine" work often cleans up, tidies, and allows the "masculine" (main) work to proceed.

> The place of women … is where the work is done to facilitate men's occupation of the conceptual mode of action. Women keep house, bear and care for children, look after men when they are sick, and in general provide for the logistics of their bodily existence.… At almost every point women mediate for men the relation between the conceptual mode of action and the actual concrete forms on which it depends."
>
> (p. 83)

The separation of gender work roles appears to be present in campus judicial processes. While judicial professionals are expected to be sensitive to the developmental needs of college students, this more emotionally related "feminine" work appears to be a responsibility delegated outside the judicial arena, as if it were not as important as the primary "masculine" work of adjudicating misbehavior. If judicial processes and outcomes are intended to be developmental, empathetic, and respectful, we must then incorporate these philosophies into the actual practices we provide. Ideally, this would include providing students with an opportunity to explore their emotional awareness and expressiveness during their judicial experience, rather than as a supplemental and subsequent process.

It would also be beneficial for student affairs professionals to recognize the overwhelming perceptions students have of the judicial process as adversarial. The judicial process is power-laden as the institution has authority to administer a code of conduct and to hold students accountable to a set of behavioral expectations. Students entering the judicial process often feel like they have less knowledge than the administrators responsible for facilitating the process, and as discussed by Foucault (1980), knowledge is a technology of power. As students perceive this power differential, the judicial process milieu may not be conducive to student development and learning in general, and emotional development in particular. Empowering students through providing opportunities to learn about judicial processes prior to participating in them may lessen the perceived power imbalance and result in a more developmental experience for these students.

Many traditional judicial programs, furthermore, espouse a philosophy that refers to procedures as empathetic and supportive of students. However, this discourse often competes and conflicts with the legalistic discourse, which can confuse everyone participating in the processes. While both these principles are deemed important, it appears that the discourses of legal versus developmental philosophy compete for status. Rather than complementing each other, these contested discourses have become a binary argument (Lather, 1991), with each discourse vying for hegemonic status in the judicial arena. These contested discourses have created tensions among judicial affairs practitioners. As described earlier, Gehring (2001) discussed the incompatibility of the legalistic nature of judicial process in higher education and the student development outcomes they intend to provide. More recently, Lake (2009) also presented an argument against the legalistic approaches used in the administration of student discipline in the college context. Campus judicial officers must review their disciplinary procedures and processes to refocus on education and student development.

It is, therefore, critical that judicial officers, at all levels, spend time discussing the competing legal and developmental goals, clarify their mission, and incorporate these values in their disciplinary processes.

Student development professionals must recognize the importance of the emotional experience of college men and develop systems and processes that encourage emotional exploration, expression, and development. If college men view the judicial process as a power-laden, adversarial process, they are less likely to experience a willingness to explore and express their emotions. Failing to incorporate what we know about the developmental nuances related to men's development noted above, may serve to simply exacerbate an already problematic disciplinary situation.

Specific Developmentally Appropriate Interventions for College Men

There are several possible judicial strategies that could be explored related to enhancing the emotional development of male college students. For example, mediation as a venue for resolution of judicial complaints empowers both the complainant and the accused students to learn from their experience. Serr and Taber (1987) stated, "In the collegiate setting, mediation provides an educational, non-adversarial method of resolving conflict" (p. 83). Warters (1995) also discussed mediation as an educational approach to conflict resolution on college campuses. The goal of mediation is to empower the disputing parties to generate alternatives regarding a resolution to their dispute (Serr & Taber, 1987).

Through the less adversarial process of mediation, judicial officers could encourage emotional awareness and expressiveness on the part of the male students, and facilitate emotional development and learning through challenging and empathetic processes. The mediator, whether a judicial officer or another trained professional, could more readily incorporate a counseling style and approach in resolving conflict or conduct code violations, and pay specific attention to opportunities for students' emotional needs and growth during the process. Through role modeling emotional expression, and encouraging and affirming emotional expression by male students, male mediators, in particular, could afford college men opportunities to successfully challenge rigid gender borders related to emotionality. For example, two roommates who had engaged in a fight in the residence halls could be brought together through mediation to discuss their emotions related to the conflict and the altercation. The mediator could work with these men to explore how their emotional awareness and expressiveness, or lack thereof, had contributed to the conflict. Through the mediation process these men could be empowered to develop insight as to how they could better understand and manage their emotions.

A second recommendation for the developmental processing of college student behavioral concerns would be to employ a restorative justice model, which would involve the victims and accused students' peers in the resolution of judicial cases. Restorative justice enables offenders to make amends to their victims and the community, builds offender and victim skills, and involves the offender, victim, and community in the process and resolution (DeVore & Gentilcore, 1999). This restorative justice model has been used as a venue for addressing at-risk youth (e.g., DeVore & Gentilcore, 1999) and community-based moral education (e.g., Schweigert, 1999) and may be more consistent with men's justice orientation (Gilligan, 1982) than traditional judicial sanctions.

A restorative justice model could be valuable in enabling college students to better understand their emotions and behavior. For example, if a male student is charged with creating excessive noise late at night on a residence hall floor, the students impacted by this disruption on the floor could be brought together to engage in a process of determining the judicial outcomes. During this process, the judicial officer could encourage all students involved to explore aspects of the case, including their emotional experiences before, during, and following the incident. As emotions are recognized and expressed by these students, the judicial officer could facilitate a developmental discussion in order to acknowledge the relationship of emotions and behavior. Through this process, students could develop insight regarding emotions and the connection they have to behavior as well the consequences of their behavior. For college men, due to gender role expectations and penalties for acting outside of them, this may be difficult. However, with a developmental focus, this process may provide men an opportunity to explore their emotionality and empower them to understand better the connection of emotions and behavior.

Another venue for facilitating male students' emotional development is a group process for male students who have participated in the judicial process. During this group process, judicial officers could share observations with these men related to their emotional awareness and expressiveness prior to and during the judicial process. Discussions regarding the negative consequences of gender role conflict, hegemonic masculinity, and restricted emotionality could be presented and discussed. Most importantly, judicial officers could develop rapport and trust to establish a safe space for these men (Harris III, 2008) that is conducive to emotional awareness and expressiveness. Rather than referring these students to a service venue away from the judicial system, judicial officers could be educated and trained to provide emotionally developmental experiences as an extension of the judicial process.

As recommended by Harris III (2008), men should be encouraged to critically reflect on their behavior and its consequences as a part of judicial sanctioning. This must include emotional reflection and the opportunity for men to connect their emotional experience to their behaviors. Providing men this opportunity for critical reflection could occur through such activities as developmental dialogue with the judicial officer, small group process, or journaling. Reflection can be followed with processing and implementation opportunities and/or referrals for additional support or learning regarding emotional development. The reflection process is more powerful if it occurs immediately following the behavioral issue. Therefore, judicial officers must be both skilled at assessing the developmental issues of college men and determining what strategies would be most effective in providing learning.

Clearly, more research and assessment regarding strategies for behavioral intervention with college men is necessary. Judicial practitioners must engage is this inquiry and exploration and involve college men in the process. The judicial process in higher education is a venue that presents significant learning and developmental opportunities for college men, but traditional approaches often fail to incorporate critical components related to men's gender role conflict and other developmental nuances. Understanding the relationships between men's gender identity, emotional development, and behavior in the college setting can provide direction toward more successful interventions.

References

Amada, G. (1986). Dealing with the disruptive college student: Some theoretical and practical considerations. *Journal of American College Health, 34*(5), 221–225.

Blazina, C., & Watkins, C. E. (1996). Masculine gender role conflict: Effects on college men's psychological well-being, chemical substance usage, and attitudes toward help-seeking. *Journal of Counseling Psychology, 43*(4), 461–465.

Boots, C. C. (1987). Human development theory applied to judicial affairs work. *New Directions for Student Services, 39*, 63–72.

Bostic, D., & Gonzalez, G. (1999). Practices, opinions, knowledge, and recommendations from judicial officers in public higher education. *NASPA Journal, 36*(3), 166–183.

Brooks, G. R., & Silverstein, L. B. (1995). Understanding the dark side of masculinity: An interactive systems model. In R. Levant, & W. Pollack (Eds.), *A new psychology of men* (pp. 280–333). New York: Basic Books.

Brown, R. (1965). *Social psychology*. New York: Free Press.

Capraro, R. L. (2000). Why college men drink: Alcohol, adventure, and the paradox of masculinity. *Journal of American College Health, 48*, 307–315.

Chickering, A. W. (1969). *Education and identity* (1st ed.). San Francisco: Jossey-Bass.

Chickering, A. W., & Reisser, L. (1993). *Education and identity* (2nd ed.). San Francisco: Jossey-Bass.

Chodorow, N. (1978). *The reproduction of mothering*. Berkeley: University of California Press.

Consolva, C., & Dannells, M. (2000). Disciplinary counseling: Implications for policy and practice. *NASPA Journal, 38*(1), 44–57.

Cournoyer, R. J., & Mahalik, J. R. (1995). Cross-sectional study of gender role conflict examining college-aged and middle-aged men. *Journal of Counseling Psychology, 42*(1), 11–19.

Courtenay, W. H. (1998). College men's health: An overview and a call to action. *Journal of American College Health, 46*, 279–287.

Dannells, M. D. (1991). Changes in student misconduct and institutional response over 10 years. *Journal of College Student Development, 32*, 166–170.

Dannells, M. D. (1997). *From discipline to development: Rethinking student conduct in higher education*. ASHE-ERIC Higher Education Report Vol. 25, No. 2. Washington, DC: Graduate School of Education and Human Development, George Washington University.

Dannells, M. D., & Stuber, D. (1992). Mandatory psychiatric withdrawal of severely disturbed students: A study and policy recommendation. *NASPA Journal, 29*, 163–168.

Davies, J., McCrae, B. P., Frank, J., Dochnahl, A., Pickering, T., Harrison, B., Zakrzewsk, M., & Wilson, K. (2000). Indentifying male college students' perceived health needs, barriers to seeking help, and recommendations to help men adopt healthier lifestyles. *American Journal of College Health, 48*, 259–267.

Davis, T. (2002). Voices of gender role conflict: The social construction of college men's identity. *Journal of College Student Development, 43*(4), 508–521.

DeVore, D., & Gentilcore, K. (1999). Balanced and restorative justice and educational programming for youth at-risk. *The Clearing House, 73*(2), 96–100.

Diamond, J. (1994). *The warrior's journey home: Healing men, healing the planet*. Oakland, CA: New Harbinger.

Fagot, B. (1985). A cautionary note: Parent's socialization of boys and girls. *Sex Roles, 12*, 471–476.

Farrell, E. F. (2008). Counseling centers lack resources to help troubled students. *Chronicle of Higher Education, 54*(25), A1.

Featherman, S. (2004). Emotional rescue: New generation of troubled students strains college services. *Connection: The Journal of the New England Board of Higher Education, 19*(1), 13–14.

Federal Bureau of Investigation. (1992). *Uniform crime reports*. Washington, DC: U. S. Government Printing Office.

Foucault, M. (1980). *Power/knowledge* (C. Gordon et al., Trans.). New York: Pantheon.

Gallagher, R. P., Harmon, W. W., & Lingenfelter, C. O. (1994). CSAOs' perceptions of the changing incidence of problematic college student behavior. *NASPA Journal, 32,* 37–45.

Gehring, D. D. (2001). The objectives of student discipline and the process that's due: Are they compatible? *NASPA Journal, 38*(4), 466–481.

Gilligan, C. (1982). *In a different voice*. Cambridge, MA: Harvard University Press.

Greenberg, B. (1982). Television and role socialization: An overview. In National Institute of Mental Health, *Television and behavior: Ten years of scientific progress and implications for the eighties* (pp. 179–190). Washington, DC: U.S. Government Printing Office.

Hanson, D. J., & Engs, R. C. (1995). College drinking: Administrator perceptions, campus policies, and student behaviors. *NASPA Journal, 32,* 106–114.

Haraway, D. (1989). *Primate visions: Gender, race, and nature in the world of modern science*. London: Routledge.

Harper, S. R., Harris III, F. H., & Mmeje, K. C. (2004). A theoretical model to explain the over-representation of college men among campus judicial offenders: Implications for campus administrators. *NASPA Journal, 42*(4), 565–588.

Harris III, F. H. (2008). Deconstructing masculinity: A qualitative study of college men's masculine conceptualizations and gender performance. *NASPA Journal, 45*(4), 453–474.

Harris III, F. H., & Struve, L. E. (2009). Gents, jerks, and jocks: What male students learn about masculinity in college. *About Campus, July–August,* 2–9.

Hartley, R. (1974). Sex-role pressures and the socialization of the male child. In J. Pleck & J. Sawyer (Eds.), *Men and masculinity* (pp. 7–13). Englewood Cliffs, NJ: Prentice-Hall.

Healy, M. A., & Liddell, D. L. (1998). The developmental conversation: Facilitating moral and intellectual growth in our students. In D. L. Cooper & J. M. Lancaster (Eds.), *Beyond law and policy: Reaffirming the role of student affairs* (New Directions for Student Services, No. 82, pp. 39–48). San Francisco: Jossey-Bass.

Hong, L. (2000). Toward a transformed approach to prevention: Breaking the link between masculinity and violence. *Journal of American College Health, 48,* 269–279.

Howell, M. T. (2005). Students' perceived learning and anticipated future behaviors as a result of participation in the student judicial process. *Journal of College Student Development, 46*(4), 374–392.

Hyde, J., & Linn, M. (1986). *The psychology of gender*. Baltimore, MD: Johns Hopkins University.

Koss, M., Gidycz, C., & Wisniewski, N. (1987). The scope of rape: Incidence and prevalence of sexual aggression and victimization in a national sample of higher education students. *Journal of Consulting and Clinical Psychology, 55,* 162–170.

Lake, P. F. (2009). Student Discipline: The case against legalistic approaches. *The Chronicle of Higher Education, 55*(32), A31–34.

Lather, P. (1991). *Getting smart: Feminist research and pedagogy with/in the postmodern*. New York: Routledge.

Levant, R. F. (1997). *Men and emotions: A psychoeducational approach*. New York: Newbridge.

Levin, B. (1993). A dream deferred: The social and legal implications of hate crimes in the 1990s. *Journal of Intergroup Relations, 9,* 3–27.

Levinson, D. J., Darrow, C. N., Klein, E. B., Levinson, M. H., & McKee, B. (1978). *The seasons of a man's life*. New York: Knopf.

Meth, R. L. (1990). The road to masculinity. In R. L. Meth & R. S. Pasick (Eds.), *Men in therapy: The challenge of change* (pp. 3–34). New York: Guilford.

Mullane, S. P. (1999). Fairness, educational values, and moral development in the student disciplinary process [Electronic version]. *NASPA Journal, 36*(2), 86–95.

Nathanson, C. A. (1977). Sex roles as variables in preventative health behavior. *Journal of Community Health, 3,* 142–155.

O'Neil, J. M. (1981a). Male sex-role conflicts, sexism, and masculinity: Psychological implications for men, women, and the counseling psychologist. *The Counseling Psychologist, 9,* 61–81.

O'Neil, J. M. (1981b). Patterns of gender role conflict and strain: Sexism and fear of femininity in men's lives. *Personnel and Guidance Journal, 60,* 203–210.

O'Neil, J. M. (1982). Gender role conflict and strain in men's lives: Implications for psychiatrists, psychologists, and other human service providers. In K. Solomon & N. B. Levy (Eds.), *Men in transition: Changing male roles, theory, and therapy* (pp. 5–44). New York: Plenum.

O'Neil, J. M. (1990). Assessing men's gender role conflict. In D. Moore & F. Leafgren (Eds.), *Problem solving strategies and interventions for men in conflict* (pp. 23–38). Alexandria, VA: American Counseling Association.

O'Neil, J. M., Helms, B., Gable, R., David, L., & Wrightsman, L. (1986). Gender Role Conflict Scale: College men's fear of femininity. *Sex Roles, 14,* 335–350.

Perry, W. G. (1970). *Forms of intellectual and ethical development in the college years: A scheme.* Troy, MO: Holt, Rinehart, & Winston.

Pollack, W. S. (1998). *Real boys: Rescuing our sons from the myths of boyhood.* New York: Henry Holt.

Pollack, W. S. (1990). Men's development and psychotherapy: A psychoanalytic perspective. *Psychotherapy, 27,* 316–321.

Pollack, W. S. (1999, Winter). The sacrifice of Isaac: Toward a new psychology of boys and men. *The Society for the Psychological Study of Men & Masculinity Bulletin, 4*(1), 7–14.

Rabinowitz, F. E., & Cochran, S. V. (1994). *Man alive: A primer of men's issues.* Pacific Grove, CA: Brooks/Cole.

Sattel, J. (1976). The inexpressive male: Tragedy or sexual politics? *Social Problems, 23,* 469–477.

Schweigert, F. J. (1999). Learning the common good: Principles of community-based moral education in restorative justice. *Journal of Moral Education, 28*(2), 163–183.

Seidler, V. (1996). Masculinity and violence. In L. May, R. A. Strikwerda, & P. D. Hopkins, (Eds.), *Rethinking masculinity: Philosophical explorations in light of feminism* (pp. 63–75). Lanham, MD: Rowman & Littlefield.

Serr, R. L., & Taber, R. S. (1987). Mediation: A judicial affairs alternative. In R. Caruso & W. Travelstead (Eds.), *Enhancing campus judicial systems* (pp. 73–83). San Francisco: Jossey-Bass.

Sharpe, M. J., & Heppner, P. P. (1991). Gender role, gender role conflict, and psychological well-being in men. *Journal of Counseling Psychology, 38,* 323–330.

Smith, D. E. (1987). *The everyday world as problematic: A feminist sociology.* Boston: Northeastern University.

Smith, D. B. (1994). Student discipline in American colleges and universities: An historical overview. *Educational Horizons, 72,* 78–85.

Stewart, A. J., & Lykes, M. B. (Eds.). (1985). *Gender and personality: Current perspectives on theory and research.* Durham, NC: Duke University Press.

Stone, G. L., & Lucas, J. (1994). Disciplinary counseling in higher education: A neglected challenge. *Journal of Counseling and Development, 72,* 234–238.

U.S. Department of Health and Human Services. (1991). *Healthy people 2000: National health promotion & disease prevention objectives.* DHHS Publication No. 91-50212. Washington, DC: U. S. Department of Health and Human Services.

Valois, R., Vincent, M., McKeown, R., Garrison, C., & Kirby, S. (1993). Adolescent risk behaviors and the potential for violence: A look at what's coming to campus. *Journal of American College Health, 41,* 141–147.

Van Kuren, N. F., & Creamer, D. G. (1989). The conceptualization and testing of a causal model of college student disciplinary status. *Journal of College Student Development, 30,* 257–265.

Warters, W. C. (1995). Conflict management in higher education: A review of current approaches. *New Directions for Student Services, 92,* 71–78.

Wechsler, H., Deutsch, C., & Dowdall, G. (1995, April 14). Too many colleges still in denial about alcohol abuse. *Chronicle of Higher Education,* B1–2.

13

EMBRACING LIBERATORY PRACTICE

Promoting Men's Development as a Feminist Act

Rachel Wagner

UNIVERSITY OF DAYTON

> You never get there by starting there, you get there by starting from some here.
>
> (Freire & Freire, 2006, p. 47)

I have attended and presented sessions at a number of professional conferences, joining with colleagues calling upon higher education to re-imagine our obligation to—and understanding of—young men. Yet there is a reluctance, in my opinion, to speak candidly about the underlying causes of the underinvolvement and underenrollment of men in college or their overrepresentation in campus disciplinary proceedings. Some scholars have begun to address the issues, including examining the situations of particular male subpopulations such as men of color or poor and working-class men (Harper 2006; Beattie, 2002). However, it appears that talking overtly about masculinity and the need to inform professional practice with scholarship about men is politically incorrect. On numerous occasions I have been in conversations or conference sessions where people reacted uncomfortably when I have spoken sympathetically about men. I have found that my being a woman brings additional complexity to these politics, particularly when I assert the need for acting more consciously to inform professional practice with scholarship on masculinity. I am convinced that as a profession we need to talk more about men as men, to speak openly and transparently about masculinity, its socialization, and its impact on individual men as well as our campuses at large.

I also know that we live in a world where differences in social group membership (gender, race, ability, etc.) are not neutral. These differences manifest in a field of power. That is, we wear our identities in public, and our culture and institutions are shaped by belief systems that afford some identities more resources and more access to opportunities than others (Adams, Bell, & Griffin, 2007). In terms of gender, men are afforded more access and opportunity than women. Given such a socio-political reality, it is worth considering the implications and consequences when women administrators choose to be invested in issues of, and scholarship about men and masculinity.

I am not suggesting that women in student affairs should spend more time thinking and reading and studying about men in general, however. Feminism clarified for us decades ago that part of the way that institutional and cultural sexism functions is to encourage women to believe that it is their obligation, their role in the world to be attentive to the needs of the men in their lives—their fathers, brothers, lovers, and sons, and the point of this chapter is not to endorse such wholesale preoccupation with men. Rather, I feel strongly that *all* student affairs practitioners should have some experience mastering a select subset of knowledge that pertains to men, such as a basic understanding of masculine gender role development, as it is integral to the development of our students who were socialized as men. Women constitute an overwhelming majority of student affairs practitioners (McEwen, Williams, & Engstrom, 1991).

As a result, there is a fundamental tension between the expectations of women in student affairs to become experts on men's development and the political reality that within patriarchy all women are coerced into being experts on men in order to survive and thrive. In this chapter I would like to explore that tension and offer some ways of thinking about and approaching our work such that we might expand the range of options for politically conscious women practitioners. Integral to that discussion is a re-evaluation of our theories of social justice.

Our current conventions in student affairs dissect oppression neatly into a binary, an either/or proposition. The dominant discourse in social justice maintains that isms are largely written on the body, and that one can easily fit into a category of "dominant" or "subordinate." Such assumptions obfuscate intersections and ignore how oppression is secured and maintained within cultural norms that render a particular view of the world as inevitable and reasonable. I hope to excavate a parallel discourse in social justice, one where our genders are raced and classed and nuanced by a number of social positions, including religion and ability, sexual orientation and professional role. I wish to expand our framework of oppression to consider implications beyond the personal or individual. This is not to suggest this level of experience is invalid, but rather it is more widely discussed than the systemic contexts which need similar analysis. I want to turn our attention to how our social justice scripts may be limiting because of my confidence that doing so might alleviate a perceived double-bind faced by women professionals. In particular, the current framing of the issues often leaves women professionals wondering if they are colluding in their own oppression when spending time and energy focused on promoting men's growth and development.

My intent for this chapter is to illuminate conceptual obstacles that women in student affairs navigate as they seek to promote men's development, and to offer insights about how to avoid having the work become personally diminishing. Some of the more obvious dilemmas may be assuaged as I examine ways in which masculine ideology harms young men, expose overly simplistic beliefs about social justice, and reconcile student development and social justice goals. I will examine the real costs associated with promoting men's development and suggest ways for women to manage their professional role without compromising their personal integrity. I will conclude by conducting a brief examination of the liberatory promise embedded in men's consciousness-raising.

Are Men Harmed by Gender Systems? The Implications of Hegemonic Masculinity

Men in the United States are subject to a confining set of expectations and gender scripts that do not allow for the full expression of their humanity. Adherence to hegemonic masculinity alienates the individual man from himself, women, and other men. As demonstrated through empirical research, male gender role conflict has been linked to a multitude of variables, including anxiety (Cournoyer & Mahalik, 1995), depression (Good, Dell, Mintz, 1989; Sharpe & Heppner, 1991), fear of intimacy (Fischer & Good, 1997), and reduced help seeking (Blazina & Watkins, 1996). Though the cost of sexism may not be as dehumanizing for men as it is for women, there is considerable evidence that men's gender socialization is harmful.

What Is Hegemonic Masculinity?

For our purposes, masculinity captures the experience, the social performance of conducting oneself in a fashion that is commonly accepted as "manly." In our society, gender is a constructed identity. That is, men and women are assigned particular roles and characteristics based on their cultural context—beyond any genetic dispositions. Because gender is socially constructed, there is no single masculinity. Rather, there are a multitude of masculinities that are reflective of the particular cultural context of the man in question. Masculinity is nuanced by race, religion, geography, ethnicity, socioeconomic status, and historical time period (Kimmel, 2001). Scholarship has begun to reflect this by examining intersectional nuances such as queer masculinities, Latin masculinities, Jewish masculinities, and a host of other identities (Barrett, 2000; Brod, 1988; Gutman, 2003; Halberstam, 1998; Heasley, 2005; Saez, Casado, & Wade, 2009). However, as Brod (1988) has argued convincingly, not all masculinities are equal in terms of their access to power and their credibility as *authentically* masculine.

Systems of domination ensure that one way of being and doing is elevated above all others. Antonio Gramsci developed a theory of hegemony to explain how consent functioned to secure systems of domination. Active in anti-fascist movements in the 1930s, he struggled to understand why people suffering under political oppression did not revolt. Though violence and the threat of violence is an effective strategy for controlling large groups, he determined it insufficient in the long term. Gramsci theorized that a force stronger than oppression, ideology, was at play. In order for people to consent to a system that did not appear to work in their best interests, they must envision their experience as somehow justified or normal. Gramsci reasoned that such justification is achieved when powerful groups dominate "the society's systems of meaning, building what he called hegemony—the way that *idea systems* come to legitimize, or support, the interests of ruling groups in society" (Kaufman, 2003, p. 258, emphasis added).

Hegemony can also be applied to our understanding of gender. Consider how a singular definition of masculinity might dominate systems of meaning. What if one way of demonstrating masculinity was embedded and valorized in our schools, our media, our parenting and even our practices of worship? Young (2000) argued that social structures could be arranged so that "everyday practices of a well-intentioned liberal society" accomplished the same outcomes as a tyrannical regime (p. 37). That particular way of doing and being masculine could become so embedded in our consciousness that we might consider it normal or natural and hardly notice it enough to question it.

Connell (1995) defined hegemonic masculinity as "the configuration of gendered practice which embodies the currently accepted answer to the problem of the legitimacy of patriarchy, which guarantees (or is taken to guarantee) the dominant position of men and the subordination of women" (p. 77). His definition makes three key points. First, that there is a constellation of attitudes, behaviors and expressions that is considered "masculine." Second, that masculinity, while a performance, is socially contingent and thus malleable. Standing in a particular way isn't innately masculine, rather it is coded by a given culture at a particular time as masculine. Finally, he argued that masculinity is the glue that keeps the institution of patriarchy intact, "a pattern of practice ... that allow[s] men's dominance over women to continue" (Connell & Messerschmidt, 2005, p. 832). A particular set of attributes and behaviors are positioned as being authoritatively "masculine" and all others don't quite measure up. Moreover, these practices are so woven into the fabric of our cultural experience that we don't question them, even when they operate to undermine the humanity of most of the men in our society and secure the domination of everyone else.

Hegemonic Masculinity in Practice

Ask a group of college students who embodies a masculine ideal and the answers are unsurprising. James Bond, Arnold Schwarzenegger, Disney princes, Reggie Bush, Alex Rodriguez, and Jay Z are frequent answers to my inquiries. A common curriculum of what constitutes masculinity lurks just beneath the surface of our everyday interactions. Tragically, the curriculum can be incredibly limiting, promoting some ways of being and doing over others. Furthermore, hegemonic masculine ideologies lead to significant psychological distress. Psychologists have had some success in enumerating what exactly constitutes problematic masculine ideology in the contemporary United States.

O'Neil was one of the first to indicate that masculine gender conflict was the source of much of men's psychological problems, "the negative outcome of adhering to or deviating from culturally defined and restrictive masculinity ideologies," (O'Neil, 2008, pp. 364–365). He originally theorized six patterns of what he called gender role conflict, contending that men in general understand that there is an accepted gender performance of masculinity, and that an individual man's ability to embody that performance or embody it too well dictates his conflict. He was able to empirically validate four patterns through repeated testing: (a) restrictive emotionality; (b) success, power, and competition; (c) restrictive affectionate behavior between men; and (d) conflict between work and family relations (1981, 1982, 1990). Essentially, define yourself in opposition to femininity, make sure you can accomplish more, make more money, risk more and succeed, don't be gay, and remain detached. In 1986 a team of researchers, O'Neil, Helms, Gable, David, and Wrightsman developed a Gender Role Conflict Scale (GRCS) to assess the degree to which an individual respondent experienced GRC in the four pattern areas.

Failure to live up to the ideal, to embody a masculinity that is implicated within the four patterns has serious consequences. GRC has empirically been associated with depression, anxiety, low self esteem, and stress across racial, cultural and sexual orientation samples, and seven separate studies have linked it to substance use and abuse (O'Neil, 2008). Furthermore, a meta-analysis of studies using the gender role conflict scale demonstrated that GRC is associated with (a) sexually aggressive behaviors and likelihood of forcing sex, (b) abusive behaviors and coercion, (c) dating violence, (d) hostile sexism, (e) hostility toward women, (f) rape myth acceptance, (g) tolerance of sexual harassment, and (h) self-reported violence and aggression.

Male Gender Role Conflict paints a detailed picture of the ideologies prized by hegemonic masculinity and their implications. These ideologies are central to the maintenance of dominant patriarchal culture; they secure the current social order that harms so many. Grounded by fear of femininity, the four patterns of hegemonic masculinity constitute an undisclosed curriculum to which all men are subjected and few succeed. Furthermore, gender role conflict, the problems accrued when one either fails to embody or embodies too well hegemonic masculinity, has been linked to a number of problems that harm men, women, queer identified people, and in my opinion, our campuses at large.

As educators and practitioners of student development it is incumbent upon us to be knowledgeable about hegemonic masculine ideology and its consequences for men students. Such work is consistent with our central values and principles as a profession. In 1994, American College Personnel Association's (ACPA) Student Learning Imperative implored the profession to affirm its fundamental commitment to student learning and development. The profession revisited that commitment in Principles of Good Practice in Student Affairs (1997) and more recently, a joint ACPA/NASPA (National Association of Student Personnel Administrators) report articulating the profession's required competencies (2010). To fulfill our responsibility to foster students' growth and development, we must be able to "articulate theories and models that describe the development of college students" (ACPA/NASPA, 2010, p. 28). A focus on development keeps us mindful that some of the troubling behaviors we encounter on our campuses are the result of social arrangements and cultural programming rather than a lack of individual principle or ethics. We live in a society that socializes and conditions men (and women and transgendered folk) to equate true masculinity with stoicism and competition and independence and indifference.

While none of the preceding qualities are inherently bad, if they exist at the expense of almost all other qualities, this is cause for concern, because the complexities of daily life require a more differentiated set of intellectual, emotional and behavioral responses. Cultural scripts encourage men to think and feel and act in compliance with the hegemonic ideal. When men exhibit negative or hurtful elements of this behavior, student affairs practitioners are socialized to attribute this to individual students' flaws. We understandably lament pro-rape attitudes and valorization of violence and wonder if there isn't something really wrong with most young men today. As an anti-racist educator and activist, I find this analogous to the shock and condemnation we might direct at someone's racist behavior despite the reality that racism is part of our societal curriculum. In that case, the exceptional situation is not when someone manifests racism, but rather when he or she does not. Imagine the transformative implications for our professional practice if we were to operate from the premise that hegemonic masculinity is also part of our societal curriculum, and that as professionals we have an opportunity (obligation) to invite young men to consciously examine their assumptions about gender and masculinity.

Competing Values? Social Justice and Student Development

When I attend a regional or national student affairs conference, the first thing I do upon registering is to skim the list of programs and workshops that will be presented. I look for anything containing diversity watchwords: multiculturalism, privilege, oppression, or social justice. Several people are doing amazing work, but I have been disturbed by the increasingly generic use of the term, "social justice." Anything and everything seems to be labeled with the title of social justice. Social Justice is a term employed to comprise both the process and goal of equitable access to the resources necessary for all people to achieve their full potential as humans (Adams et al., 2007). It includes the area of study that actively seeks to identify and dismantle injustices associated with social group membership, such as racism, sexism, and homophobia. As a discipline and practice, social justice seeks to understand and undermine the individual, group and systemic forms of oppression that are enacted in society. A few erroneous assumptions about social justice have emerged that suggest the pursuit of social justice is in opposition to promoting men's learning and development. I shall chronicle a few in particular that surface most frequently.

Individuals and Systems

If you participate in a workshop on sexism or social justice, you will often find that significant time is focused upon individual experience. While this can be a powerful teaching tool, allowing the learner to situate the construction of knowledge in their own experience (Freire, 1970; Shor & Freire, 1987), it often becomes an end unto itself; failing to illuminate the systemic, or to value change, increased awareness and personal growth as outcomes of the learning process (Adams et al., 2007). Overattention to the individual level can monopolize our analysis, creating distinct villains and victims. Those who are privileged by their social group identity are rendered one dimensionally evil or ignorant. Perhaps more insidiously, this robs already marginalized groups of their agency.

Focusing on individual acts of oppression is appealing precisely because it provides a clear-cut bad guy. Noting the way White men might have been dominating the air time in a given college class meeting can be exhilarating. Giving voice to tangible evidence of the existence of oppression has a certain allure. Compound that with the opportunity to place the grievance at the feet of an individual present in the room, and its temptation increases. I admit that I have at times been vigilant about interrupting individual acts of oppression in the classroom or a training session. But, I have come to the belief that such a pedagogical technique, while congruent in principle with my political agenda, can actually be at odds with fostering an environment that is conducive to student learning and development. Providing a feminist lens, a substantive cultural critique, is emotionally taxing for both students and the instructor (Lewis, 2000). It is therefore critical to establish "the conditions of learning that enable [students] to locate themselves in history and to interrogate the adequacy of that location as both a pedagogical and political question" (Giroux & Simon, 1998, quoted in Lewis, 2000, p. 3). We need to move away from dualistic political positions in the classroom that are either "right" or "wrong" and embrace pedagogies that are effective for student learning. I have had success creating conditions that afford students dignity and encourage them to look at cultural and institutional culprits more so than individual ones.

I recognize and grieve the insidious impact of oppressive acts that occur within familiar relationships and everyday interactions with stunning regularity. But I do not wish to fetishize such occurrences, paying them excessive attention because their incidence provides a clear view of an unacceptable behavior or attitude—and perhaps more to the point, a tangible opponent. Such reductionist tendencies are ineffective in the pursuit of real change. They incline us to focus exclusively on the individual while the systemic eludes us.

This is particularly concerning when "isms" are physically tied to and located upon the body. It is not uncommon for practitioners to see patriarchy manifested in a person, a man for instance, or White supremacy embodied by a White man. To be sure, a White person can be racist. In fact, Tatum (2003) makes a compelling analogy of a moving walk way, arguing that unless a White person is actively cultivating an anti-racist identity they are susceptible to employing racist attitudes and behaviors. However, racism, and in particular, White supremacy, does not require White bodies to be present. A cultural imperialism of Whiteness exists within the academy (and within student affairs) regardless of whether White bodies happen to be occupying space in a given classroom or club meeting. Similarly, men need not be present in a room in order for a culture of male dominance—a patriarchy—to persist in our meetings and our classrooms. It dictates "linguistic forms, communicative strategies and presentation of the self; that is, ways of talking, ways of writing, ways of dressing, and ways of interacting" (Delpit, 1995, p. 25).

Refraining from associating oppression with a person offers tremendous possibility in the classroom the workshop. It is much less threatening to deconstruct an idea than a person, making it easier for someone to consider thoughtfully. Taking the time to disentangle the theory and materiality of oppression from an individual's conscious acts is a necessary first step. Once students understand that powerful cultural forces are at play, their participation in the system can be critically considered and they are more present to learn, and less distracted by notions of personal failings that are exposed at every opportunity.

Beyond Dualism

A second way in which we misconstrue social justice is by employing a dualistic theory of oppression that divides the world into oppressed and oppressor, powerless and powerful, good and bad. This presents problems for a number of reasons. First, as discussed earlier in this chapter, cultural hegemony encourages consent to oppression and domination by employing the tools of ideology. Applying a moralistic view, that is, judging one group as good and one group as bad is both overly simplistic and ignorant of the way hegemony functions. Furthermore, dissecting oppression into powerful and powerless undermines the agency of historically marginalized groups. To say that women are powerless ignores the creative and ingenious ways in which women (and other subjugated populations) have historically wielded power through individual relationships and strategic resistance movements (Conquergood, 2002; Scott, 1990). Finally, adherence to a strictly dualistic view of oppression divides the world into dominant and subordinate, and it can't help but do so one identity at a time. Men and women, of color and White, able-bodied and not, people are distilled down to a singular identity.

What's particularly problematic about this are the identities that we tend to forget. As an educator, I have authority in a classroom or a residence hall program. As an adult, I have access and influence and agency unavailable to youth. I have often been in environments where the young man in front of me seemingly represents every dominant group; he is White, affluent, heterosexual, able-bodied, etc. And yet, by his status as a youth and a student in my office or classroom, a power dynamic exists that I cannot readily dismiss.

In my experience, we who hold marginalized identities often navigate our surroundings from the positions of our subordinated identities, largely unaware of how others holding privileged identities might also be doing so. Consider applying this to a situation that commonly occurs in student affairs. For instance, in a judicial proceeding or while advising a student group, a female professional might be meeting with a male student. It is not as immediately evident that an administrator with authority is meeting with a young student without it. One can imagine the swirl of identity politics that might ensue. As a woman, I might be frustrated with the young man's sexist behavior. Rather than inquire beneath the surface level of his language or actions, I may respond instead to his lack of reflection about how misogyny is the tool of a system that regularly hurts me. Engaged in my own psychic distress, I might abdicate my responsibility towards effectively engaging the young man in his learning.

Liberatory Practice ... or Why Engaging in Men's Development Undermines Patriarchy

A cursory examination of workshops at national conferences and articles in professional journals in student affairs indicates that much of the professional discourse of social justice seeks to illuminate the various manifestations of privilege and oppression. While describing the interlocking nexus of power and dehumanization that marginalizes, co-opts, wields violence, and renders groups powerless is indeed essential, as activists and individuals committed to access and equity it is incumbent upon us to envision liberatory environments, and the strategies necessary to make them actionable. I propose that sexism is rendered invisible, and thereby secured, by rigorous scripts that naturalize some men's domination of other men, women, children, animals, and the environment. As Gramsci and Foucault suggested, systems of ideas maintain systems of domination (Kaufman, 2003). As such, providing opportunities for young men to interrogate the normative scripts offers intriguing options for upsetting the conditions that endorse sexism.

There are costs and trade-offs to such work, however, for women and queer people. Men's socialization into hegemonic masculinity is intense; young men have been overwhelmed with stimuli that tell them to simultaneously take risks and be in control. Providing opportunities for young men to question their cultural conditioning can demand a great deal of patience and tolerance. When their decisions and actions have put them in a precarious position, such as happens in a campus disciplinary proceeding, their fear and sense of inadequacy might manifest as arrogance or apathy. In this situation, it is incumbent upon the professional to tap their own professional knowledge of masculinity and developmental theory, and the wisdom of their experience in fostering conditions of learning. For example, they might slow things down and look beneath the surface swagger to the vulnerability and insecurity which often lies under it. I have found that some of the precepts of intergroup dialogue, suspending judgment, and practicing inquiry provide tools that increase my effectiveness as an educator in such circumstances (Teurfs & Gerard, 1993).

I won't suggest that doing this is easy. For me, doing so taps internal reserves of mental and intellectual energy that are already taxed by sexism and misogyny. When I feel diminished by the forces of sexism that are interwoven in the relationships and locations I negotiate in the course of a day, I recognize that I may not be in the best state of mind to exert the energy required to extend the benefit of the doubt or loving compassion. It is a daily decision, and sometimes I choose to hand off responsibility to trusted allies to do the work when I cannot. I have learned that I am more of a magnet for displaced anger than are my male colleagues. Cultural programming has instilled in our students that it is more dangerous to challenge a male instructor or administrator than a female one, so there are moments when I take an internal inventory and assess whether or not I am able to effectively engage someone else in their learning. I don't believe making that choice is shirking my duty; on the contrary, it is responsible professionalism. Fortunately, I have taken time to cultivate relationships with colleagues who are men capable of effective strategies for promoting men's development.

Another difficulty I have encountered involves noticing how my marginalized identities are significant to an encounter and then setting them aside and managing the ways in which I am privileged as a result of my group memberships. This is difficult. I have walked into classrooms and shown up as a queer, mixed-race woman with a hearing disability and failed to situate my dominant group memberships as a Christian, as someone with White skin privilege, as an adult, and as the only person in the classroom who is being paid to be there, and has power over grades or future recommendations. More often than not individuals are more conscious of the identities they have that are marginalized by the dominant culture. Young men in my office may have access to power through their membership in the category men, but still may feel powerless when faced with the institutional power I wield. Being conscious of how my identities surface and act as a lens through which I see and hear the world can offer insight into an interaction that has quickly deteriorated.

Finally, similar to theorizing oppression and women's subjugation (feminist theory), naming, and critiquing masculine ideology is new intellectual terrain for many students. Feminists have long articulated the consequences of surfacing oppositional knowledges, those that contradict conventional wisdom, in the classroom (Gore, 1992; Lather, 1991; Lewis, 2000). Ultimately transformative, new understandings can be painful. We are attached to our view of the world, and rather than see it as a product of society's messages, or as funneled through the lens of our own identities and experiences, we tend to view it as objectively true or natural. Disentangling how one has been duped by a required social curriculum that encourages many men to actively work against their best interests or to achieve their goals at the expense of the subjugation of mothers, sisters, lovers and friends is not welcome knowledge. It is not unusual for students to be resistant to such content and to transfer feelings of anger, confusion and frustration to the instructor.

Suggestions for Practice

It's important that we develop relationships and coalitions in the work of student affairs and in the work of social justice. Acting individually, against a political and cultural tide that is overwhelming and unceasing, ensures failure. Social justice has taught us that our lives and our fates are tied up in one another, that my struggle is your struggle. For instance, there is much we can learn from feminist scholars and theorists and liberation workers about the power of surfacing the complexity of identity in a field of power. "The challenge of feminist teaching is in finding ways to make speakable and legitimate the personal/political investments we *all* make in the meanings we ascribe to our historically contingent experiences" (Lewis, 2000, p. 101). Lewis notes the necessity of exploring with women the paradox of living in a world where it is both in their best interests and against them to comply with the dominant group. Similarly, men both benefit from and are harmed by patriarchy. Encouraging men to explore the contradictions can foster the necessary dissonance for growth and development.

The sex/gender system needs to be troubled. It is standard practice to assume a biological sex binary, a gender binary, and to link one to the other, so that males grow up to be (masculine) men. The system requires us to ignore a physiology that offers far more than two options and demands that arbitrary patterns of performance are associated with anatomy. We can note gender performances that "work" and "don't work" and then deconstruct why, illuminating our underlying assumptions and exposing them as anything but fact.

Somewhere along the way in the social justice movement we decided that it is our responsibility to tell the "truth" about the relative oppression index of every interaction in and out of the classroom every single second of the day. The numbers of times I have sat in a classroom and pointed out how someone else's behavior was racist or sexist are too numerous to count. The implication here is that I know what someone else thinks or believes. I have learned that it is more productive to comment on my own racist behavior, because I am powerfully aware of when I have enacted a troubling script that is part of the cultural curriculum. To assume anyone else's action is racist is arrogant. In a workshop or office or classroom, I am confident it is an abuse of power. I can note when something bothers me, and I can make transparent my own susceptibility to an oppressive system, but I have found that when I presume to know another's motive, conscious or unconscious, I am usually wrong and rarely effective.

Hegemonic masculinity is reinforced by men and women and gender queer individuals. *Patriarchy can exist even without men in the room.* This is important because we all contribute to the socialization of gender. It's active in our relationships, in how we teach, how we play, how we worship, our media outlets, and our families. The social rewards for those who successfully perform the gender commonly associated with their assigned sex are tremendous. Approval, visibility, attention, affirmation are a few; for those who violate gender convention, disapproval, avoidance, invisibility and violence are not uncommon.

Finally, like a qualitative researcher, as professionals in a field of student learning and development, we are often the instruments used in our work. We need to give care and attention to our psychological and spiritual fitness. There is much we can learn from the fields of psychology and counseling about effective practice. Issues of self-awareness and transference should be addressed through preparation programs and supervision. Being emotionally fit for duty can be the difference between success and harm.

Summary and Conclusion

Feminists have long enumerated the possibilities and costs of introducing students to oppositional knowledges that problematize the status quo (Gore, 1992; Lather, 1991). This chapter has acknowledged both and offers considerations for the practitioner to inform their decision making. By troubling the sex/gender system and re-evaluating professional assumptions about social justice we can design strategies and interventions that foster men students' development. For women practitioners in student affairs, there are real costs to promoting men's development. These concerns are mitigated somewhat by a re-evaluation of our professional assumptions about social justice. Re-conceptualizing the aims and purpose of social justice also offers opportunities for liberatory practice that eclipse the costs.

References

ACPA. (1997). *Principles of good practice in student affairs.* Washington, DC: Author.

ACPA/NASPA. (2010). *ACPA/NASPA professional competency areas for student affairs practitioners.* Washington, DC: Author.

Adams, M., Bell, L. A., & Griffin, P. (2007). *Teaching for diversity and social justice.* New York: Routledge.

Barrett, D. (2000). Masculinity among working-class gay males. *Gay Masculinities, 13,* 176–205.

Beattie, I. R. (2002). Are all "adolescent econometricians" created equal? racial, class, and gender differences in college enrollment. *Sociology of Education, 75*(1), 19–43.

Blazina, C., & Watkins, C. E., Jr. (1996). Masculine gender role conflicts: Effects on college men's psychological well-being, chemical substance usage, and attitudes toward help-seeking. *Journal of Counseling Psychology, 43*(4), 461–465.

Brod, H. (1988). *A mensch among men: Explorations in jewish masculinity.* Freedom, CA: Crossing Press.

Connell, R. W., & Messerschmidt, J. W. (2005). Hegemonic masculinity: Rethinking the concept. *Gender & Society, 19*(6), 829–859.

Connell, R. W. (1995). *Masculinities.* Berkeley: University of California Press.

Conquergood, D. (2002). Performance studies: Interventions and radical research. *TDR, 46*(2), 145–156.

Cournoyer, R. J., & Mahalik, J. R. (1995). Cross-sectional study of gender role conflict examining college-aged and middle-aged men. *Journal of Counseling Psychology, 42*(1), 11–19.

Delpit, L. (1995). *Other people's children: Cultural conflicts in the classroom.* New York: The New York Press.

Fischer, A. R., & Good, G. E. (1997). Men and psychotherapy: An investigation of alexithymia, intimacy, and masculine gender roles. *Psychotherapy: Theory, Research, Practice, Training, 34*(2), 160–170.

Freire, P., & Freire, A. M. A. (2006). *Pedagogy of hope: Reliving pedagogy of the oppressed.* New York: Continuum.

Good, G. E., Dell, D. M., & Mintz, L. B. (1989). Male role and gender role conflict: Relations to help seeking in men. *Journal of Counseling Psychology, 36*(3), 295–300.

Gore, J. (1992) What we can do for you! What *can* "we" do for "you"? Struggling over empowerment in critical and feminist pedagogy. In C. Luke & J. Gore, (Eds.), *Feminisms and critical pedagogy* (pp. 54–73). New York: Routledge.

Gutmann, M. C. (2003). *Changing men and masculinities in Latin America.* Durham, NC: Duke University Press.

Halberstam, J. (1998). *Female masculinity.* Durham, NC: Duke University Press.

Harper, S. (2006). *Black male students at public universities in the U.S.: Status, trends and implications for policy and practice.* Washington, DC: Joint Center for Political and Economic Studies.

Heasley, R. (2005). Queer masculinities of straight men: A typology. *Men and Masculinities, 7*(3), 310–320.

Kaufman, C. (2003). *Ideas for action: Relevant theory for radical change.* Boston: South End Press.

Kimmel, M. (2001). Masculinities and femininities. In Neil J. Smelser, & Paul B. Baltes (Eds.), *International encyclopedia of the social & behavioral sciences* (pp. 9318–9321). Oxford, UK: Pergamon.

Lather, P. A. (1991). *Getting smart: Feminist research and pedagogy with/in the postmodern.* New York: Routledge.

Lewis, M. (2000). Interrupting patriarchy: Politics, resistance and transformation in the feminist classroom. In I. Shor. & C. Pari (Eds.), *Education is politics: Critical teaching across differences, postsecondary* (pp. 82–106). Portsmouth, NH: Boynton/Cook.

McEwen, M. K., Williams, T. E., & Engstrom, C. M. (1991). Feminization in student affairs: A qualitative investigation. *Journal of College Student Development, 32*, 440–446.

O'Neil, J. M. (2008). Summarizing 25 years of research on men's gender role conflict using the gender role conflict scale: New research paradigms and clinical implications. *The Counseling Psychologist, 36*(3), 358–445.

O'Neil, J. M., Helms, B. J., Gable, R. K., David, L., & Wrightsman, L. S. (1986). Gender-role conflict scale: College men's fear of femininity. *Sex Roles, 14*(5), 335–350.

Saez, P. A., Casado, A., & Wade, J. C. (2009). Factors influencing masculinity ideology among Latino men. *The Journal of Men's Studies, 17*(2), 116–128.

Scott, J. (1990). *Domination and the arts of resistance: Hidden transcripts.* New Haven, CT: Yale University Press.

Sharpe, M. J., & Heppner, P. P. (1991). Gender role, gender-role conflict, and psychological well-being in men. *Journal of Counseling Psychology, 38*(3), 323–330.

Shor, I., & Freire, P. (1987). *A pedagogy for liberation.* Granby, MA:Bergin & Garvey.

Tatum, B. D. (2003). *Why are all the black kids sitting together in the cafeteria?": And other conversations about race.* New York: Basic Books.

Teurfs, L., & Gerard, G. (1993). *Reflections on building blocks and guidelines for dialogue.* Laguna Hills, CA: The Dialogue Group.

Young, I. M. (2000). *Democracy and inclusion.* Oxford, UK: Oxford University Press.

INDEX

Page numbers in italic refer to figures or tables.

A

Aberrant male hypothesis, men's misbehavior, 197–198
Academic identity, 89–90
Acceptance, 161
Activity sharing, hegemonic masculinity, 150
African American men, peer circles, 53
African American women
  double discrimination, 91–92
  identity, 91–92
Alcohol, social norms, 173
Athletic teams, 154–156
  leadership, 154–155
  masculine script narratives, 76
Authenticity, student affairs, 76–77
Autonomy, 30–31

B

Biracial identity, identity intersections, 85–87
Bisexual, *see* Lesbian, gay, bisexual and transgendered students
Boy code, 7–8
  masculinity, 7–8
Boys' career day, 69–72
Bystander behavior, rape, 169–171

C

Campus culture, 65–66
  disabled men, 140–141
  diversity, 66
  identity, 66
Change, 187–188
Change agents, 161–173
  skills training, 173
Chickering and Reisser's identity vectors, 27–33
Class, *see* Low socioeconomic status; Socioeconomic status
Class identity
  duality, 87–88
  identity, 87–88
College men
  assumptions, 50–51
  being queer and male, 103–106
  coming out process, 103–104
  completeness of knowledge about, 58–59
  degree attainment, declining, 55–56
  engagement in college settings, 65–69
  enrollment, declining, 55–56
  false perceptions, consequences, 166–167, *167*
  gender and support responsiveness, 58
  gender equity, 56–57
  health, 177–191
    assuming worst, 184–185
    educational campaigns, 187–191
    evidence-based strategies, 180–191
    gender-specific health care needs, 177–191
    harnessing patient's strengths, 186–187
    health beliefs and behaviors, 177–178
    health education interventions, 183
    health promotion strategies, 190–191

humanizing, 181–183
learning unhealthy beliefs and behaviors, 178–180
marketing, 187–191
outreach, 187–191
poor health explained, 177–178
Six-Point HEALTH Plan, 180–187
supports, 185
tailoring plan, 185–186
history, 65–69
how men feel about being men, 162–166, *163–165*
myth *vs.* reality, 55–59
positive aspects, 59–60
rape, 67
research limitations and opportunities, 54
risky and objectionable behavior unavoidable, 57, 67
service delivery, 38–45
  autonomy, 30–31
  Chickering and Reisser's identity vectors, 27–33
  competence, 28–29
  conformity, 20–23
  conformity to masculine norms paradigms, 21–22
  denial, 18–19
  developing mature relationships, 31–32
  dubious assumptions, 18–19
  emotion management, 29–30
  empirical case for campus programming, 23–27, *24–26*
  gender role conflict, 20–23, *25,* 27–33
  gender role transition, 36–38
  help seeking, 36–38
  history, 17–18
  identity, 33
  integrity, 33
  interdependence, 30–31
  lack of consciousness about men, 18–19
  male role norms, 21–22
  masculine norms, 20–23
  masculinity ideology, 20–23, 27–33
  men's programming (1979-present), 17–18
  men's programming challenges, 36–38
  Pleck's gender role strain paradigm, 21, *24*
  politics of gender, 36–38
  power loss, 36–38
  prevention, 38–44, *39, 42–43*
  psychoeducation, 38–44, *39, 42–43*
  psychology of men–Chickering and Reisser's identity vectors integration, 33–36, *35*
  psychology of men–student development theory link, 27–33
  purpose, 33
  research on boys and men, 23–27, *24–26*
  service delivery model, 38–44, *39, 42–43*
  statistical findings on problems, 20
  theoretical case for campus programming, 20–23
  sexual harassment, 67
  situating, 50–61
  student development theory, 196–197
College success
  gender, access, 114–115
  habitus, 117–119
  Head Start, 123
  importance, 112
  socioeconomic status
    access, 114–115
    college counseling, 123–124
    curriculum, 124
    gender, 124
    gender disparities, 113–117
    low, 112–117, 121–122
    parents, 124–125
    peer influence, 121–122
    recommendations, 122–125
    widening gap, 112–113
College women, history, 65
Coming out process
  college men, 103–104
  lesbian, gay, bisexual and transgendered students, 103–104
Competence, 28–29
Complex individuality, 81–94
  educational practice implications, 91–94
  good practice, 93
  large-scale programming, 93–94
  problematizing identity ranking, 90–91
Consciousness groups, 150–154
Critical, meanings, 4
Critical reflection, student affairs, 73
  student affairs, 73
Critical theory
  masculinities, 4
  men, 4
Culture of entitlement, Guyland, 10–11
Culture of protection, Guyland, 11
Culture of silence, Guyland, 11
Curriculum, 124

D
Degree attainment
  college men, declining, 55–56

Degree attainment (*continued*)
  identity, 66
  race, 65
  socioeconomic status, 111–126
Developing mature relationships, 31–32
Developmental Concept of Queer-Authorship, 84
Disabled men, 131–142
  alternative forms of masculinity, 141
  campus culture, 140–141
  disability awareness and pride, 141
  disability identity intersections with masculinities, 131–142
  gender performance, 136
  individual in social context, 139
  intersection of masculinity and physical disability, 135–142
  not a primary identity, 141
  outreach and mentorship programs, 141–142
  population characteristics, 131–134
  population size, 131–134
  recruiting, 140
  research agendas, 139–140
  secondary to postsecondary education transition, 134–135
  stigma, 135–136
  student affairs, 137–142
    training, 139
Diversity, campus culture, 66
Double discrimination, black women, 91–92

E
Emotion management, 29–30
Empathy, student affairs, 76–77
Enrollment
  college men, declining, 55–56
  identity, 66
  race, 65

F
Factor Model of Multiracial Identity, 84
Faculty, role modeling, 53
False perceptions, college men, consequences, 166–167, *167*
Femininity
  characterizations, 98
  fear of, 7
Fraternities, 154–156
  leadership, 154–155
  masculine script narratives, 76

G
Gay, *see also* Lesbian, gay, bisexual and transgendered students

Gay bashing, 68–69
Gay identity, masculine identity, juxtaposing, 88–89
Gender, 124
  college success, access, 114–115
  false gender binary of male/female, 102–103
  identity intersectionality, 82–83
  low socioeconomic status white males, intersections in educational success, 119–121
  power dynamics, 109
  sexual identity, 97
Gender differences, 148–149
Gendered identities, low socioeconomic status men, 116
Gendered norms, 97
Gendered pedagogy, 63–64
  history, 65–69
Gender equity, college men, 56–57
Gender gap, mortality, 177
Gender-informed pedagogies, 74
  men's identity, 74
  student affairs, 74
Gender performance
  disabled men, 136
  gender performance education, 109
  hegemonic masculinity, 136–137
Gender role conflict, 13, 22–23, *25*, 27–33
Gender Role Conflict Scale, 214
Gender role strain paradigm, 21, *24*
Gender role transitions, 36–38
Greek organizations, 154–156
  leadership, 154–155
  masculine script narratives, 76
Guy code, 7–9
  consequences of breaking, 7
  elements, 8
  interventions and practical suggestions, 12–13
  learning, 7–9
  maintaining, 9–11
  selling, 9–11
  unifying emotional subtext, 8–9
Guyland
  culture of entitlement, 10–11
  culture of protection, 11
  culture of silence, 11
  interventions and practical suggestions, 12–13
  three intersecting cultures, 10
  time to rebel, 11–12

H
Habitus
  college success, 117–119

defined, 117
low socioeconomic status men, 117–119
socioeconomic status, 117–119
Hate speech, 68–69
Head Start, college success, 123
Health
college men, 177–191
assuming worst, 184–185
educational campaigns, 187–191
evidence-based strategies, 180–191
gender-specific health care needs,
177–191
harnessing patient's strengths, 186–187
health beliefs and behaviors, 177–178
health education interventions, 183
health promotion strategies, 190–191
humanizing, 181–183
learning unhealthy beliefs and behaviors,
178–180
marketing, 187–191
outreach, 187–191
poor health explained, 177–178
Six-Point HEALTH Plan, 180–187
supports, 185
tailoring plan, 185–186
masculinities, 178
conflicting messages about manhood and
health, 180
Hegemonic masculinity, 50–51, 70–71
activity sharing, 150
characterized, 212–213
defined, 98
forms, 98–99
gender performance, 136–137
identity development, coming out process,
104
implications, 212–215
men harmed by gender systems, 212–215
men's misbehavior, 197
physical body, 136–137
in practice, 213–215
reinforced, 221
script, 71–72
violence, 197
Hegemony
defined, 9–109
masculinity, relationship, 9–10
Help seeking, 36–38
Higher education, history, 65
Homophobia, social norms, 169
Homosexuality, *see also* Lesbian, gay,
bisexual and transgendered students;
Queer
identity, 88–89

I
Identity, 33, *see also* Specific type
academic identity, 89–90
black women, 91–92
campus culture, 66
class identity, 87–88
degree attainment, 66
dominant or one-dimensional, 91
enrollment, 66
homosexuality, 88–89
men's groups, 153
multiple dimensions, 83–85
one-identity-at-a-time approach, 92
performances, 97
problematizing identity ranking, 90–91
race, 85–87
socioeconomic class, 87–88
spiritual identity, 90
Identity development, 82
hegemonic masculinity, coming out process,
104
reimagining masculinities, 148–149
Identity intersectionality, 81–94
biracial identity, 85–87
case study, 85–91
educational practice implications, 91–94
gender, 82–83
Identity vectors of student development, 27–33
elements, 28–33
Integrated identities
helping students navigate, 106–109
lesbian, gay, bisexual and transgendered
students, 106–109
Integrity, 33
Interdependence, 30–31
Intersecting authorities, large-scale
programming, 93–94

J
Judicial interventions, 200–207
characterized, 201–202
history, 200–201
specific developmentally appropriate
interventions, 205–207
traditional, 202–204

K
K–12 school system, 65

L
Lesbian, gay, bisexual and transgendered
students
being queer and male, 103–106
coming out process, 103–104

Lesbian, gay, bisexual and transgendered
     students identity
  development, 99–103
     D'Augelli's model, 99–102
  integrated identities, 106–109
  performances of diverse masculinities,
     104–107
  residence halls, 108
  safe space training, 108–109
Liberatory practice, 218–220
Low socioeconomic status
  college success, 112–117
     access, 114–115
     class, 119–121
     gender, 119–121
     men *vs.* women compared, 113–117
     peer influence, 121–122
     race, 119–121
     widening gap, 112–113
  gendered identities, 116
  habitus, 117–119
  intersections in educational success, 119–121
  peers, 118–119

M
Male bonding, 150
Male Gender Role Conflict, 82, 195, 214
Male gender role socialization, 194–195
  parents, 194
  peers, 194
Masculine identity, gay identity, juxtaposing,
     88–89
Masculine script narratives
  fraternities, 76
  student affairs, 75–76
  teams, 76
Masculinities
  conflicting messages about manhood and
     health, 180
  consequences of non-conforming, 162
  critical approach, 148–159
  critical theory, 4
  different meanings as embodied by different
     people, 99
  multiple intersections of identities, 52
Masculinity
  boy code, 7–8
  characterizations, 98
  dominant norm, 98–99
  health, 178
  hegemony, relationship, 9–10
  mental rules, 7–8
  performance, 98

public discourse, 12–13
  social norms, 173
Masculinity ideology, 27–33
Mature relationships development, 31–32
Media, health messages, 179
Men
  critical theory, 4
  development
     conceptual basis for understanding, 6
     cultural influence, 4
  ideal sense, 152
  individually accountable, 13
  multiple intersections of identities, 52
  patriarchy, differentiated, 3–4
  potentiality, 53–54
  statistical findings on problems, 20
Men's groups, 148–159, *see also* Specific type
  critical approach, 148–150
  history, 151–152
  identity, 153
  misinformation and ridicule, 153–154
  need for, 153
  rites, 152–153
  working effectively with, 150
Men's identity, gender-informed pedagogies, 74
Men's misbehavior
  aberrant male hypothesis, 197–198
  biological etiologies, 198
  etiology, 197–199
  gender role strain/conflict paradigm, 198
  hegemonic masculinity, 197
  social construction hypothesis, 198
  social-developmental hypothesis, 198
Men's rites of passage, new rituals and
     ceremonies, 13
Middle 60, student affairs, 73–74
Mortality, gender gap, 177
Multiple Dimensions of Identity, 84, 148–149
Multiracial college students, 93
  Factor Model of Multiracial Identity, 84

O
Occupation
  boys' career day, 69–72
  role models, 69–72
Offensive speech, 68–69
O'Neil's Gender Role Conflict construct, 7
Oppression, positionality, 5–6
Outdoor learning programs, 156–158

P
Parents, 124–125
  health messages, 179

male gender role socialization, 194
Patriarchal hegemony, unequal male benefits, 151
Patriarchy
  characterized, 3
  men, differentiated, 3–4
  men's development undermining, 218–220
  who benefits, 3–4
Peers
  health messages, 179
  low socioeconomic status men, 118–119
  male gender role socialization, 194
  peer circles, African American men, 53
  pressure on low socioeconomic status white
    males, 121–122
Performativity
  context, 149
  history, 149
Physical body, hegemonic masculinity, 136–137
Pleck's gender role strain paradigm, 21, *24*
Pluralistic ignorance, 161
Politics of gender, 36–38
Positionality, 5–6
  oppression, 5–6
  privilege, 6
  in relation to others, 5
Power
  enforcers, 162
  men's contradictory experience, 151
Power dynamics, gender, 109
Power loss, 36–38
Privilege, positionality, 6
Psycho-educational groups, 150–154
Public discourse, masculinity, 12–13
Purpose, 33

Q

Queer, *see also* Homosexuality; Lesbian, gay,
  bisexual and transgendered students
Queer-authorship, 84–85
Queer masculinities, 97–109
Queer studies, 98–99

R

Race
  degree attainment, 65
  enrollment, 65
  identity, 85–87
  low socioeconomic status white males,
    intersections in educational success,
    119–121
Racial identity, factors, 84
Rape
  bystander behavior, 169–171

college men, 67
  social norms, 167–169
Residence halls, lesbian, gay, bisexual and
    transgendered identity, 108
Role models
  faculty and staff, 53
  occupation, 69–72
Role socialization, 68–59

S

Safe space training, lesbian, gay, bisexual and
    transgendered identity, 108–109
Sensation seekers, 189–190
Service delivery, college men, 38–45
  autonomy, 30–31
  Chickering and Reisser's identity vectors,
    27–33
  competence, 28–29
  conformity, 20–23
    masculine norms paradigms, 21–22
  denial, 18–19
  developing mature relationships, 31–32
  dubious assumptions, 18–19
  emotion management, 29–30
  empirical case for campus programming,
    23–27, *24–26*
  gender role conflict, 20–23, *25,* 27–33
  gender role transition, 36–38
  help seeking, 36–38
  history, 17–18
  identity, 33
  integrity, 33
  interdependence, 30–31
  lack of consciousness about men, 18–19
  male role norms, 21–22
  masculine norms, 20–23
  masculinity ideology, 20–23, 27–33
  men's programming (1979-present), 17–18
  men's programming challenges, 36–38
  Pleck's gender role strain paradigm, 21, *24*
  politics of gender, 36–38
  power loss, 36–38
  prevention, 38–44, *39, 42–43*
  psychoeducation, 38–44, *39, 42–43*
  psychology of men–Chickering and
    Reisser's identity vectors integration,
    33–36, *35*
  psychology of men–student development
    theory link, 27–33
  purpose, 33
  research on boys and men, 23–27, *24–26*
  service delivery model, 38–44, *39, 42–43*
  statistical findings on problems, 20

Service delivery, college men (*continued*)
  theoretical case for campus programming, 20–23
Service learning programs, 156–157
Sexism, 210–222
Sexual activity, social norms, 166, *167, 167*–168
Sexual harassment, college men, 67
Sexual identity, gender, 97
Six-Point HEALTH Plan, 180–187
Skills training, change agents, 173
Social identities, 83
Social justice
  beyond dualism, 217–218
  individuals *vs.* systems, 216–217
  social norms, *167,* 169
  student development, 215–221
  Universal Design, 52
  University Instructional Design, 52
  values, 215–221
Social norms
  alcohol, 173
  homophobia, 169
  masculinity, 173
  rape, 167–169
  sexual activity, 166, *167,* 167–168
  social justice, *167,* 169
  student affairs
    normative feedback, 172–173
    research agenda, 172
  violence against women, 167–171
Social norms marketing campaign, 188–189
Socioeconomic status
  college success, 111–126
    access, 114–115
    college counseling, 123–124
    curriculum, 124
    gender, 124
    gender disparities, 113–117
    parents, 124–125
    recommendations, 122–125
  degree attainment, 111–126
  habitus, 117–119
  identity, 87–88
Spiritual identity, 90
Staff, role modeling, 53
Stages-of-change model, 187–199
Student affairs, 38–45, 66–69
  authenticity, 76–77
  autonomy, 30–31
  budgets, 138
  case example, 68

Chickering and Reisser's identity vectors, 27–33
competence, 28–29
conformity, 20–23
  masculine norms paradigms, 21–22
critical reflection, 73
denial, 18–19
developing mature relationships, 31–32
disabled men, 137–142
  training, 139
dubious assumptions, 18–19
emotion management, 29–30
empathy, 76–77
empirical case for campus programming, 23–27, *24–26*
gender-informed pedagogies, 74
gender role conflict, 20–23, *25,* 27–33
gender role transitions, 36–38
help seeking, 36–38
history, 17–18
identity, 33
integrity, 33
lack of consciousness about men, 18–19
male role norms, 21–22
masculine norms, 20–23
masculine script narratives, 75–76
masculinity ideology, 20–23, 27–33
men's programming (1979-present), 17–18
men's programming challenges, 36–38
Middle 60, 73–74
one-identity-at-a-time approach, 92
Pleck's gender role strain paradigm, 21, *24*
politics of gender, 36–38
power loss, 36–38
prevention, 38–44, *39, 42–43*
psychoeducation, 38–44, *39, 42–43*
psychology of men–Chickering and Reisser's identity vectors integration, 33–36, *35*
psychology of men–student development theory link, 27–33
purpose, 33
research on boys and men, 23–27, *24–26*
role, 68–69
service delivery model, 38–44, *39, 42–43*
social norms
  normative feedback, 172–173
  research agenda, 172
statistical findings on problems, 20
theoretical case for campus programming, 20–23
vulnerability, 76–77

Student conduct codes, *see* Judicial
        interventions
Student development
    identity vectors, 27–33
    social justice, 215–221
Student disciplinary systems, 200–207
    characterized, 201–202
    history, 200–201
    specific developmentally appropriate
        interventions, 205–207
    traditional, 202–204
Student services budgets, 138

T
Teams, 154–156
    leadership, 154–155
    masculine script narratives, 76
Theory
    need for, 4–5
    uses of, 4–5
Transgendered, *see also* Lesbian, gay, bisexual
        and transgendered students
Transgender identity
    development, 102–103
    discrimination, 102
Transtheoretical model, 187–199

U
Universal Design
    characterized, 52–53
    social justice, 52
University Instructional Design
    characterized, 52–53
    social justice, 52

V
Values, social justice, 215–221
Violence, *see also* Judicial interventions
    hegemonic masculinity, 197
Violence against women, social norms,
        170–171
Vulnerability, student affairs, 76–77

W
Women
    developmental processes, 196
    low socioeconomic status men,
        postsecondary success compared,
        113–117
Women's studies, 70–71
    rationale, 97–98